Drawn into the Mystery of Jesus

through the Gospel of John

Jean Vanier

Drawn into the
Mystery of Jesus
through the Gospel of John

DARTON·LONGMAN+TODD

© 2004 Novalis, Saint Paul University, Ottawa, Canada

The right of Jean Vanier to be identified as the author of this work has been asserted in accordance with the Copyright, Designs and Patents Act 1998.

Cover design: Christiane Lemire

Cover and interior images are from *La Cappella Redemptoris Mater del Papa Giovanni Paolo II* [The Redemptoris Mater Chapel of Pope John Paul II], edited by Apa-Clement-Valenziano, and are reprinted here with the kind permission and co-operation of Libreria Editrice Vaticana.

Layout: Christiane Lemire and Francine Petitclerc

Published in Canada by Novalis
Business Offices:

Novalis Publishing Inc.
10 Lower Spadina Avenue, Suite 400
Toronto, Ontario, Canada
M5V 2Z2
Phone: 1-800-387-7164
Fax: 1-800-204-4140
E-mail: books@novalis.ca
www.novalis.ca

Novalis Publishing Inc.
4475 Frontenac Street
Montréal, Québec, Canada
H2H 2S2

National Library of Canada Cataloguing in Publication: C2004-900725-4

ISBN 10: 2-89507-482-8
ISBN 13: 978-2-89507-482-3

Published in the United States by
Paulist Press
997 Macarthur Boulevard
Mahwah, New Jersey 07430
Phone: 1-800-218-1903 or (201) 825-7300
Fax: 1-800-836-3161 or (201) 825-6921
E-mail: info@paulistpress.com
www.paulistpress.com
A catalog record for this book is available from the Library of Congress.

ISBN 10: 0-8091-4296-1
ISBN 13: 978-0-8091-4296-5

First published in Great Britain in 2004 by
Darton, Longman and Todd Ltd
1 Spencer Court
140-142 Wandsworth High Street
London SW18 4JJ

A catalogue record for this book is available from the British Library.

Reprinted 2005 and 2006

ISBN 10: 0-232-52572-2
ISBN 13: 978-0-232-52572-4

Published in Australia by
John Garratt Publishing
32 Glenvale Crescent
Mulgrave Vic 3170

ISBN 10: 1-920721-09-6
ISBN 13: 978-1-920721-09-1

Printed in Canada.

We acknowledge the financial support of the Government of Canada through the Book Publishing Industry Development Program (BPIDP) for our publishing activities.

8 7 6 5 4 3   08 07 06

Contents

Foreword

This book is the fruit of many years of reflection, study, prayer and living in community, which began in 1950 when I left the navy to follow Jesus more closely. At that time, I met Père Thomas Philippe o.p., who became my spiritual father and encouraged me to let myself be drawn into the mystery of Jesus through the Gospel of John.

Over these years my friendship with Jesus and my understanding of this gospel have deepened. I have read books and commentaries on John's gospel written by many distinguished biblical scholars, all of which have helped me to understand better the context, the language, symbolism, historical setting and biblical roots of various passages. Thomas Brodie's commentary in particular led me to see the inner flow of this gospel, what gives it its unity and how each chapter grows out of another; how everything is oriented so that the reader may believe and trust in Jesus and have life through his name.

In 1999, Dick Nielsen of Norflicks, with whom I had done a television series on l'Arche and its vision entitled *Images of Love and Hope*, approached me to see if we could work together again on another program. I responded to his call by suggesting that we do a series on the Gospel of John. Dick talked with Susan Morgan, who had been of significant help on the first series, and they accepted the challenge. So in September 2001, we completed twenty-five talks on the Gospel of John for Vision TV. Susan helped me in a particular way to make more accessible the beauty, wisdom and relevance of this gospel to people today. I am deeply grateful to her.

This television series, entitled *Knowing Eternity*, became the basis for this book. I reworked the material and asked many wise friends, such as Susan Morgan and Kevin Burns of Novalis, to review the manuscript; they have helped to sharpen and clarify it and make it more alive and true. My deepest thanks go out to them.

The style of the book is what I call "meditative prose," written in a way that I hope will lead people to be drawn slowly and prayerfully into the mystery of Jesus.

In quoting from Scripture I use mainly the New Revised Standard Version (NRSV) and sometimes the Revised StandardVersion (RSV); often I use my own translation from the Greek.

The Gospel of John is like a mine of precious stones. I have extracted but a few; other people have extracted many more. And in the years to come, still other precious stones will be uncovered. There is such life and wisdom contained in this gospel that no one person can discover or hold on to it all.

Jean Vanier
November 20, 2003
Trosly-Breuil, France

Introduction

Our world is entering a new era.
Never before have we had at our disposal
such technology.
We can visit space, isolate the origins
of life, and even manipulate genes.
We have new medications for psychotic illness.

The last century was a century of hope, an immense hope in science.
We thought we could at last bring peace to the world
and that everyone's needs could be attended to.

But what do we see at the beginning of this new millennium?
War, genocide, new forms of destructive weapons, HIV/AIDS,
an ever-increasing gap between wealthy and poor countries.
A world governed more and more by an economy that is
disrespectful of minority cultures and of the deepest human needs.
An aggressive individualism that fosters selfishness prevails;
each for his or her own self.
We face a breakdown of what holds people together
in family and cultural groups.
Our poor earth is abused by greed.
The weak are easily crushed and put aside.
We all want to be winners,
though in reality so few can be.
Many will lose, only to become victims.

Where are there signs of hope today?
More than ever before there is a consciousness
of the importance of each and every human being,
whatever their race, culture or religion,
their abilities or disabilities.

We are becoming more conscious
of the vulnerability of our earth and of human life.
Yet depression, oppression, anguish and death
seem to loom everywhere.
Where to turn? What direction to take? Have we lost our way?
What is the meaning of our world and of our lives?

Many today seek to discover meaning in spirituality.
They seek inner healing and wholeness, inner peace and tranquillity
to taste the infinite and the divine within them.
This spirituality can, however, close some people up in themselves
and cut them off from the pain and the oppressed of this world.

My hope in sharing the Gospel of John with you
is to reveal what I am discovering in it:
a spirituality that gives me the light, the strength and the love
to live my life in l'Arche
with my brothers and sisters who have disabilities,
and to live an experience of communion with God
through a personal relationship with Jesus.
Jesus is at the heart of the spirituality of the Gospel of John.
He came to unveil lies, illusions and hypocrisy,
to give witness to the truth,
to lead people to the God of compassion and forgiveness.
He sends his disciples into our world of pain and conflict
to bridge the gap between the powerful and the powerless
and between people of different cultures
and to reveal a way to universal peace.

But Jesus not only committed himself to healing people
and doing works of justice.
He offered his love, trust and friendship to each person,
revealing to each one – Jew, Samaritan or Gentile –
how beautiful and valuable each one was
and how each one was loved by God.

In this way he awoke and fulfilled in people
their deepest need to be loved without limits
and to be creative and compassionate in loving others.
His healing and forgiving love called them forth to wholeness
and to the discovery of how beautifully human
and beautifully divine they were,
that they were beloved of God.

The Gospel of John is different from those of Matthew,
Mark and Luke.
It does not give facts about the life of Jesus
in the same way the other gospels do.
It does not provide the different elements of his message
through parables.
The author, under the guidance of the Holy Spirit,
chooses certain moments and signs, or miracles,
not only to help us believe Jesus is the Son of God
and the Son of Man,
but also to lead all the disciples of Jesus
into an experience of communion with God.
At the end of this gospel the evangelist says that he has written it

> *that you may believe that Jesus is the Messiah, the Son of God*
> *and that believing you may have life in his name.*   *Jn 20:31*

This "life" is the very life of God, which Jesus came to give us
through a new birth and growth in the Holy Spirit.
It is a life of friendship with Jesus
that brings us out of self-centredness
to a centredness in God and in others
and into a new knowledge of God.

This gospel was written in Greek,
somewhere around the end of the first century.
The author refers to himself as the "beloved disciple."
He never calls himself by his name, and that is significant;
he speaks of himself only in relationship to Jesus,
as if his real value and identity flow from this relationship.

A long tradition going back to the second century names him:
"John," son of Zebedee and brother of James,
although one of his disciples may have served as a secretary
and actually transcribed it.
This gospel reveals few personal details about him, only a few incidents:
during the last supper he was reclining on the heart of Christ,
he was at the cross where he received Mary,
given to him by Jesus as his spiritual mother.
We see him again in the last chapters,
where he and Simon Peter seem inseparable.
By signing the gospel as the "beloved disciple,"
perhaps the author wants to reveal that each one of us
can identify with him
and become a "beloved of Jesus."

The Gospel of John gives some facts about the life of Jesus,
although every fact leads further into a mystery
revealed in a symbolic way
that tells us something about who *we* are called to be.
Thus, the Gospel of John is not only about the disciples
at the time of Jesus,
their growth in faith and trust,
and the passages and crises of faith they had to live.
It is also about the growth in faith and trust
of all the followers of Jesus,
and the crises and passages *we* have to go through
in order to become beloved disciples.

One may ask why the Gospel of John did not find its final form
until some sixty years after the death and resurrection of Jesus.
Why is it so different from the other three gospels,
which John obviously knew?
During all those years he must have told over and over again
what he had lived and seen about Jesus
and what he had heard from Jesus.
But why did he wait so long for the gospel to become complete?

We can only make suppositions, of course.
Mine is that there was a special need at the end of the first century
to make better known what I call
the mystical element of this gospel,
which was lived and announced in a special way
in the community over which John presided.
This mystical element is the call of Jesus
for his followers to become one with him
and to live with him as a beloved friend.
The message of Jesus was beginning to spread
throughout Asia Minor, Greece and other parts of the world.
Followers of Jesus were becoming more numerous.
The structures of the church were being put into place
and the theology of the church was developing.
History has shown that as a group grows larger,
discords and conflicts arise,
rules and regulations become necessary,
and then structures can take precedence over the spirit.
The mystical and the spiritual tend to take a back seat.
No wonder John wanted to complete his gospel!

At the same time, at the end of the first century,
a new doctrine concerning Christ
was being propagated in Asia Minor.
It claimed that Christ was not really human,
that his body was of no importance.
In his three letters to his disciples,
John struggled against this doctrine,
which had become for some the basis of a "pseudo" mystical life,
cut off from human realities and from the human body.
The Gospel of John reveals that the body of Jesus,
his incarnated person,
is at the heart of the mystical life
and of a new knowledge of God.
This life is not a *flight from* the world of pain and of matter
but a *mission into* it,
to love people as Jesus loves them.

Mary, the mother of the Word–made–flesh,
who was bonded in such an intimate way to the body of Jesus,
formed and sanctified by his presence and love for many years,
must have guided the heart of the "beloved disciple,"
her spiritual son,
in his inner journey of union with Jesus.
With the mystical realism of a woman filled with the Spirit of truth,
she must have helped him to discover the deep significance
of many of the words and gestures of Jesus during his life on earth,
even all the details concerning time, dates and places,
which then became the basis for this gospel.
She must have helped him to see
how the life of communion with God
flows from this union with the humanity of her son.

André Chouraqui, the former deputy mayor of Jerusalem,
translated this gospel into French. He writes in his introduction:

> A book like this fourth gospel seems to flow from a deep silence,
> there where the Word of God is revealed as logos, the living word.
> And it is from this silent contemplation that we are called
> to read, understand, interpret and translate this work of John.

That is why I propose that we do not read this gospel simply
as someone wanting more theological,
historical and biblical knowledge,
but rather as someone who desires to be *drawn into a mystery*.

Perhaps many people today have never read the four gospels,
particularly the Gospel of John.
Some may have found this gospel too complicated.
The thread of wisdom that brings it together as a coherent whole
and makes it meaningful
has been hidden from them.
My hope is that as we go through it together as pilgrims –
those of us who find a home in a church and those who do not,
those of us who are immersed in our societies

or are marginalized by them –
we will discover the journey of the first disciples
and our journey as well.
These disciples were attracted by Jesus
and sometimes shocked by him,
but they let themselves be drawn, little by little,
into the mystery of the Word-made-flesh.
So, too, may we all let ourselves be attracted and shocked by Jesus
and so discover what it means to be a friend of Jesus.

What I share in these pages is the music I have heard
behind the words and the flow of the Gospel of John.
I have listened to the song,
which warmed and stirred my heart,
opened up my intelligence,
gave hope, meaning and orientation to my life,
with all that is beautiful and all that is broken within me,
and meaning to this world of pain in which we live.

I want to sing this song, too,
even if my voice is weak and sometimes wavers
so that others may sing it
and that together we may be in the world
singing a song of hope
to bring joy where there is sadness and despair.

1

To lead us into love

John 1:1-18

In the beginning,
before all things
communion was:
communion between God
and the "Logos"
– the "Word."

At one moment in time
the "Logos"
became flesh
and entered history.
He came to lead us all
into this communion,
which is the very life of God.

The Gospel of John begins with an extraordinary poetic,
mystical vision of the healing of humanity,
which in some way condenses the history of salvation
and serves as a capsule version of the whole of this gospel.
It is called the "Prologue."
It is centred on the Greek word "*Logos,*"
which is normally translated as
the "Word."
This is not incorrect, but "Logos" has a much wider meaning,
referring not only to the spoken word
but also to *the idea* and *thought* behind the spoken word,
the *vision*, the *plan* and the *wisdom* that inspire it.
It is the "Word" that has the power to change, create and transform.
"Wisdom" and "Word" both describe divine activity.

Before reading the Prologue of this gospel,
let us look at a text from the book of Proverbs,
written a few centuries before the birth of Jesus.
It tells about the wisdom of God at the heart of creation:

> *The Lord created me [wisdom] at the beginning of his work...*
> *Ages ago I was set up,*
> *at the first, before the beginning of the earth.*
> *When there were no depths, I was brought forth...*
> *Before the mountains had been shaped,*
> *before the hills, I was brought forth...*
> *When he established the heavens, I was there...*
> *Then I was beside him, like a master worker*
> *and I was daily his delight,*
> *rejoicing before him always ...*   *Prov 8:22-30*

In writing this magnificent Prologue in the Gospel of John,
the author had certainly contemplated this form of wisdom.
Here is a rather free translation from the Greek
of this hymn of the wisdom of God:

Before all things were,
the Word was
and the Word [or Wisdom] was with God,
[or turned towards God,
present to God,
in communion with God].
He was God.
Before all things were he was in communion with God.

All things were made through him
and without him nothing was made that was made.

In him was life,
and life was the light of every person
and the light shines in the darkness
and the darkness does not overcome it.

The light which was God was in the world
because all things were made by the light of the Word;
he was hidden and yet revealed in all of creation.
But people did not welcome this light and wisdom.

He came also among his own people through prophets
and holy people,
but they did not welcome him either.
All those who did receive the light which was God,
hidden in the conscience of each person,
became children of God, children of the light.

Even though the world was filled with violence,
engulfed in darkness,
the God of light and of creation was with his people
as they spread and evolved throughout the world.
God was revealing the Word and Wisdom to holy men and women,
to prophets, over the centuries and throughout the world,
showing them how to live in the ways of God.

Socrates, a wise and holy man in ancient Greece,
said he would rather die a thousand times than disobey God,
who revealed himself in the light of his conscience
and in his desire for truth.
But people did not listen to these prophets:

> *The Word of God came unto his own,*
> *but his own received him not.*

Then, at one moment in time and space,

> *the Word became flesh and dwelt amongst us.*   *Jn 1:14*

Here is the heart, the centre, the beginning and the end of the gospel:
the heart, the centre, the beginning and the end of history.
God, the eternal God, Creator of the heavens and the earth,
became like us, a vulnerable, mortal human being.
He became as a baby needing a mother,
conceived in her flesh
nourished at her breast
needing her love and the love and presence of Joseph
in order to grow and develop as a human being.
He "dwelt amongst us,"
which can be translated "put up his tent amongst us."
He became a pilgrim and a brother,
walking through the desert with us.
He became part of history
revealing to us a way to God
and to universal peace.

The "beloved disciple," the author of this gospel, adds:

> *We have seen with our eyes his glory*
> *the glory of the only begotten Son of the Father*
> *who was full of love and of truth.*   *v. 14*

Yes, the disciples have now seen that God is no longer distant
or set apart from our world.
They have seen him and received so much from him.

> *From the fullness of life and of love in Him*
> *we have received love upon love.*
> *The Law was given through Moses*
> *but love and truth came through Jesus, the Messiah.*
> *No one has ever seen God*
> *except the only begotten Son who is in the womb of the Father.*
> *He has made God known.*   *vv. 16-18*

Or as Luc de Villers, a professor at L'École Biblique de Jérusalem
translates it,

> *The only Son of God who came to lead us*
> *into the womb of the Father.*

What is clear in this magnificent movement or flow of the Prologue
is that in God
there is communion, unity, love and light,
and from this communion, all creation flows.
And this movement finds its fulfillment
as the Word became flesh
to lead human beings into a new communion with God,
to become one with God.

Let us pause a moment here.
Jesus reveals himself in the Prologue
as the unique Son of the Father.
He alone can witness to who God is
because he knows God intimately,
has seen God,
is with God,
and is in God.
He alone shows us the road to oneness with God.

Perhaps we have difficulty with language
when we speak of God as "Father."
Words are so limited.
How can finite words describe the Infinite?
For us humans, a "father" is a man.
But is God masculine? Of course not!
God is God, Creator of heaven and earth.
God created human beings; man and woman, God created them.
God transcends any notion of feminine or masculine.
God is neither one nor the other.
God is the source of all life and of all that is masculine and feminine.
Over the centuries, however, some men with power and influence
have equated God with manhood
and have tried to make women feel inferior,
as if women could not live a relationship with God.
Each of us can, in one way or another, use or manipulate religion
to exert power and make others feel inferior.
If Jesus speaks of God as "Father,"
it is because the Son flows from God.
God is the source of all life.
God is the Source of the Word or Wisdom that flows from God,
is born of God.
So when Jesus speaks of his "Father,"
he is speaking of the Infinite Source of Life, God,
from whom the very person of Jesus flows.
That is why John speaks of the womb or innerness
(in Greek, *kolpos*) of the Father
in which Jesus lives and abides.
The Father is Source of Life from whom the Son flows;
through the Son flows all life and all creation.
Through the Son we are drawn into God
and become children of God;
we receive the very life of God within us.

The origins of Jesus

The Gospel of John begins by leading us to contemplate
the origin of all things.
Some of the religious authorities of his time
were continually inquiring about the origins of Jesus:
where he came from, who his parents were.
Where other gospels tell us more about the human origins of Jesus,
John speaks about his *divine origin*:

> **Before all things, the Word was.**

Jesus comes from God and is going to God.

But Jesus also had *very human origins.*
He was a Jew, the son of a Jewish mother; his upbringing was Jewish.
He went to the synagogue.
On feast days he went to the Temple in Jerusalem to worship God.
The Jewish people are steeped in Scripture;
their culture and way of life are moulded by their history
from Abraham to Moses and on through the prophets.
They love to tell their story, how God watches over them,
loves them and guides them through all their joys,
suffering and infidelities,
for they are a people who have lived and suffered
through many invasions and oppressions.

To understand the Gospel of John
we have to go back to the history of the Israelite people
in which it is rooted.
Abraham is our father in faith.
The words of Jesus frequently flow
from the words of Moses and the prophets.
To let this gospel unfold in us, we have to claim and love this heritage.
People reach greater maturity as they find
the freedom to be themselves
and to claim, accept and love their own personal story,
with all its brokenness and its beauty.

So, too, Christians reach greater maturity in Jesus
and advance into the new
as they claim, accept, love, honour and forgive
all that is beautiful and all that is broken in their heritage.
This heritage is their Jewish origins.
It is also the evolving history of Christianity and of the Church,
with all that was and is broken and beautiful in it.

The Gospel of John, then, is the story of how the Eternal Word
became flesh, was born a Jew, immersed in the Jewish culture.
The story of how he leads us all
from behind the barriers of fear and indifference
into a new unity, a new peace
through a relationship with him
which flows from God
and brings us into the heart of God.

2

Preparing to meet Jesus

John 1:19-34

In the Prologue of the Gospel
of John
we learn that the Word
became flesh
to lead us into communion
with God.

John the Baptizer was sent
to prepare people to welcome
the Word-made-flesh
who appears as a gentle lamb.

We, too, need to prepare
ourselves to meet Jesus
the Lamb of God.

John the Baptizer

Aﬆer the Prologue, this gospel opens with a man called John.
He came to prepare the way for Jesus
by baptizing people in the river Jordan, near Jerusalem.
He would pour water over each person
as a sign that he was cleansing them
and calling them to repent
from all that was corruption, violence and evil in them.
To distinguish him from the John who wrote this gospel
he has been called "John the Baptist."
I like to call him "John the Baptizer,"
because this is what he did.

To understand the mission of John
we must remember that the people of Israel
were a humiliated people.
For centuries they had been ruled by various conquerors:
the Assyrians, the Babylonians, the Greeks and then the Romans.
The Romans had spread their empire all over the known world.
They had power, technology, armies;
they felt that their mission was to create peace
through power and domination.
They were proud and scornful
of this little, seemingly superstitious, people.
For the Romans, their emperor, Caesar, was a god.

But the Jewish people believed in the one and only God,
the Creator of heaven and earth,
the God of Abraham, Isaac and Jacob,
the God who had chosen them, who loved them,
the God who had brought them out of Egypt,
from slavery to freedom.
They were waiting for a prophet –
even more, the Messiah, the anointed one –
who would come to liberate them
and give them back their dignity and freedom.

Some were waiting for a strong, victorious Messiah sent by God,
who would unite the people and drive out the Romans.
He would reveal the glorious power of their God,
the Holy One, the Mighty One, the Almighty.

As the chapter opens, John the Baptizer is causing quite a stir.
People wonder if he is the Messiah.
Naturally, the religious authorities send a delegation
of priests and Levites
to find out if John really is the Messiah.
He makes no bones about this, and the gospel insists:

> *He confessed, he did not deny, he confessed:*
> *"I am not the Messiah."*　　　　　　　　　　　*v. 20*

But the priests and Levites want to know why he baptizes people
and with what authority he is doing this.
They must report back to the authorities who sent them.
The Baptizer answers in an ambiguous way by quoting
the words of the prophet Isaiah:

> *I am the voice of the one crying out in the wilderness:*
> *make straight the way for the Lord.*　　　　　　*Is 40:3*

As the rest of this text from Isaiah reveals,
he is but a voice, a voice that announces that God is coming.

> *"Behold your God!"*
> *He will feed his flock like a shepherd.*
> *He will gather the lambs in his arms.*
> *He will carry them in his bosom*
> *and gently lead those that are with young.*　　*Is 40:9-11*

The "one who is to come" is coming!
He is coming like a gentle, compassionate shepherd.

The mission of all the prophets was
to awaken people to the coming of the Messiah,
to prepare their hearts to receive him,

to call them to be faithful to God and the Laws of God,
to encourage them to have compassion for the weak and the poor,
and to warn them not to fall into idolatry.

John was the last of the great prophets of Israel.
His mission, given by God, was to prepare the way
for the immediate coming of the Lord,
to point to Jesus and to say: "Behold, it is he!"
This preparation began, however, with Abraham
and continued with the prophets.
The whole majesty of the Jewish faith is a preparation
to welcome the Messiah
just as Abraham, through his son Ishmael,
was a preparation for Islam.
As disciples of Jesus
we are indebted to our mothers and fathers of the Jewish faith,
for their familiarity with God,
who have led us into a knowledge of God.

But why did the Word-made-flesh
need someone to prepare the way for him?
Wasn't it because he did not want to be seen first of all
as a powerful person, creating fear and awe in people?
He did not come in power and majesty
but as a lamb, in humility and littleness.
John the Baptizer was a spectacular person.
He attracted people because he lived like a prophet,
austerely in the desert.
He dressed in a special way:

> *Now John wore clothing of camel's hair*
> *With a leather belt around his waist...*　　　　　　　*Mt 3:4*

He cried out and challenged people as other prophets did.

Jesus was not spectacular. He dressed simply.
He did not live in the desert but in an obscure village
with ordinary people like us.

He loved to be with people who were poor, or sick,
people who felt rejected and excluded from society.
He became their friend.
He went to the synagogue, to celebrations and wedding feasts
like ordinary people of his time.
He drank wine and ate normally, like us.
Jesus, seemingly so ordinary, simple and humble,
needed a John the Baptizer
to prepare the way for him,
to awaken the hope and hearts of people,
to point to him.
It is Jesus who will lead us all in and through the dailiness of life
and the darkness of the world
into something new:
a simple, loving friendship with God
where we will be free from fear, hatred and violence:
free to love people,
particularly those who are weak and suffering.

His coming was prepared for not only by John the Baptizer,
but also by his mother.
To become flesh, he needed the womb of a woman,
Mary, married to Joseph.
The Word did not appear out of the skies as a powerful superman.
The Word became flesh, conceived by the Holy Spirit
as a tiny human being,
invisible, hardly formed, yet totally prepared for growth.
He came out of the womb of this woman
and lived in a deep relationship with her.
He needed her presence, her love, her warmth,
the nourishment that flowed from her breasts.
He became part of the history of the human race.
The Word who became flesh needed this double preparation,
one *very hidden,* the other *very visible.*

John the Baptizer: a witness to God

One of the characteristics of this gospel
is the way it introduces the importance of witnessing or testifying.
In the Prologue we read:

> *There was a man sent by God, his name was John.*
> *He came as a witness to testify to the light.*
> *He was not the light*
> *but he came to testify to the light.*   *vv. 6-8*

John the Baptizer was able to witness to Jesus
because God had spoken to his heart
and revealed his mission to him:

> *"I myself did not know him*
> *but the one who sent me to baptize with water said to me:*
> *'He on whom you see the Spirit descend as a dove from heaven*
> *and dwell upon him*
> *is the one who baptizes in the Holy Spirit.'*
> *And I myself have seen and have testified*
> *that this man is the Chosen One of God."*   *Jn 1:33-34*

John the Baptizer and the beloved disciple,
and the first disciples,
and all the disciples of Jesus throughout the ages,
are called to be witnesses and to point towards Jesus, saying:
"He is the chosen one of God."
He is the one who came to heal our broken hearts,
to give us peace
and to lead us further into the truth.
Those who are witnesses to Jesus do not give out ideas,
ideologies or even doctrines.
They do not seek followers for themselves and their own glory.
Rather, they seek to lead people to Jesus.
They do not manipulate people
or impose their ideas or way of life on others.
They believe in the compelling power of the truth

and the freedom of people to welcome the truth or not.
They speak of what they have lived, experienced,
seen and heard in their hearts.
They speak out clearly, truthfully and with courage,
even in the face of opposition or mockery.
They tell their story.
They tell how Jesus is healing their hearts of stone,
giving them hearts of flesh,
leading them into the world of universal love and compassion
and breaking down barriers of culture, fear and sin
that close them up in themselves.
Witnesses tell how Jesus is transforming their lives
and bringing them a new inner freedom, peace and joy.
People in our world find hope when they find credible witnesses,
men and women with a living faith,
bearing witness to the presence of God –
more by their lives, their growing compassion
and their dynamic love
than by their ideas or their words.
Jesus said that people will know his disciples
by the love they have for one another.   *Jn 13:35*

During the war in Kosovo a few years ago,
as the Serb army advanced into the country,
an Orthodox priest protected and hid certain Kosovars
who were in danger.
Later, when the tide had turned
and the Serbs were obliged to pull back,
some Kosovars sought revenge.
This same priest then protected and hid
the Serbs who were in danger.
He walked a thin, dangerous line
between two warring, fearful peoples.
He was witnessing to the love of Jesus, the God of peace,
who weeps as people seek to kill each other.
He was witnessing to the love of God
for each and every human being.

A humble witness

John the Baptizer was a humble witness.
If he attracted people from Jerusalem and also from Judea
it was not to satisfy his own spiritual ego but to bring people to Jesus.
It was Jesus who was important; he was nothing compared with Jesus.

> *"He who comes after me, ranks ahead of me,*
> *because he was before me."*   Jn 1:15

> *"I am not worthy to undo the thongs of his sandals."*   v. 27

Later, he named Jesus the "Bridegroom,"
saying that he is but the friend of the Bridegroom
who must decrease

> *and Jesus increase.*   Jn 3:30

What a beautiful man! What transparency! What humility!
If only we could all be like that,
not pointing to ourselves and to our own spiritual power,
but pointing to Jesus, who draws us to a new and deeper love.
A witness is only a witness if he or she is humble.

In l'Arche and in Faith and Light,
we are called to witness in a special way
to the gift of people with disabilities.
So often they are looked down upon, cast aside,
seen as being without value.
In l'Arche and in Faith and Light we see their value and their beauty
and can bear witness that not only are they fully human,
but also they are loved by God in a special way.
We want to be witnesses not only through our words,
but through the life we share with them.
Witnesses, then, are there to tell us where to find
inner healing and liberation,
what is the road to God,
and how God is hidden in love, not in power.

Jesus: the Lamb

The revelation that Jesus was the Chosen One of God,
the Son of God,
was given while John was baptizing Jesus.
It was because of this experience that, later on,
when he saw Jesus coming towards him, he prophesied:

> *"Behold the Lamb of God*
> *who takes away the sin of the world."*   *v. 29*

Isn't it strange that John the Baptizer should declare solemnly
that Jesus is a lamb,
the Lamb of God,
such a meek and gentle little animal?

In some way, the cry of John the Baptizer announcing

> *"Behold the Lamb of God"*

is like a mysterious answer to the question
asked by Isaac, the beloved son of Abraham.
God had promised Abraham that he would be
the father of a multitude of people,

> *more numerous than all the stars of the sky.*   *Gen 22:17*

Yet God asked him to sacrifice his own beloved son.
The two of them went up the mountain, Isaac carrying the wood,
Abraham carrying the knife and the fire.
Isaac said:

> *"Father, the fire and the wood are here,*
> *but where is the lamb for the burnt offering?"*
> *Abraham replied: "God himself will provide the lamb, my son."*
> *Gen 22:7-8*

The answer came through John the Baptizer:

> *"Behold the Lamb of God."*

To understand the deep significance of the lamb
for the Jewish people,
we must remember the Book of Exodus.   *cf. Ex 11–15*
The blood of the lamb saved the Israelites from slavery
and permitted them to walk forward to freedom,
to the Promised Land.
During the feast of the Passover, the Israelites celebrated this freedom
by eating a lamb "roasted over the fire."
Later, the prophet Isaiah spoke of the "suffering servant"
who was pierced because of our faults and who brought us peace:

> *He was led like a lamb to slaughter...*
> *and did not open his mouth....*
> *He bore the sin of many*
> *and made intercession for our transgressions.*   *Is 53:7, 12*

In front of the power and armies of Caesar,
in front of their mighty weapons,
stands a lamb, the lamb of God.
What can this lamb do?
The lamb will break down the walls of fear, of aggression,
of violence, of sin
which imprison people in themselves
and incite them to seek their own glory.
He will liberate in each person a new life of communion with God,
with other people and with what is deepest in the self,
sowing seeds for universal peace.

In our world today there are some prophets like John the Baptizer
who are spectacular.
They prepare our hearts to receive Jesus.
But when Jesus comes, he comes not as a spectacular God of power,
but as a gentle lamb,
the Chosen One of God, the Beloved.
He comes in a very simple way, opening our hearts to people
with the breath of peace and a quiet shaft of light, a gentle kiss.

He comes into that part of our being that is our treasure,
that sacred space within us,
hidden under all the fears, walls and anger in us
so that we may grow in the spirit of love.

Yesterday, as today, John the Baptizer is calling people to be attentive
to the quiet voice and presence of Jesus,
calling us to trust him
and to enter into friendship with him.
We are being called to be gentle followers of the Lamb,
not people of power.

Even though John recognizes Jesus
as the Lamb and the Chosen One of God,
he does not stop baptizing in order to follow Jesus.
He continues to baptize and to attract disciples.
It would have seemed normal for him to send all his disciples to Jesus.
But the fact is that John, the last of all prophets in the Bible,
inspired by God,
continued to live his mission as a Jewish prophet.
Isn't that a sign of the importance of this faith
and the need for it in our world?

3

Meeting Jesus the first time

John 1:35-51

*Jesus attracts a few people who start to walk with him
on a journey of faith and transformation.*

*Many young people today are searching for authentic models
who open their hearts and minds to a new vision
and start them off on this journey of faith
and transformation.*

What are we looking for?

John the Baptizer is with two of his disciples.
Fixing his eyes on Jesus, he says:

> *"Behold the Lamb of God!"*   *v. 36*

On hearing this prophetic cry, the two disciples leave him
and begin to follow the Lamb, the "Lamb of God."
It is not Jesus who calls these two men towards him,
it is John who guides them to Jesus,
and through John it is the Father who is drawing the hearts
of these two men to meet Jesus.
Later, Jesus will insist on this when he says:

> *"I have revealed your name to those*
> *whom you took from the world to give to me.*
> *They were yours and you gave them to me."*   *Jn 17:6*

We are beginning to see the unfolding plan of God.
Jesus is going to gather around him a core group of people
who will continue his work after his departure.
Jesus will preach only for a short time, about three years,
in a small land.
Yet his message is for the whole world and for all the ages to come.
What is important for him is to form the hearts of a few disciples
who will travel, as poor pilgrims, throughout the world,
to announce and communicate his message of love and forgiveness.
These few disciples will break down the barriers
that separate people and cultures
from one another and so bring peace.

Many young people today, like these first disciples of Jesus,
are disillusioned by our rich societies.
They are looking for an ideal,
a vision that gives meaning to their lives.
They search, but what do they find?
A world where material success has become

the most important thing in life.
Many seek to break through the competition and rivalry,
greed and corruption
that they see and hear everywhere.
They are often shocked by the way our beautiful, fragile earth is treated
and depressed by the continuing armed conflicts.
Some slip into a world of drugs, searching for an experience
that takes them away for a few moments
from our rigidly structured society.
They hope to find relief from the pain of despair, to taste the "infinite"
and forget the harshness of our world.
Many are waiting to meet men and women who
are actually living what they are saying.
They seek authentic models and witnesses
who will lead them from a road of sadness, despair and death
to a path of hope and life
where they can live a true experience of God.
They yearn to find a place in the world
where, with others, they can give and receive new life,
struggling for justice and peace.

Jesus, the Lamb, turns towards these first two disciples and asks:

"What are you looking for?"   Jn 1:38

These are the first words of Jesus in this gospel.
Perhaps they are the first words of Jesus to each one of us.
Jesus does not want to impose on us an idea,
a doctrine or an ideology.
He wants people to follow him and his path of love freely.
He calls us to look into our own hearts
and to become aware of our fundamental desires.
What do we really want for our lives? What are we looking for?
Are we prepared to believe in ourselves and to make clear choices?
By asking this question, Jesus enters into a relationship,
a dialogue, with these two men.
Little by little, he will draw them deeper into the mystery

and show them how to live their lives.
He will do this with us, too.
It all begins with a personal relationship with Jesus.

The two men, perhaps taken by surprise,
not knowing clearly what they want, ask Jesus:

> *"Rabbi, teacher, where do you live?"*   *v. 38*

They do not want ideas or theories. They do not want to be students.
They want to enter into a relationship with Jesus,
to *be with* him, stay with him.
They want to let themselves be touched by his life
and by all he is and has.
They want to become his disciples or followers.

> *"Come and see,"* says Jesus.

This word "come" from the mouth of Jesus
flows throughout the gospel of the beloved disciple.
Jesus does not impose or force anything on anyone.
He gently *invites* each one of us to move forward.
He says "come," come and see,
come and live an experience of love, healing and a new inner freedom.
The two men follow Jesus,
see where he lives
and choose to dwell with him.

This Greek word *menein*, to "*stay*," to "*abide*," to "*dwell*,"
is special in the Gospel of John and in his letters to his disciples.
He uses it sixty-three times!
We have already seen this word when John the Baptizer said that
he saw the Spirit,
like a dove, *"dwell"* upon Jesus.
If John uses this word to signify "staying" in a particular place,
he uses it even more to signify a friendship
where we "dwell" in another person.

A *"mutual in-dwelling"* is a permanent, deep friendship.
It is an intimate, dynamic relationship between two people
dwelling in one another.
So when the evangelist says here,

> They [the two men] came and saw where he was dwelling
> and they dwelt with him that day,   v. 39

this has special significance.
It certainly means the actual, physical place where Jesus was staying,
but it also suggests what we will discover in a more explicit way
later on:
that the *real home of Jesus is in the Father.*
He dwells in the Father's presence.

Words and events in this gospel are frequently symbolic.
For example, the evangelist gives a precise time:
it was four o'clock in the afternoon.
The author also wants to show that Jesus is grounded
in a particular space and time,
rooted in history.
It was perhaps for him a moment and a date that he will never forget:
the moment he met Jesus for the first time.

We are told that one of these two men is Andrew,
Simon Peter's brother.
The second remains anonymous.
Perhaps it was John himself.
If we are not told the name of this disciple
maybe it is to show that each one of us can identify with
the unnamed disciple.
In order to follow Jesus and dwell with him,
each one of us is called to let go of the search for power,
wealth and reputation that our culture tends to impose.

After *dwelling with* Jesus, Andrew goes and finds his brother Simon
and says to him:

> "We have found the Messiah."   v. 41

"Messiah" means the "Anointed One," "the Christ."
Before dwelling with Jesus, the two disciples had called him "Rabbi."
Now Andrew calls him the "Anointed One,"
the one chosen by God to bring liberation to the people.

What happened during this time with Jesus
that makes Andrew now call him the "Messiah"?
Did they pray together?
Did Jesus speak of his vision and love for the Father?
How did he reveal to them that he was the Messiah?
That remains their secret.
We all have our secret,
a secret meeting with God, with truth, with another,
a peak moment that has touched and opened our hearts to God.
I can imagine, however, that these two men,
while they "dwelt" with Jesus,
were enveloped in an immense inner peace.
The very presence of Jesus, his love for them,
his words of truth and of love,
brought them a new inner joy, a sense of freedom,
and inspired in them a new hope and creativity.
They must have felt a mixture of awe and love in his presence
that in some way transformed them.

I lived something similar with Père Thomas Philippe,
a Dominican priest with whom I started l'Arche.
When I left the navy in 1950,
I went to a small community founded by him near Paris.
His presence changed my life –
or rather orientated my life in a new way.
By his very presence, Père Thomas seemed to communicate
a presence of God
that filled me with inner peace and silence
and drew new life from within me.
I knew very quickly that I was called to become his disciple,
or spiritual son.

It was because of our relationship that l'Arche began many years later.

Andrew, filled with awe and love, goes and finds his brother, Simon,
and brings him to Jesus. Jesus says to him:

> *"You are Simon, son of John;*
> *You shall be called 'Cephas,'*
> *which means Peter* [the Rock]. *"*　　　　　　　　　　*v. 42*

When God changes someone's name, as he did with Abram,
who became Abraham,
or Sarai, his wife, who became Sarah,
or Jacob, who became Israel,
it has a special significance.
Simon is called to be a rock of faith and strength,
the rock upon which the house of God would be built.
In the Gospel of Matthew, Jesus speaks about a house
built upon a rock that did not collapse
in spite of the winds and torrential rains.　　　　　　　*Mt 7:24-25*
An assembly of believers needs the rock of faith.
As the psalmist prays:

> *O Lord...be for me a rock of refuge*
> *A strong fortress to save me,*
> *for you are my rock and my fortress.*　　　　　　　*Ps 71:3*

Simon is now "Peter," the "Rock."
A mission is being suggested to him.
This mission will become clearer later.
Doesn't a new identity emerge within each one of us
when we live a deep, personal relationship with Jesus
and discover in a new way who we are called to become?

The next day, Jesus goes to Galilee with the three new disciples.
There he meets Philip,
who is from the same town as Andrew and Peter.
The name of the town is Bethsaida,

which means the "House of fishermen."
Jesus says to him:

> *"Follow me."*   *v. 43*

Philip then goes off and finds Nathanael and tells him:

> *"We have found him of whom Moses*
> *in the law and the prophets wrote,*
> *Jesus of Nazareth, the son of Joseph."*   *v. 45*

Philip and Nathanael, both from Galilee,
obviously knew Jesus' family in Nazareth,
a village that did not have a particularly good reputation.
Nathanael answers cynically:

> *"Can anything good come from Nazareth?"*   *v. 46*

Philip, touched by Jesus, touched also by his two friends,
Peter and Andrew,
does not try to prove anything.
He simply says:

> *"Come and see,"*

implying, "Come and see for yourself.
Come and live the experience I have lived."

As Nathanael approaches, Jesus says to him:

> *"Behold I tell you there truly is an Israelite*
> *in whom there is no guile."*
> *"How do you know me?" asks Nathanael.*
> *"Before Philip called you, when you were under the fig tree,*
> *I saw you."*   *vv. 47-48*

Nathanael is shocked and surprised:
how could Jesus have seen him there?
What was he doing or saying at that moment?
Certainly something significant.
Praying? Yearning to see the Messiah?

Making a special promise to God if he found the Messiah?
Anyway, the words of Jesus bring forth a cry of faith and of praise
from Nathanael:

> *"Rabbi, you are the Son of God, the king of Israel!"*

Jesus says to him:

> *"Do you believe because of what I have told you,*
> *that I saw you under the fig tree?*
> *You will see greater things than that.*
> *I tell you, you will see the heavens opened and the angels of God*
> *ascending and descending upon the Son of Man."*   *vv. 50-51*

Here we have a clear reference to the great Patriarch Jacob,
son of Isaac, the beloved son of Abraham.
Jacob

> *dreamed there was a ladder set up on the earth*
> *and the top of it reached the heavens*
> *and the angels of God were ascending and descending upon it.*
>   *Gen 28:12-13*

When Jacob awoke from his sleep, he said:

> *"Surely the Lord is in this place and I did not know it."*

Then he added:

> *"How awesome is this place!*
> *This is none other than the house of God*
> *and this is the gate of heaven."*   *Gen 28:16-17*

The cry of humanity expressed by the prophet Isaiah has come true:

> *O, that you would tear open the heavens*
> *and come down!*   *Is 64:1*

The Word has become flesh; the heavens have opened
and God has come down to walk with us as a pilgrim.
Yes, he is the Son of God, as Nathanael cried out,
but he is also very human, vulnerable and weak.
He is the Son of Man
who came to lead us into a new vision for humanity.

These words of Jesus to Nathanael may appear strange to us
at first reading,
but they are pregnant with meaning, echoing Jacob and the prophets.
They reveal the whole reality
of how the Word came down from heaven, became flesh,
and will return to the Father with all his brothers and sisters in
humanity.

Yes, Nathanael will see greater things: the final liberation of humanity
when we will all see and enter the heavens of love.
These heavens have been opened up for us.
We have found the gate: Jesus.

The first five

Let us come back to these five men whom Jesus called.
First, they are friends; they come from the same place.
Through their friendship, they attract and call each other to Jesus.
Friendship is a deeply human reality,
the treasure of each person and the basis of community,
as people with the same hope and vision seek meaning to their lives.
Friendship is helping each other,
giving each other support when one or the other is in difficulty,
working and struggling together,
moving forward to new things together.
Friendship is fidelity.
Aristotle says that without friends, nobody would want to live.
Cicero says that friendship is like the sun
that gives warmth and light to us.
Jesus, the Word-made-flesh, knows the importance of friendship.
Friendship is at the heart of his message.
He wants to become the friend of each one of us
so that we become friends of God.

He calls each one personally to follow him.
Each one is special; each one is unique.
It is not a collective call.
Jesus is not seeking votes like a politician in an election.
He calls each one to follow him and to become his disciple.

What is so special about these five men?
Why are they so prominent at the beginning of this gospel?
As we enter the Gospel of John we will meet other disciples
who seem to be closer to the heart of Jesus,
and who understand him better than these men,
who quarrelled among themselves,
each one wanting to be the most important.
There is Martha, Mary and Lazarus of Bethany, for example,
and of course Mary and Joseph, the family of Jesus.
Why are we introduced to these five men so early in the gospel?
Here they are five, but later they will be twelve.
They are the ones that Jesus will send out
to the four corners of the world
to announce and reveal his presence and love.
They will be the shepherds to tend and guide the flock of believers,
and to nourish them with the word and presence of Jesus.

Other disciples will be called to live with Jesus in community,
as Mary and Joseph did,
to live the pains and joys of community life,
to live community as a place of worship and prayer,
a place of hospitality and welcome,
especially for those who are weak and in need,
a place of sharing and receiving the word of God,
a place of celebration and growth towards forgiveness.
These five chosen ones will have a special role
as servant-leaders of the budding church,
and so they will carry a certain authority.
They will be called to guide, to tend, to nourish the people of God
and to continue the mission of Jesus to the whole world.

They are not necessarily closer to Jesus because of their mission.
Only one of them will remain with Jesus at the cross.
It is Mary of Magdala, not Peter,
who will be the first to see the risen Jesus.
All the disciples of Jesus are called to live his message.
Each one has his or her specific mission, hidden or visible;
each one is called to be with Jesus in a particular way,
according to his or her call.

To follow Jesus

This gospel begins with two disciples following Jesus
and it ends with Jesus saying to Peter, "Follow me."
They are called to learn from him
to discover little by little who he is,
his vision of love,
and who *they* are.
They do not always know where he is leading them
but they trust him
and walk with him.
We, too, are called to follow Jesus
day by day,
not always knowing where he will lead us
but trusting in him, seeking to become like him.

In Greek the word "*to follow*" not only means
"*to walk in the footsteps*" of a master
but also *to accompany*, to *be with*.
For the moment, these five men are called to be disciples of Jesus;
later, Jesus will call them "friends."
The prophets of Israel were chosen by God and sent out immediately.
Their call was to be sent.
Their mission was clear from the beginning.
But for these five men it is not so.
Jesus wants first of all to form their hearts and minds and attitudes
so that they become good servant-leaders.

We know, however, the difficulties and dangers for those of us
who carry any responsibility.
We can get caught up in our own need for spiritual power,
seeking to protect ourselves.
We so easily forget the compassion and humility of Jesus.
That is why, before sending forth these men,
Jesus wants them to *be with* him,
to *dwell with* him and become his friends
so that they do not so much announce a theology or a doctrine
but *a person: Jesus.*
A person they love,
a person with whom they have a living relationship,
a person who is transforming their lives.

Jesus spent about thirty years living the good news
in Nazareth with Mary and Joseph before announcing it.
We too are called to live and be with Jesus before speaking about him.
But how can we speak of him if we do not know him personally?

The gospel of growth

In this chapter of the Gospel of John,
Jesus gathers around him a little group.
This is the beginning of their journey with Jesus.
It begins with enthusiasm: they have found the Messiah,
the "one who was to come" to liberate their people.
This enthusiasm grows as Jesus does wonderful things.
They believe in him more and more.
He is truly the Messiah.
Many of us live this enthusiasm
when we begin in a community and with friends to follow Jesus.
We give ourselves to an ideal.
We admire our leaders
and we want to become like them.
This is the period of childhood in our spiritual journey.
Later we will experience all that is broken in our community,
in the church and in us.

We will live conflicts and opposition.
We will discover that it is not going to be easy to live the ideal.
We will have to struggle to be truthful and free
and to be servant-leaders like Jesus.
We have to grow from spiritual childhood and adolescence
to spiritual maturity,
and discover the presence of God in the pain of reality.
Later, as we move into old age,
we will encounter physical weakness and even failure.
Like Jesus, and with Jesus, we will be called to enter
into the pits of pain, failure and rejection
and into a new communication with God.
We will discover the weakness and foolishness of God.

The journey is just beginning for the first disciples.
So, too, we are called to begin a journey of faith
with Jesus.

4

A wedding feast

John 2:1-12

*Jesus reveals
that our final destiny
is love
and that we are all called
to a wonderful
sacred wedding feast.*

*But to live this celebration
the waters of our humanity
have to be transformed into
the new wine of divine love.*

Jesus, the Lamb of God, brings his disciples to a wedding feast

The very first thing the Lamb of God does in this gospel
is to choose five companions or disciples from Galilee,
where he lived, had his home and was well known.
These Jewish men were destined to be sent out
to the four corners of the world
to announce the love of God revealed in Jesus.
They did not have any special education,
but were open and well disposed.
Some of them had been awoken in their faith and hope
by John the Baptizer
and were waiting for the Messiah
who would liberate them from the yoke of the Romans,
who were the masters of the world.

One could imagine that Jesus would have wanted
to give these men a spiritual and intellectual formation,
especially since they would be called to assume an important role
in the future.
It would have been normal for Jesus to take time with them,
to share and pray with them,
to bring them into the desert for a spiritual experience,
or to a school to deepen their knowledge
of the Torah, the scriptures and the prophets.
But where does Jesus take them first of all?
To a magnificent celebration, a wedding feast in Cana of Galilee!
It is there that they begin their journey of faith.
At that time, wedding feasts lasted about a week.
In Aramaic, the word for "wedding feast"
has the same roots as the word "drink,"
a sign that it was a time of great revelry and rejoicing.
People would come from near and far to meet friends
and family members.
Weddings were great occasions for a huge family
and village gathering.

Weddings are a wonderful human reality.
People dress up in their best clothes, they rejoice, sing, dance,
joke, laugh and have fun together.
And so Jesus plunges his new disciples
into the fullness of their humanity.
I cannot imagine Jesus sitting alone with a serious face,
talking quietly with just one or two people,
or just coming in at the last moment to perform a miracle.
Instead, I see him as a part of the celebration,
singing with everybody else, rejoicing in the festivity,
profoundly happy to celebrate with people he knows and loves.
He is especially present to the poorest, the weakest
and the loneliest of those who are there.
Jesus is so beautifully human!
Jesus is celebrating because a wedding is a celebration of love.
And Jesus has come to reveal, strengthen and deepen love.
For Jesus, marriage is not a prison of wearisome fidelity,
but the sign of a sacred union, enfolded in love,
that enables people to grow in forgiveness, tenderness,
kindness and compassion.
For some today who are not officially or legally married,
they still discover that their union is sacred.
It is a covenant of love.

In this story of the wedding feast in Cana,
Jesus is going to perform a miracle:
he is going to change water into wine.
Some people today may snicker and laugh at such an idea.
Changing water into wine!
How many would love to have Jesus around all the time
to change water into alcohol!
May I ask you for a moment to suspend disbelief
and not let the miracle undermine your understanding
of the depth of what is being revealed to us in this story.

Aren't many of us caught up in weary lives of work,
needing to find the stimulation of alcohol
and the distraction of television
to help us forget the dreariness of life when we return home?
Water is "dailiness," but wine is for rejoicing.
If we have seen religion as something dreary,
we will have difficulty imagining Jesus
changing dreariness into fullness of joy.
Aren't we all seeking this miracle?
Behind this event in Cana, Jesus is offering in the form of a symbol
a transformation from the drudgery of duty to a new passion of love.

There is no more wine

Yet, in the middle of all the festivities
there is a moment of crisis and panic.
There is no more wine!
What a terrible humiliation for the two families of the married couple
to be unable to provide enough wine for their guests.
It seems that the mother of Jesus is at the wedding
more as a helper than as an invited guest.
She plays an important role in this story;
her name comes up three times.
When she sees the humiliation of the wedding couple
and their families,
she is moved by compassion, and says to Jesus:

> *"They have no more wine."*

Jesus knows immediately what that means for these poor people,
but he is seemingly not ready to do anything about it.

> *"Woman," he says to his mother,*
> *"what is there between you and me?"*

This is a Semitic way of expressing a refusal to act.
And he adds:

> *"My hour has not yet come."*   vv. 3-4

This event is the first great event of the public life of Jesus
in the Gospel of John.
It has great significance.
Mary, interceding for the poor and the humiliated,
is present at the beginning of his public life,
just as she will be present at the end, at the cross,
where Jesus once again will call her *"Woman,"* a sign of respect.

His apparent refusal brings forth in Mary a gesture and words
which seem not to heed the refusal.
She goes to the servants and tells them:

> *"Do whatever he tells you."*   vv. 9-10

She has total confidence in Jesus.
She knows his love for the weak and the poor.
She knows he will do something.
So perhaps the apparent refusal of Jesus to Mary –

> *"What is there between you and me?"* –

has some deeper meaning.
Maybe Jesus is saying that now he must leave Nazareth
and be separated from her
in order to announce his message of love throughout Israel.
It is a new stage in his life as well as in hers.
But it will lead to his being rejected
and put to death,
at the "hour" of the cross, where the new wine of divine love
will be poured out,
and again she will be present.

Water transformed into wine

Jesus tells the servants to fill six huge jars with water.
These jars were used for the rituals of purification
and each contained a hundred litres or more.
This must have taken some time and many buckets of water.
Then Jesus tells them to draw the water

and bring it to the chief steward.
What faith and trust those servants – surely simple, humble folk –
had in Jesus.
It must have seemed crazy to them to take "water"
to the chief steward.
Imagine their surprise when they discover it is wine!
Jesus uses the faith of humble people to do beautiful things.

> *When the chief steward tasted the water that had become wine,*
> *and did not know where it had come from*
> *(although the servants who had drawn the water knew),*
> *the steward called the bridegroom and said:*
> *"Everyone serves the good wine at first*
> *and the inferior wine after the guests have become a bit drunk.*
> *But you have kept the good wine until now.*

An incredible amount of wine is presented,
an abundance of excellent wine: hundreds of litres of it!
And people had already drunk quite a bit!
Today, we humans would be more prudent…perhaps.
However, God does things abundantly.
God loves us abundantly
and wants to give us more and more life and joy.
God is continually and unendingly pouring out love and light to us,
stretching our being
so that we can receive always more, infinitely more….

The abundance of wine was a sign
that the Messianic time had arrived.
That is why the prophet Amos had cried out:

> *Behold the days are coming, says the Lord,*
> *when the mountains shall drip sweet wine*
> *and all the hills shall drip sweet wine.*
> *I will restore the fortunes of my people Israel*
> *and they shall rebuild the ruined cities and inhabit them.*
> *They shall plant vineyards and drink their wine.*   *Amos 9:13-14*

Our final destiny: to live the eternal wedding feast of love

In his gospel, John wants to reveal to each of us in a special way
the significance of this wedding feast,
so he leads us gradually towards it.
He begins with John the Baptizer and the act of baptizing.
Then, *the next day,* John the Baptizer sees Jesus and says:

> *"Behold the Lamb of God."*   *v. 29*

Then again the next day the two disciples begin to follow Jesus,
the "Lamb."   *v. 35*
Then again the next day Jesus goes to Galilee.   *v. 43*
Four days.
And then at the beginning of this chapter we read,

> *"On the third day."*

So this situates the wedding day on the seventh day.
Of course "the third day" is a symbol of the resurrection.
It was on the third day that Jesus rose from the dead.

This "third day" was prefigured in the prophet Hosea:

> *Come let us return to the Lord*
> *for it is he who has torn and he will heal us;*
> *he has struck down and he will bind us up.*
> *After two days he will revive us;*
> *on the third day, he will raise us up*
> *that we may live before him.*   *Hos 6:1-2*

These six days leading up to the wedding feast
echo the six days of creation.
The seventh day is the day of fulfillment;

> *On the seventh day, God finished the work he had done*
> *And he rested on the seventh day from all the work he had done.*
> *So God blessed the seventh day and hallowed it*
> *because on it God rested*
> *from all the work he had done in creation.*   *Gen 2:2-3*

"The seventh day" echoes the final day when God will be all in all,
and we will rise up in his glorious presence
and be held in his intimate love.
This day will be the revelation of the wedding feast of the Lamb,
to which we are all invited
and which is announced in the last book of the Bible.

> *Then I heard what seemed to be the voice of a great multitude,*
> *like the sound of many waters and like the sound of mighty*
> *thunderous crying, "Halleluiah! For the Lord our God,*
> *the Almighty reigns.*
> *Let us rejoice and exult and give him glory, for the marriage of*
> *the lamb has come and his bride has made herself ready."*
> *And the angels said to me, "Write this:*
> *'Blessed are those who are invited*
> *to the wedding feast of the lamb. '"* Rev 19:6-9

The very last words of the Bible are

> *"The Spirit and the Bride say 'come'!*
> *Come, Lord Jesus!"* Rev 19:17, 20

It is the cry of humanity yearning for the promised fulfillment of love.
Our final destiny is the marriage feast of the Lamb of God.
John the Baptizer had pointed to Jesus and prophesied:

> *"He who is with the bride is the bridegroom;*
> *the friend of the bridegroom, who stands and hears him,*
> *greatly rejoices at the bridegroom's voice.*
> *Therefore this joy of mine is now full."* Jn 3:29

In one of his parables,
Jesus says that the kingdom of God is like a wedding feast
where those who were invited, people well positioned in society,
refused to come.
They were too busy with their short-term projects. *cf. Mt 22:2*
The rest of the parable, as shown in Luke's gospel *Lk 14:15 ff.*
is very significant for us in l'Arche and in Faith and Light.

The master of the household is terribly upset.
He tells the servants to go out onto the highways and byways
and to bring in "all the poor, the lame, the disabled and the blind."
They, of course, hungry and thirsty for relationship,
affirmation and food,
come running to the banquet of love!
How difficult it is for those who thrive on success,
admiration and power to accept the invitation.
They have no time.
Those who are rejected have time on their hands.
They are not yearning for success but for love and community.

How is it, then, that a wedding feast symbolizes
the kingdom of God?
At the time of Jesus,
a wedding was an immense celebration of unity.
It still is so today in many cultures and for many people,
although for some it has lost its symbolism and meaning.
For many, marriage is seen solely as a legal contract
and not as the sign of man and woman celebrating their unity.
The wedding feast is the sign of communion
between man and woman who give themselves to each other
in their littleness, vulnerability and humility.
It is a promise of fidelity over time, until death:
the place of our final nakedness.
They are secure in their commitment to each other.
In this way, the wedding feast is a taste and sign of eternity,
a sign of the covenant that bonds God to his people.
Did not God create man and woman,
through their love for one another,
to be the image of the Trinity: Father, Son and Holy Spirit
and to give life to their children through this love?

Even as this desire for a covenant of love
still exists today for many people,
there is a fleeting suspicion that long-term fidelity
is unlikely and in danger.

Wedding celebrations are now often clouded
by the spectre of easy divorce.
Something has gone wrong; the initial symbol has been destroyed.
In all cultures, over and over again,
the equality of the love
of man and woman
has been radically hurt by men's need to dominate
and to use a woman as a sexual servant.
She has not always been seen as the beloved, a beloved friend.

But Jesus came to renew all things,
to change our broken humanity into a new unity
as he changed the water into wine.
If he brings the disciples first of all to a wedding feast,
it is not only to affirm the importance and beauty
of the bonding of man and woman in the oneness
of human sexuality,
but also to reveal to his disciples and to each one of us
the deepest thirst in us: our desire and need to love and be loved.

The need to be loved

This is the deepest yearning within each one of us,
deeper even than our need to appear strong and powerful,
or to have a spiritual consciousness of self,
a feeling of the infinite within us.
Aristotle says that when people do not feel loved,
they seek to be admired.
Those who work in the field of publicity and public relations
know well this deep yearning for love and unity.
They use images of beautiful women and strong, handsome men
to sell cars or to draw people to a particular bank.
Our thirst for love, to be "beloved," can be easily diverted
and become perverse through a world of fantasies and images.
We are all more or less broken and wounded in our affections
and in our capacity to relate.

We want a unity of love but are frightened of commitment
and even of relationship.
Our sexual desires can be cut off from committed relationship.
It is as if anguish is planted in our sexuality,
a sexuality that seems to have lost its meaning
and can become a game
where one person – or both – lose.

Many people today find true, rewarding love,
yet others are frustrated in love.
Many people with disabilities cannot live a deep, intimate,
faithful relationship in marriage.
Other people have known painful, broken relationships.
For many, marriage has ended in divorce.
Some seem unable to find the right partner for their lives.
For others, sexual relationships are a continual search
for a fulfillment they seem unable to find,
because they are frightened of commitment
and afraid of true, healing relationships.
So many people are caught up in a terrible loneliness,
a feeling of not being loveable.
They live in unresolved anguish, feeling guilty for existing.

A journey of hope

Jesus leading his disciples to this wedding feast is our hope.
He is leading us all to this final, wonderful celebration of love.
Our desire for love is not a hoax,
awakening in us a thirst for an unattainable, infinite, eternal love
that can be quickly crushed by the limits and brokenness in us all.
We are not cheated of love; love is possible.
In changing the water into wine,
Jesus reveals that he wants to change
the waters of our broken humanity into the joys of wine – today!
In order to be able to do this, Jesus needs our co-operation,
just as he needed the faith, trust and hard work of those servants

who filled the six jars to the brim with water.
He needs our trust and our belief.
He needs us to work at this inner transformation
and to live our humanity to the brim.
The "eternal" wedding feast into which Jesus is bringing us
is not just the ecstasy that we will live after death;
this eternal wedding feast can begin as we enter today
into a personal relationship of trust and of friendship with Jesus.
This can gradually grow and deepen into a song of songs
where we discover we are beloved of Jesus. He is our beloved.

Let us celebrate life

If this gospel begins with a beautiful, marvellous
and very human celebration
where there is song, laughter and wine,
isn't it also to remind us of the importance of meals and celebrations
in our lives?

Religion is not just "serious" business, doing good, learning theology,
carrying out our duty, separating ourselves from greed.
The heart of the religion of Jesus is relationship, celebration
and communion in the joy of love.
We human beings are made for celebration.
Isn't the Eucharist the place of such celebration,
communion and togetherness?

"Dailiness" can often become drudgery; there is work to be done.
But there are also meal times, leisure hours,
when we come together not to *do* or *produce* things,
but to *be* together, to celebrate our friendship.
Today many of us have experiences of parties
where we can drink a lot, maybe even too much.
But we can forget what a real celebration is.
A celebration is a moment of the fulfillment of joy,
a deeply human time,

where we give thanks to God for having brought us
out of the depths of loneliness
and into togetherness: community and faithful friendship.
We celebrate our bonding.
We reveal to each person their value and importance –
particularly to those who are weaker, more fragile, more vulnerable
because of their age, sickness or disability.
Sunday as a day of rest is a day for celebration
and for deepening relationships.
Throughout the year we celebrate special days:
birthdays, anniversaries, Christmas, Easter, births and even deaths.
We are called to live these special days as times when
the God of love and of joy is present to us, calling us to a greater hope
of the final celebration to come.
We are all made for happiness and a fullness of joy.

Permit me to tell you a story that illustrates this special time.
A community of l'Arche was founded in Kerala, India,
twenty-five years ago.
Ramesh, a young Hindu man with intellectual and psychological
difficulties, was one of the first men welcomed.
A few months ago, he went to his brother's place for a couple of days.
When he left his brother's house, he said to him and to the
neighbours and friends:
"Today is my wedding day. Come!"
People just smiled at him.
He got on the bus and when he arrived back in the community,
he told the community leader: "Today is my wedding day!"
He went to the workshop for awhile, but was feeling a bit tired.
He went to his bedroom to lie down, had a heart attack and died.
"Today is my wedding day!"
Yes, it truly was the day of his wedding feast!

5

Is the world only a marketplace?

John 2:13-22

Jesus reveals to us
that his body
is the dwelling place of God
where we can find life.

But we often seek life
in the culture of money
and forget
that we too
are the dwelling place of God.

In his Father's house

The first place Jesus visits when he goes to Jerusalem
is the Temple, the "house of his Father."
For the Jewish people, the Temple
is the sign of the presence of God:
God's "dwelling place" among them.

But what does Jesus find in the Temple?

> *people selling cattle, sheep and doves*
> *and money changers sitting at their tables.*

People had changed his Father's house into a place of commerce!
Jesus was enraged:

> *making a whip of cords, he drove them out of the temple,*
> *both the sheep and the cattle.*
> *He overturned the tables of the money changers*
> *and threw out the coins.*   *vv. 14-15*

Jesus was fulfilling the prophecy of Malachi:

> *I send my messenger to prepare the way before me,*
> *and the Lord whom you seek will suddenly come to the Temple....*
> *He will purify the sins of Levi and refine them like gold and silver*
> *until they present right offerings to the Lord.*   *Mal 3:1-3*

Instead of worshipping God, people were making an idol of money.
They were selling animals for sacrifice at an unjust price.
The money changers were taking a big commission,
impoverishing those who were already quite poor
because of the temple tax they had to pay
with temple money, not Roman money.
Isn't this thirst for money at the heart of so many injustices
in our world?
Money brings power and power brings money.
People, even children, can be used as slaves,
exploited by money-makers,
ruining their health and lives.

Civil wars and conflicts are so often caused
by the desire for greater wealth.
Money beguiles and can even seduce in the name of "doing good."
In Matthew's gospel, Jesus says that we cannot serve two masters:
God and money;

> *we will either hate the one and love the other*
> *or we will be devoted to one and despise the other.*   Mt 6:24

Today we are surrounded by a particular culture of money.
Instead of using money as a means to help people to grow
and have access to essential cultural goods,
money has become an end in itself.
In the business world some years ago,
people spoke about ethical trading
and the "just" or "fair" price of goods.
Now the price of goods is "whatever sells" –
and if the profits are greater, so much the better!

The threat of today's world
with its globalized economy is not just unfettered capitalism
but overwhelming commercialization.
Advertising and public relations try to shape our cultures,
thoughts, imaginations and lives.
Seductive and closely studied images and clichés,
which seem to awaken in people chaotic elements of sexuality,
violence and a thirst for power, are being used to sell goods.
The mission statement of one corporation
affirms that they should evoke the desire and need for
"non-essential things: easy to use, hard to resist."
Corporations do not try to sell what is best for people,
for their growth to maturity and to greater humaneness.
They sell whatever will make more money,
what will give the corporations and their shareholders
more benefits…
more, more, more….

Commercial television is similarly in the hands of big corporations
that offer security and the promise of instant happiness.
Advertisers are trained to use psychological techniques
in order to create even more consumers
willing to spend even more of their money.
No wonder there is so much cynicism and corruption
in the world of commerce, industry and politics –
even in those who are officially called to oversee, control
and verify the accounts of corporations.

Huge shopping centres,
however convenient they may be for people
to save them time and money,
seduce people to keep buying more than they actually need.
They are replacing churches and temples
as the places where people gather together.

It is greed and rampant consumption that have led to
the destruction of important species of
animals, insects, birds, fish and plants
that are necessary for people's health and for the delicate balance
of climate and the welfare of our beautiful planet.

Money has become the focus of cultures worldwide.
It is being used to cultivate an acute individualism:
"wealth, all the signs of wealth, houses, cars, gadgets,
for *me* and for *my* family and *my* group!"
If money was better distributed,
if we sought to use it to bring greater justice and peace
to other people,
our world could become a better place.
Misdirected and misspent, it fuels greater injustices,
conflicts and destructiveness.

At the beginning of the Gospel of John
we see Jesus celebrating a very human reality:
a wedding feast, a celebration of love.
Now he reminds us of the danger of worshipping
money and commerce.

Jesus reveals that his body is the new Temple of God

We can imagine the commotion, the screaming,
the noise of the animals,
the sound of money falling to the ground
as Jesus chases the animals out of the Temple.
The money changers and those trying to hold on to their animals
shout in fury.
The whole place is in chaos!
Jesus with a whip, filled with the "zeal of his Father's house,"
cannot bear to see this holy place –
where the Jewish people were called to listen to God
and be faithful to God's covenant of love –
turned into a place of commerce.

In their resentment, the merchants and money changers
rush to find the Temple priests.
The priests want to know what right Jesus has
to make such a commotion.
With what authority is he acting like this?

> *"What sign can you show us for doing this?"*
> *Jesus answers: "Destroy this sanctuary*
> *and in three days I will raise it up!"*
> *"This sanctuary has been under construction for forty-six years,*
> *and you will raise it up in three days?"*
> *they responded mockingly.*   *vv. 18-20*

Then John gives us the clue to understand Jesus:

> *He was speaking of the sanctuary of his body.*   *v. 21*

The disciples will come to an understanding
of the meaning of these words
but not until after the resurrection,
when the body of Jesus will rise up on the third day after his death.
Jesus is shifting the conversation from the sacredness of the Temple
to the sacredness of his own body.

He is revealing something totally new.
The Temple of Jerusalem is, and always will be, a place of holiness.
Now his body, his very being, is the new Temple,
the place of holiness where God dwells.
Jesus is indicating that life and love and healing and forgiveness
will flow from him, through his body,
his broken and risen body,
for he is the Word-made-flesh
as was prophesied by Ezekiel,
who saw life-giving and healing waters
flowing abundantly out of the new Temple.   *cf. Ez 47:9-11*
Jesus is at the centre of this new way of life
that he has come to bring.
God has become one of us through the body of Jesus.
God is no longer far off in the heavens,
symbolized by the great beauty and majesty
of the Temple of Jerusalem.
God has pitched his tent among us.
God is a fellow pilgrim, with all the vulnerability of a human being,
walking through the desert of life with us.
This new sanctuary is not made of precious stones
but of flesh and blood,
which permit a meeting, a presence to people
and a presence that will be relationship,
a communion of hearts,
a community.

Our bodies are the Temple of God

Jesus, hurt and angered by the desecration of the Temple of Jerusalem,
"his Father's house," is also crying out
against the desecration of the temple of our own bodies.

We human beings are also called to be the home,
the dwelling place, of God.
In this gospel Jesus says that if we keep and love his words,
he and the Father will come and dwell in us.
Paul says:

> *Do you not know that your body is a temple of the Holy Spirit*
> *within you and which you have received from God?...*
> *So, glorify God in your body.*   *1 Cor 6:19*

Etty Hillesum, a young Jewish woman in Holland
who was later gassed by the Nazis in Auschwitz,
had a deep sense of the value of each person as the "home" of God.
At one time, when she was in Westerbork,
waiting with other Jews for their final hour of deportation
to Auschwitz,
she wrote that her only desire was to help people to discover
the treasure of their personhood,
that each person is called to be the "home of God":

> And I promise you, yes I promise you, my God, that I shall try to
> find a "home" and a roof for you in as many houses as possible.
> There are so many empty houses, where I will bring you in as
> guest of honour.

Today we seem to have lost a sense of the role and place of our bodies.
Many of us are not aware of the sacred space within us,
the place where we can reflect and contemplate,
the space from which wonderment can flow
as we look at the mountains, the sky,
the flowers, the fruits and all that is beautiful in our universe,
the space where we can contemplate works of art.

This place, which is the deepest in us all,
is the place of our very personhood,
the place of inner peace where God dwells
and where we receive the light of life and the murmurings
of the Spirit of God.
It is the place in which we make life choices
and from which flows our love for others.

As our societies become noisier and busier,
we may forget this silent, sacred space within us.
It can be desecrated.
It becomes like a marketplace, a shopping centre,
invaded by superficial needs and all kinds of trivialities.
But even worse, we can desecrate the bodies of others.
We no longer see them as a sacred dwelling place of God
calling us to deep respect,
but rather as objects of desire and fantasy,
as commodities to be bought.

And as we treat others, so do we treat our mother earth.
The earth entrusted to us as a home,
given to us to cultivate and to make more beautiful,
is being desecrated through greed.
In his Prologue, John tells us that the "Word is hidden in creation.
Creation is also the Temple of God.

The pain in the heart of Jesus
as he saw the Temple of Jerusalem turned into a marketplace
is the same today
as he sees hearts and bodies that have become like a marketplace,
that are no longer a source of life and of love for others.

Conflict between Temple and mercy

In Jewish history, the story of the Temple of Jerusalem
is both beautiful and sad.
At times, rituals and external worship, even theological discussions,
took precedence over the love of God and works of mercy.
The Temple became defiled; the sacrifices emptied.
The prophet Jeremiah raved against such situations:

> *Do not trust in these deceptive words:*
> *'This is the Temple of the Lord,*
> *the Temple of the Lord, the Temple of the Lord.'*
> *For if you truly amend your ways and your doings,*
> *if you truly act justly with another,*
> *if you do not oppress the alien, the orphan,*
> *the widow or shed innocent blood,*
> *then I will dwell with you in this place....*   *Jer 7:4-7*

God cannot bear rituals that are empty acts,
that do not flow from the heart.
That is why Isaiah told the people, and tells us all,
that the fasting and rituals that please God are those when we
loose the bonds of injustice, liberate the oppressed,
share our bread with the hungry,
and bring the homeless poor into our home.   *Is 58:6-7*
In Matthew's gospel, Jesus cites the prophet Hosea,
who cried out on behalf of God:

> *I desire mercy and not sacrifice.*   *Hos 6:6*

The same is true in the history of Christianity,
when people want to worship God in their church on Sunday
but do not share their bread or their love
with the needy and the lonely.

Church is the place where,
in the midst of the demands of our daily lives,
we can come together with others, as a community of believers,
to a place of silence, our inner sanctuary,
to listen to the word of God, to hear the murmurings of the Spirit
and to welcome into our being the presence of
the Word-made-flesh, Jesus.
As we welcome Jesus and become one with him,
we seek to welcome each other
and together to go forth
to welcome others,
revealing to them the compassion and forgiveness of God.

6

Born in the Spirit

John 3:1-21

To live the message of this gospel
we must be reborn in the Holy Spirit.

Then we begin to grow in a relationship of trust
with Jesus
and to love people as God loves them.

Open to a new love

The Gospel of John introduces a question
that is pertinent for us all.
We all need security,
and yet to be fully alive we also need to take risks.
Too much security stifles us,
while too much insecurity brings fear and anguish.
How can we plan for the future and yet be open to the unforeseen?

While Jesus was in Jerusalem,
Nicodemus, one of the religious leaders, a Pharisee,
came to him *"at night."*
The evangelist mentions *"at night"* probably to signify
that Nicodemus was in the dark,
afraid that other religious leaders might know about this visit.
Perhaps some of them were already getting upset about Jesus' activities
and the miracles he was accomplishing.

Nicodemus is sure of himself. He *knows.*
He is a leader and is secure behind his power and certitudes.
He is a bit like the priests and Levites
sent by the authorities in Jerusalem
to investigate John the Baptizer:
Nicodemus wants to make a judgment about Jesus.
He begins the conversation with respect, but as a man in authority:

> *"Rabbi, we know you are a teacher who has come from God;*
> *for no one can do the miracles that you do*
> *unless God is with him."*   *v. 2*

In the face of these certitudes, Jesus is going to lead Nicodemus
into another way of *being and living*.
He replies in an ambiguous way:

> *"Truly, truly, I tell you no one can see the Kingdom of God*
> *without being born from above."*   *v. 3*

In a very Semitic way, Nicodemus replies by asking a question:

> *"How can anyone be born after having grown old?*
> *Can one enter a second time into our mother's womb*
> *and be born?"*   *v. 4*

Jesus repeats:

> *"Truly, truly, I tell you, no one can enter the kingdom of God*
> *without being born of water and the Spirit....*
>
> *"Do not be astonished that I said to you,*
> *'you must be born from above.'*
> *The wind blows where it chooses*
> *and you hear the sound of it,*
> *but you do not know where it comes from*
> *or where it goes.*
> *So it is with everyone who is born of the Spirit."*   *vv. 5, 6-8*

In the face of the certitudes, the *"we know"* of Nicodemus,
Jesus proposes another way:
the way of *"not knowing,"*
of being born from "above."
That means becoming like a child again, a child of God,
a new person,
listening to the Spirit of God and letting ourselves
be guided by the Spirit.

Isn't this desire to be born again in many of us?
Don't we often want to start anew,
to leave behind past hurts, habits and old ways
that imprison us in the values of our society
and prevent us from growing towards greater freedom?
The message of Jesus is about transformation.

Intuition and reason

Ever since we were young, we have been taught to be autonomous,
and to work towards independence.
We have been taught to be competent
and to plan our way through life,
sometimes with clear moral and religious certitudes.
Such certitude gives security.
We are encouraged to take control of things
and have power over our lives,
and this is both important and necessary.
However, Jesus is affirming a new path that implies risk,
insecurity and vulnerability.
It implies intuition and trust more than reason.

Once, a television reporter asked me how I knew
that I should leave the navy and follow Jesus,
how I knew that my vocation was to live with people with disabilities.
I surprised him by asking in reply, "Are you married?"
He seemed embarrassed by the tables being turned
and by my questioning him.
To ease the situation I followed by asking another question:
"Why did you ask this particular woman to be your wife?"
He was still a bit confused.
I told him, "There are moments in our lives
when we do not reason things out,
we just know in our heart of hearts that this or that
is the right thing to do."

There is such a thing as *intuition*.
We feel or sense things. They are not planned.
That is where the Spirit intervenes,
inspiring us to say or do things we had not planned.
Paul, in his letter to the Galatians, gives us some guidelines:

> **Walk in the Spirit and do not gratify the desires of the flesh....**

The fruit of the Spirit is love, joy, peace, patience, kindness
goodness, faithfulness, gentleness, self-control;
against such, there is no law.   *Gal 5:16, 22-23*

The Spirit calls us to follow Jesus more totally
and to become like him.
The Spirit calls us to live in communion with God
and with each other.
We do not always know where she is leading us.
We cannot control the Spirit, we must let ourselves be guided by her.
This can lead us to take risks,
sometimes even to risk the disapproval of our family
or our Church authorities.

God intervenes in our lives precisely when we open up
and let God show us the way.
It is into the place of our poverty and insecurity that God comes.
It is when we do not know what to do and ask God for light
that God gives us light.

Every time we enter into a relationship,
we take a risk.
Love is the gift of self to another.
We have no certitude of how everything will turn out,
whether we ourselves or the other will remain a faithful friend.
When we enter into a relationship with a person who is fragile,
wounded or with disabilities, who is in dire need,
we do not know where that relationship will lead us.
When we love, we accept not to control another;
we become vulnerable.
That is why it is important to discern with a holy, wise person
whether a certain gesture or activity, plan or inner experience
is from God
rather than just something springing from our own need or desire
to prove ourselves or to feel important.

God is not only leading and guiding us individually,
God is leading us *with* others in community, and in church.
God is guiding the Church and humanity as a whole,
just as God led the Israelites through the desert.
The pillar of fire shone through the night
and the pillar of cloud led them through the day.
Today, however, the pillar of fire is less visible;
it is hidden in people's hearts.
That is why we need to discern with others
what God is saying to our world and to our churches today.
Where is God leading us?
Where should we put our energies today
so that the God of peace may be revealed?

Some cultural and economic certitudes
contained in our liberal economies,
which encourage greed, individualism
and the concentration of power,
have to be challenged when over half the planet lives in dire poverty
while others live in luxury.
Certain ecclesial structures that strengthen clerical power
are also called to evolve under the inspiration of the Spirit
in order to discover the Church as a body.
We all need to move in the direction of the gentle wind of God.

Certitudes and risk

Nicodemus had certitudes. He knew the law.
Clearly, theological certitudes and laws are important and necessary.
We need to know Scripture.
We need a community of faith, a place of belonging.
We need church.
We need teachers.
We need a vision that flows from those of the past who have lived
and loved Jesus.
All this gives us a solid foundation

that enables us to love in truth
and to live a deep spiritual and mystical life.

But certitudes and law can also close us up in ourselves
in the self-satisfaction of knowledge,
of feeling righteous and superior.
They can prevent us from listening to people,
and being open to new ways of God.
They can wound the childlike attitudes of wonderment
and stifle the longing for the Spirit.
Those who live only out of certitudes and the law,
who hide behind the law,
tend to control others,
fearing that all that is "new" will lead to a loss of control.
They fear change and risk stifling the Spirit
in their own hearts and in the hearts of others.
Certitudes and power are seductive.
They give security and a feeling of existing, even an identity;
we are *someone* if we have certitudes and power.

On the other hand, some people want to prove that they are free,
which for them means being able to do whatever they want,
regardless of the impact it might have on others
and on their deeper self.
They want to act without any reference to the word of God
or to a community of believers
or without any true, wise vision of what it means to be human.
Some can even see their freedom as the freedom to transgress the law,
to shock people in order to prove that they are someone.

True freedom needs to be rooted firmly in faith,
in the word of God,
in community.
It implies humility and a submission to God and to truth.
It implies help from others
as we discover together what is from God.

This gospel reveals the tension that exists between
certitudes and power on one side,
and littleness, openness and love on the other;
between being a teacher who knows
and being a disciple who is open and searching.
The answer Jesus gives us is this:
We cannot be good shepherds and teachers
unless we are reborn in the Spirit
and allow ourselves to be led by God,
open to the new ways of God and truly open to people.
This means that we are dying to our own ego
and our need to be in control,
but also to our need to rebel and prove ourselves.

How is this new birth going to come about?

Nicodemus, this Jewish teacher who is
sure of himself and of his theology,
now opens up humbly and asks Jesus:

> *"How is this to be?"*   *v. 9*

Jesus is shocked at his question:

> *"Are you a teacher in Israel*
> *and yet you do not understand these things?"*   *v. 10*

Had not all the great Hebrew prophets announced
the gift of the Spirit of God
that would renew people and change their hearts?

This gift of the Spirit and of life announced by the prophets
is often symbolized by water.
Water cleanses, purifies and gives life.
The prophet Ezekiel saw the waters flowing
from the New Temple, healing and giving life,   *Ez 47:9-12*
and in the name of God he announced:

I will sprinkle clean water upon you
and you shall be cleansed from all your uncleanliness
and from all your idols I will cleanse you.
A new heart I will give you
and a new spirit I will put within you
and I will remove from your body the heart of stone
and give you a heart of flesh. *Ez 36:25-26*

The prophet Joel had announced that the Spirit of God
would be poured out –
not just on the religious leaders, prophets and theologians,
but on all the people. *Jo 2:28*

How could Nicodemus forget all the promises of God
revealed through the prophets?
What made him cling to human religious ways
and theological certitudes
devoid of the wind, of the breath, of the Spirit,
and made him blind to the new ways of God?
What makes us blind to the ways of God and to the new?
What makes us cling desperately to our own ideas and plans,
to legal forms of religion devoid of life?
These are the same things that make us hold on to
the values of society,
to the idols of power, competition and money,
and that prevent us from discovering alternative ways of living
and struggling for greater justice in the world.

A new gift

Jesus reveals that it is he who has come
to fulfill the promised word of God
announced by the prophets.
It is he who will give us this new life in the Spirit.
Baptized in water and the Spirit, reborn,

we enter into the kingdom of God
and become children of God like him.
We become part of a new people: the people of God, the Church.
Little by little we are cleansed of our blocks and our sinfulness.
We are called to let go gradually of old ways, certitudes and securities,
to die to self-centred needs,
in order to live by the Spirit of Jesus
and become men and women of compassion.
Together we are called to work for peace,
in community and as church.

Through our trust in Jesus we will be reborn in the Spirit

In this meeting with Nicodemus, Jesus refers to himself as
the one who has descended from heaven: the Son of Man.
He reveals that *we will live* if we look at him and believe in him
when he is lifted up on the cross,
just as Moses promised the Israelites bitten by serpents
that they would live if they looked at the bronze serpent
set on a pole.   *cf. Num 21:9*

> *No one has ascended into heaven*
> *but he who descended from heaven, the Son of Man.*
> *And as Moses lifted up the serpent in the desert*
> *so must the Son of Man be lifted up*
> *so that whoever believes in him may have eternal life.*   *vv. 13-14*

It will be through our belief and trust in Jesus
that we receive the gift of eternal life
and are born "from above," in the Spirit.

Trust

I like to think of Antonio, a young man with profound disabilities.
He could not walk, talk or use his hands.
He came to our community after twenty years in hospital.
He had accepted his disabilities in a beautiful way.
His face shone with peace and joy,
except at times when he felt lonely or upset.
He showed incredible trust in the assistants
who cared for him, who gave him his bath, who fed him.
His way of showing love was not through generous gifts
but through his marvellous trust, which grew little by little.

There are different forms of trust
and different levels in the depths of trust.
There is the trust children have in their parents or teachers,
the trust between a patient and a doctor,
the trust of a congregation in its church leader,
the trust among friends,
the trust between lovers, the trust between an elderly married couple.

Trust is a dynamic relationship that grows and evolves.
It is an openness to another.
It is a gift of self.
Trust can begin quite naturally:
when we are attracted to someone, we become friends.
Then something happens.
The other person is not what we originally thought.
We don't seem to understand each other and conflict arises.
Then we need to find deeper roots of trust.
Growth in trust comes frequently as the result of a crisis, an ordeal,
a test of our trust.

This gospel is about growing in trust,
growing in a relationship of love with Jesus.
Belief is not trusting and adhering to an abstract doctrine,
it is believing and trusting in the person of Jesus and in his words.
This belief and trust begins
as people see Jesus doing things no one else can do
and are attracted to him;
they realize he must come from God and are in awe in front of him.
Then their experience of Jesus changes and deepens.
It becomes a relationship of trust in Jesus, who offers his friendship
and reveals a new vision for humanity.
The relationship grows.

There may be times when we do not understand Jesus,
perhaps times of doubt, anger and rebellion.
Little by little, however, trust grows
until it becomes an unconditional trust in Jesus,
Son of Man and Son of God.
We become more open to him and to his love and friendship,
whatever happens, whatever the cost or pain.
Whatever the apparent silence or absence of Jesus,
we give him our trust and believe in him.
This is the gift of God, the gift of new life,
given to us as a tiny seed when we are baptized,
cleansed by water and the Spirit.
This seed needs to be nourished in order to grow gradually,
often through pain,
into an unconditional surrender to God.
This is the story of the Gospel of John,
the story of disciples' growth in faith and trust.
It is our story, too.

This new life is eternal life

In the passage with Nicodemus,
Jesus tells us that if we believe and trust in him,
we will have *eternal* life.
Eternal here does not refer to something we will live after death,
it is the life of God given to us *today*.
It is the life of the Eternal One that is in each of us,
flowing in and through us,
given to us as we are born from above through baptism
and through our trust in Jesus.

As we enter into relationship with Jesus and follow him,
we receive the life that is in him,
which is his relationship with his Father.
We are led towards the wedding feast of the Lamb.
As we grow in friendship and oneness with Jesus,
we begin to recognize the eternal life within us and
are less attracted by the idols of money or power.
We begin to see people as Jesus sees them;
we begin to love them as Jesus loves them
and to see and love ourselves as Jesus sees and loves us.
Life and trust bring us to dwell in Jesus and Jesus in us, and
as they grow and deepen, they lead us into a transformation in God.
Transformed, we can do things
that, humanly speaking, we could not do by ourselves:
love our enemies, forgive and forgive indefinitely,
be with the poor and the weak,
be compassionate as the Father is compassionate.

No wonder the evangelist reveals that

> *God so loved the world that he gave us his only Son*
> *so that everyone who believes [trusts] in him*
> *may not perish but may have eternal life.*
> *Indeed God did not send the Son into the world*
> *to condemn the world,*
> *but in order that the world may be saved through him. vv. 16-17*

To "*save*" someone means "*to pull that person out of danger*"
so that he or she is not hurt and a life is not lost.
It means "*to liberate*" from oppression
or "*to open the doors of a prison*" and let the prisoners go free.
It means "*to heal*" or "*to make whole*."
Jesus came to save us from all those fears that close us up in ourselves.
He came to liberate us and open us up to love.
He came to give us the very life of God
so that it may flow in us and through us.
It flows in us because Jesus was lifted up on the cross,
lifted up in his resurrection,
lifted up in the glory of the Father.

To open ourselves up to this new life
is like making a journey or going on a pilgrimage.
We are walking towards a holy land, led by the Spirit of Jesus.
The road can sometimes be rough and tortuous.
There can be stress and heavy winds.
We have to struggle with pain.
The road ahead is not always clear.
Some of us can be quite closed for a variety of reasons.
Perhaps as children or adults we had to protect ourselves
and prove our worth,
or perhaps we felt rejected because we had a disability,
or lost self-esteem and did not know who we were.
Some of us had to protect ourselves from a false notion of God,
an "Almighty," "all-powerful" God
who made us feel guilty or who judged us harshly.
Many have been hurt by their own church,
by a lack of understanding and compassion.
We were not always told of the humble Lamb
who came to lead us to freedom.
It can take time for our protective walls to weaken
and for the journey to openness to begin.
Born from above by water and the Spirit

we are called to gradually grow in love.
The seed of the Spirit has been planted in us.
We must learn how to nourish this seed
so that it can grow and bear much fruit.
This journey, our pilgrimage of love, begins and deepens
as we hear God murmur within our hearts:
"I love you just as you are.
I so love you that I come to heal you and to give you life.
Do not be afraid. Open your hearts.
It is all right to be yourself.
You do not have to be perfect or clever.
You are loved just as you are.
As you become more conscious that you are loved,
you will want to respond to that love with love,
and grow in love."

Why some refuse life

To have life, then, is to welcome Jesus, who comes to save us
and to liberate us from fear, violence and the walls of sin.
If we remain fixed behind the walls of our certitudes and power
and our need for security,
we will remain closed up in fear, violence
and the powers of darkness within us,
closed up in depression and guilt;
we refuse to grow and to let ourselves be led by the Spirit.

Why do we refuse the Light?
What are we frightened of?

> *All who do evil hate the light and do not come to the light,*
> *so that their deeds may not be exposed.*   *v. 20*

Yes, we are all frightened of being shown up as evil and guilty.
We do not want people to see the shadow areas in us.
We hide all the dirt inside us behind our apparent goodness,
certitudes and power.

If we do not want our bad deeds to be exposed,
perhaps it is because we are frightened of being rejected,
of falling into a pit of loneliness and anguish,
when people see who we truly are, with all our poverty and brokenness.
Maybe we cannot accept our poverty and frailty
unless we discover that we are loved just as we are.
When we realize that we do not have to be clever,
powerful or successful
in order to be loved, then we can live in truth,
come to the light and be led by the Spirit of God.
We are no longer fearful:

> *Those who do what is true, come to the light*
> *that it may be clearly seen that their deeds*
> *have been done in God.*   *v. 21*

7

Jesus came to bring us life

John 4:1-42

*Jesus meets a broken woman
and gives her new life.*

*Transformed,
she then gives life to others.*

*Jesus comes to give us life
so that we may communicate
life to others.*

*This life is one of communion
and relationship.*

Jesus meets a broken woman

Jesus came into the world to lead us all
into communion with God, to bring us new life.
Jesus begins his mission not by going first to those who are rich,
or even to the poor and broken of Israel.
Instead, he goes to a woman of Samaria,
a woman who has had many broken relationships,
a woman belonging to what the Jewish people
considered a heretical group.
The Samaritans were a break-off group
from the traditional Jewish religion.
They worshipped God on Mount Gazarim
and refused to recognize the Temple of Jerusalem
as the central place of worship.
They recognized the word of God in the first five books of the Bible,
the Torah or the Pentateuch, but they did not accept the prophets.
Although they, too, were children of Abraham,
there was a lot of fear and hatred between these groups.
At one time, wanting to insult Jesus and to affirm that he was heretical,
some Pharisees shouted at him:

> *"You are a Samaritan and the devil is in you!"*   Jn 8:48

It is never easy to belong to a minority group
that is despised and powerless.
Feeling pushed down and without value
can result in a form of collective despair or anger in the group.
We are going to discover that this woman
has a history of broken relationships.
She has lived with five men,
and the man she lives with now is not her husband.
She is not only part of a despised minority,
she is also rejected by her own people.
She is a woman with a broken self-image
who has deep feelings of guilt, of worthlessness,

who feels that nobody could ever really love her.
Is it because she feels rejected and mocked by her people
that she comes to draw water all alone, at midday,
when the sun is at its highest?
Most women come to the well early in the morning,
but a woman who feels rejected and ashamed
will probably try to avoid meeting the other women of the village.
She will come to draw water when nobody else is likely to be there.

Jesus, we are told, is tired, and is sitting by the well.
This is the only time in the gospels that we hear that Jesus is tired.
He is alone; the disciples have gone to buy food in the nearby village.
He is tired from the long walk in the sun of Judea.
Perhaps he is also tired of being with these men
who do not seem to understand him
and who quarrel among themselves.
The Samaritan woman approaches to draw water.
Jesus turns to her and says:

> *"Give me to drink."*   Jn 4:7

He is thirsty and begs for water.
She is surprised and shocked: a Jew would never speak to a Samaritan;
and a Jewish man would never speak to a woman alone!
From his accent and the way he is dressed,
Jesus is obviously a Jew from Galilee.
He is acting in a surprising way, against all cultural norms.
He is breaking down the walls of division
that separate the Jews and Samaritans.
He is thirsty for unity between all the children of Abraham.
He yearns for people to come together.

> *"How is it that you, a Jew, are asking of me,*
> *a Samaritan woman, to drink?"*   v. 9

she responds with vivacity.
John notes that Jews normally do not have any contact with
Samaritans.

How to approach those who are broken

I find it very moving how Jesus meets and welcomes
this fragile, broken woman.
He knows the depth of her negative self-image.
He does not judge or condemn her.
He does not condescend or give her any moral lessons.
He approaches her like a tired, thirsty beggar,
asking her to do something for him.
He begins to dialogue with her and creates a relationship with her.
She who has lost all trust in her own goodness is trusted by Jesus.
In trusting her, he uplifts her and gives her back her self-esteem.

Jesus is showing us how to approach people
who are broken and wounded:
not as someone superior, from "above,"
but humbly, from "below," like a beggar.
Such people who are already ashamed of themselves
do not need someone who will make them feel even more ashamed,
but someone who will give them hope and reveal to them
that they have value, they are unique, precious and important.
To accept and love broken people in that way
is the surest way to help them to grow.
We witness this so often in l'Arche and in Faith and Light,
where we welcome men and woman with disabilities
who have lost all self-confidence and self-esteem.
What they need to begin their journey of growth
is someone who appreciates, affirms and loves them
just as they are, in all their weakness and brokenness.

Meetings at the well: meetings of love

Jesus meets this woman at the well.
In Scripture, meetings at the well have a deep significance.
Rebecca, who became Isaac's bride,
was found at a well by Abraham's servant,
who went in search of a bride for Abraham's beloved son.

When the servant arrived at the well he prayed to the Lord,
asking that the first girl to come to the well
to whom he would ask for something to drink,
and who replied "yes" and gave water to the camels also,
would be chosen to be Isaac's bride.   *cf. Gen 24:10-14*

Jacob also met his future bride, Rachel, at a well.   *Gen 29*
Moses met Zeppora, his future wife, at a well.   *Ex 2:16-20*
The meeting of Jesus and this Samaritan woman at the well
is a meeting of love.
Jesus, the divine Bridegroom, came to reveal his love
to all who are seeking to draw water from the well of love.

Water gives life

Jesus continues to dialogue and tells this woman:

> *"If you but knew the gift of God
> and who it is who is saying to you: 'Give me to drink,'
> rather you would have asked him
> and he could have given you living water"*   *v. 10*

She answers with her usual vivacity:

> *"Lord, you have nothing to draw from the well
> and the well is deep.
> Where will you find the living water?
> Are you greater than our father Jacob who gave us this well,
> drank from it himself and gave water to his family and all the
> animals?"*   *vv. 11-12*

Jesus answers:

> *"Whoever drinks of the waters that I will give
> will never be thirsty.
> The waters that I will give will become in them a spring of water,
> welling up in eternal life."*   *vv. 13-14*

Water gives life.
When there is no rain, the land is dry, the crops die
and people die of hunger.
How many days can anyone live without drinking water?
The symbolism is striking.
Jesus came to quench our thirst for presence and acceptance,
the thirst for meaning, when we feel confused.
The waters Jesus gives us are the waters of his light and his presence
that will take away the pangs of loneliness and give new life.
Water is the symbol of the Spirit,
of the very life of God that Jesus came to give us.

Jesus is revealing that if we drink from the fountain
of the love and compassion of God,
we become a fountain of love and compassion.
If we receive the Spirit of God, we will give the Spirit of God.
The life we receive is the life we give.

Relationships

In his book *I and Thou*, Martin Buber, the Jewish philosopher,
tells us how in civilizations or cultures where there are a lot of *things*,
we can become less available to *people*,
to be with them, understand them, share with them.
We get too caught up with *things:*
having things, doing things, selling and buying things.
We risk forgetting that the joy and treasure of human beings
is to be with other human beings and to celebrate life together.
The heart of relationship
is not to *do things for* people.
It is not to possess them
or to use them for our satisfaction, to fill our emptiness.
It is to reveal to them that they are unique, precious
and have beautiful gifts.
It is to live a communion of hearts with them
where we help each other to grow to greater freedom.
Life flows from one to the other.

Jesus is truly a man for others.
Knowledge, competence, things are not important in themselves;
they are for relationship.
It is people who are important – you, me, each person –
whatever our origins or culture.
That is what Jesus is revealing through this encounter
with the Samaritan woman.
He is revealing that at the heart of everything –
of creation, human life and his message of love –
is the heart made for relationship, heart to heart, person to person,
where we give to and receive from each other
and help each other to be.
Jesus came to give us life – eternal life, the very life of God –
through a personal relationship with each one of us.
We are called to communicate this life to others.

Accept our brokenness in truth

The promise of Jesus to the Samaritan woman, and to each one of us,
to become a source of life for others
can only come about if we are humble and recognize our poverty
and brokenness,
and accept ourselves just as we are.
Jesus invites her, and each one of us,
to revisit our past in truth:
not just to analyze it or remain trapped in it
but to be liberated from its hold.
Jesus gently and lovingly touches this woman's inner wound
or brokenness:

> *"Go and call your husband and come back."*   *v. 16*

That is the place of her poverty and feelings of guilt:

> *"I have no husband," she replies.*
> *"You are right in saying 'I have no husband,'" says Jesus,*
> *"for you have had five husbands*
> *and the man you have now is not your husband.*
> *What you have said is true."*   *vv. 17-18*

The story of the Samaritan woman is a true story.
She was a broken woman: broken in love.
She is also a symbol. She represents each one of us.
We are all this Samaritan woman.
We are all wounded in some way in love,
and have a history of broken relationships.
Many of us hide our difficulties in relationships,
behind cleverness and power.
We crave admiration and do not want to recognize our vulnerability,
the hidden handicap of our incapacity
to love and forgive some people.
We can be imprisoned in the chaos of sadness, anger and even hate.

When I hear the woman in the gospel saying "I have no husband,"
I hear the terrible and painful cry of humanity, of so many of us:
"I feel lonely and guilty. Nobody is really committed to me."
It is a cry of anguish.
In order to receive of the living waters that flow from Jesus,
we must recognize all that is chaotic and dead in us.
We can only come to Jesus to drink if we are thirsty.
When we are full of ourselves, our power and certitudes,
we think we can do it on our own and fend for ourselves.
We do not recognize our need for new life.
It is only when we present to Jesus our emptiness,
helplessness and broken hearts
that he can fill us with the strength of the Spirit and the touch of
his love.

But the One who comes to give us new life is tired.
He comes to us and asks us for help as a little one.
It is a vulnerable God who comes
as a beggar, asking us for help.
It is he, the Broken One, who will awaken us in love
and give us new life.

Who is right or who is wrong?

The woman, certainly surprised by the way Jesus knew her, says,

> *"I see you are a prophet."*   *v. 19*

So she asks him a burning question
that was in the heart of many Samaritans
and that can only be asked of a prophet.
Who is right: the Jews or the Samaritans?
Should we worship God in the Temple or on Mount Garazim?
Which religion is right? Which one has the truth?

Jesus tells her that this is not the important question.

> *"The hour is coming and is now here,*
> *when the true worshippers will worship the Father*
> *in Spirit and in truth."*

Their prayers will be inspired by the Holy Spirit,
for the Holy Spirit will be dwelling in them.
Jesus is revealing to her in a few words
what will become clear to Paul many years later
when he writes to the disciples in Rome:

> *For all who are led by the Spirit of God are children of God.*
> *For you did not receive a spirit of slavery to fall back into fear,*
> *but you have received a spirit of adoption.*
> *When we cry "Abba, Father," it is that very spirit bearing witness*
> *with our spirit that we are children of God.*   *Rom 8:14-16*

We are called to worship God in our hearts
through the Holy Spirit given to us.

The Samaritan woman cannot really understand
what Jesus is getting at.
She says:

> *"I know the Messiah is coming.*
> *When he comes he will proclaim all things to us."*

Jesus answers:

"I AM speaks to you."

This is sometimes translated as "I am he" or "It is I the Messiah."

This expression "I AM" is pregnant with meaning.
As we will see later, it reveals the very name,
the sacred name, of God
given in the Book of Exodus.   *Ex 3*

We have known Jesus as
the Lamb,
the Chosen One,
the Bridegroom,
the Messiah,
the son of Joseph of Nazareth,
the Son of God,
the Son of Man,
the King of Israel.
Now his divine name is revealed.

"I AM" begs for water
from one of the most despised and broken women,
who is no one, with no name, who is nothing in the eyes of society.
Jesus reveals to her who she is and who she will become –
a source of the waters of life of God –
if she opens up her heart to him and receives his love.
Misery and mercy meet in love.

The woman transformed

Just then his disciples arrive;
they are astonished that he is speaking with a woman.
They want him to eat some of the food they bought in the village,
but Jesus tells them:

"I have food to eat that you do not know about....
My food is to do the will of Him who has sent me
and to accomplish his work."

The work of Jesus is to bring people together in unity
and to lead them to the Father.
We are invited to live a communion of hearts with each person.
Jesus has lived something profound with this woman,
a personal encounter of love.
His heart has been touched and nourished by her,
and she has begun to trust him.
Love has been born between them.
At times like that we do not want to eat.
A communion of hearts is food for them and for us.
Jesus must have been moved also because the Father had inspired him
to reveal to this broken woman, a Samaritan woman,
his secret, his secret name: "*I AM.*"
Jesus does not reveal this to anyone else in the gospel.
To the disciples this revelation comes from the Father;
it is only to this woman, the most broken and lonely of women,
that he reveals his secret name, who he is.
She is transformed in love.
How could she have imagined that the Messiah, the One sent by God,
would speak to her, a poor, broken woman,
banished by her own people.
Not only did he speak to her, he humbly asked her for water.
It is not possible! She must be dreaming! Yet he is there.
He has told her all she has done,
without any condemnation or judgment.
In fact, she has seen through his eyes, his attitude,
the tone of his voice not only respect but love for her.
How could this be?

She runs off to the village in excitement, leaving the pitcher of water
(for now the living waters have filled her heart).
She finds a whole lot of people and tells them:

> *"Come and see a man who has told me everything I have done!*
> *Could he be the Messiah?"*   *v. 29*

The waters of life are flowing forth from her just as Jesus had promised.
She has received life from Jesus, and now she is giving life.
The people are amazed and astonished by the transformation
that has taken place in her.
They follow her, go and meet Jesus
and ask him to stay with them.
The gospel tells us:

> *He dwelt with them for two days.*

Then they said to the woman:

> *"It is no longer because of what you said that we believe.*
> *We now believe for ourselves.*
> *We know that he is truly the saviour of the world."*   *v. 42*

For those of us who realize that we are broken, lost, unloved,
the revelation of the love of Jesus is wonderful news.
When we become aware of how lonely and thirsty we are
and how much we need the love of God,
then we shall ask as this woman did:

> *"Give me those waters that I may not thirst!"*   *v. 15*

8

From despair to life

John 5

The first time Jesus journeys with his disciples to Jerusalem
he goes to the Temple, his "Father's House."

The second time
he goes to an asylum
where rejected people
are lying around unwanted.
This is also his Father's home.

Jesus is calling his disciples
to follow him
as he goes towards
the most rejected of people.
He is revealing
that he comes to heal
the paralysis of our hearts
and to lead us all
into life.

Jesus in the local asylum

J esus is in Jerusalem.
He does not go first to places of learning and power
but to the local asylum,

where there was a multitude of people with disabilities:
lame, blind and paralyzed   *v. 3*

lying around, living in *dis-grace*.
They were no doubt dirty and ugly,
according to the values of the world,
shunned and despised:
neither beauty nor comeliness in them.
Yet it is to them that Jesus goes first.

I have visited many such asylums throughout the world,
where people with physical and mental disabilities are in bed
or lying around on the floor or wandering aimlessly.
These asylums are dismal places of despair and violence.
The people have been put there by their families
who were ashamed of them or could not cope,
or did not want to look after them.
In the culture of that time, children born with a handicap
were seen as a punishment from God.
They or their parents must have sinned.
A disability was a sign of evil.
No wonder such people were hidden away!

Jesus probably enters this asylum with some of his disciples.
He wants them to realize that their first calling will be
towards those who are broken and rejected.
For Jesus each person, whatever his or her abilities or disabilities,
is unique and important;
each one is a child of God, loved by God.

The place of the poor and the broken

Paul realized this with great clarity
when he wrote to the communities he had founded in Corinth.
He affirmed that God had chosen the weak
and the foolish of the world
in order to confound the powerful and the wise. *1 Cor 1:27-28*
Many in our societies and churches have difficulty believing this.
Our cultures favour the clever, the strong,
the productive, the beautiful.
Perhaps now and again they bend down to help
the weak and the poor,
but they do not really believe that the latter are fully human,
children of God,
and that they have something to contribute to society
and to their church.
Our productive cultures see no meaning to their lives.
Today in rich countries,
many elderly people are also put away in homes,
seen as "useless," as no longer productive.
We should of course "be good" to them,
but it is assumed that their time has passed
and they have nothing more to give to others.

Frequently, those who are well positioned in society
can be so taken up with seeking honour, riches,
power and respectability
that they tend to ignore or avoid the dis-graceful and the weak.
Those who are shunned and excluded from society,
who are crushed by despair, desperately seek relationship.
It is not power they seek but understanding,
tenderness and friendship.

A huge gap separates the "haves" from the "have-nots."

"There is a deep pit lying between us,"

says Abraham, talking to the rich man about the beggar Lazarus,

> *"so that those who want to cross over from here to you*
> *cannot do so,*
> *nor can anyone cross over to us from where you are."*   Lk 16:26

By entering into the asylum Jesus is revealing the deep desire of God
to bridge the gap that separates people,
to bring together, in unity and harmony, people who are different:
the foolish, the wise, the powerful and the powerless.

The meeting with the man in despair

Recent excavations in Jerusalem have uncovered this asylum
with its huge pool.
It seems to have been a place of healing, revered not by the Jews
but by those who were frequently called "pagans"
and who worshipped other gods.
It is to this pagan place with its therapeutic waters   Jn 5:3
that Jesus comes.
Imagine Jesus going from one person to another,
gently and compassionately touching each one,
seeing each one as a person,
giving a word of encouragement and peace to each one.
He comes to a paralyzed man who has been there for thirty-eight years.
Jesus is moved by this man who is crushed by despair
and says to him:

> *"Do you want to be healed?"*   v. 6

This man, closed up in pain,
responds not from a place of faith but from a place of despair.
He has no friends, no close family. Nobody cares for him.
He is alone and abandoned to his dismal fate.
In some ways he echoes the Samaritan woman who said,

> *"I have no husband,"*

I am alone; nobody loves me or wants me.

> *"Sir," he says, "I have no one to put me in the pool*
> *when the water is stirred up*
> *and when I am making my way*
> *someone steps ahead of me."*   *v. 7*

He seems to be referring to a belief that
the first person who entered the water when it was stirred up
would be healed.
But he has no one to help him.
His cry is a cry of loneliness.

Jesus is so moved by the despair and the powers of death in this man
that he says:

> *"Rise up and take up your mat and walk!"*   *v. 8*

It is as if Jesus cannot contain himself;
he loves this man as he is, just as he loved the Samaritan woman.
He yearns to liberate him from all the powers of despair within him,
that he be fully alive.
In this story, Jesus is not responding to a man's cry of faith, "Heal me!"
but to his cry of despair, the cry of humanity in despair!
Jesus is responding also to a pain within his own heart:
the pain of seeing the loneliness and despair of this paralyzed man.
Nobody wanted to see this man, but Jesus sees him.
Nobody loves him, but Jesus loves him.

Healing in l'Arche

Jesus healed one man in this asylum
as a sign of his love for all in the asylum.
Jesus' attitude touches me in a particular way,
as we in l'Arche often visit asylums.
Among so many crying out in need,
we are able to welcome only a few of the people with disabilities.
Our communities are not a "solution" for all people with disabilities;
they can only be a sign that those we welcome are important
– so all are important.

We can sometimes heal hearts, but not bodies.
In our l'Arche community in Honduras,
Nadine welcomed Claudia from the local asylum.
She was seven years old then: blind, autistic, closed up in anguish.
It took Claudia quite a few years in the community
to become convinced that she was loved
and to find peace and healing for her heart.
Those who are weak and in need of help like Claudia
can call forth compassion in those who are stronger,
if they but listen and open their hearts.
When the weak and the strong come together in mutual friendship,
they bridge the gap and become bonded together
in a common humanity.

Despair

A few years ago, I visited a large institution in Brazil.
It was about ten in the morning.
I was surprised to find a room with about forty children with
disabilities still in their beds
and not one of them was crying.
Children only cry out when they know and hope
that someone will answer;
they will not waste their energies
if they are certain that nobody will hear.
They will close up in despair; they have no hope.

People in slum areas, in prison cells or in institutions
can at certain moments
cut themselves off from others;
they may even cut themselves off from their own anger
and hide behind thick walls of despair.
They know that nobody will come to their help.
They are convinced that they are of no interest to anyone
and that they are not loveable.

They become apathetic.
They shut off all the energies of life in them
and become like robots.
They may survive but they are not living.

If and when someone does approach them with love and respect,
it can take a long time to awaken new life and hope in them.
They have been disappointed so many times.
They are afraid of entering into any new relationship
and then being put aside once again.

In India in 1975,
at the beginning of our community of l'Arche in Chennai,
we welcomed Sumasundra, a young man of twenty
from the local psychiatric hospital,
where he had been abandoned as a child.
He was physically quite handicapped,
dragging himself on his two very deformed legs.
He could say only a few words, but he was mentally quite alert.
His arrival in the community was a joy for him
and he made much progress.
He used to drag himself into the village
and order a drink in the tea shop.
When other members of the community received family visits,
he received none,
and he gradually began to realize that his parents were not there;
he became jealous of the others.
His despair returned because he wanted his mother.
In his despair, he would throw himself on the road nearby.
A cry for attention. A cry of pain. A desire to kill himself?
The assistants who were with him did not know,
but they redoubled their efforts to find his mother,
and they eventually did find her.
She came to see him; it was a beautiful reunion.
Sumasundra found new hope.
His mother promised to come back to see him the following month,

but she never returned
and Sumasundra fell into an even deeper despair,
throwing himself more frequently on the road.
It became too difficult for the community to keep him.
The risk of his killing himself was too great, his despair was too great.
He was sent back to the psychiatric hospital
where he still resides today.
His despair came because he realized that
his mother did not want him,
could not accept him with his broken body.
So he himself began to hate and reject his body.
If people are not loved,
they think it is because they are not loveable,
that there is something evil and ugly in them.
Why continue to live?

Many people today live in despair

Many people today are overwhelmed by despair
– and not only in asylums.
It is as if they are paralyzed in mind and heart,
like this man in this story.
They do not know where to turn or what to do
in front of all the divisions, wars, corruptions, injustices,
poverty, hypocrisy and lies of our world.
They have lost hope.
Others are paralyzed because they feel unwanted, put aside;
they are imprisoned in loneliness and anguish.
Many young people feel they have no place
in our overly structured and competitive societies.
They seek to escape through drugs, alcohol, violence and sex.
We are all in some way blocked by walls of fear and prejudice,
unable to love and respect others and to share with them.

This chapter of the Gospel of John reveals how Jesus comes to us
and meets each one of us
in those places of blockage and despair in us,

where we are paralyzed by our own needs and weakness.
He says to each one of us:
"Do you want to be healed?"

Some people do not want to be healed.
For thirty-eight years that man in the asylum
had learned to survive as he was.
Now he has to rise up, make choices,
find new friends, find work, go to the Temple.
He has to learn how to use this newly given freedom
and become responsible for his life.
Before, he could accuse and blame others
because nobody wanted to help him in his infirmity.
Now that he has been healed,
he can only accuse and blame himself!

A miracle is a sign of the love of Jesus,
who yearns to heal each one of us
so that we can become truly alive and grow in love.
We do not easily accept the risk of being healed in our hearts
and of changing in order to become more loving and open to others.
Do we believe that we are called also to become healers
through our love?
People in despair need to find men and women filled with hope,
fully alive,
who can reveal to them that they are important and loveable
and help them to discover meaning to their lives.
This paralyzed man, like the children in the Brazilian institution,
was in despair.
When people are in despair they have no hope,
they see no meaning to their lives.
But then something can happen;
they have an experience of love:
the love of a new friend, the love of God.
Despair seems to disappear; they discover a meaning to their lives.

Depression, on the other hand, is a sickness
that needs a medical response or therapy.
You may have wonderful friends, a good job
and still be in a depression.
Depression has deep physical and psychological ramifications.
The causes of depression can be multiple,
from our fundamental make-up to hidden wounds in childhood,
or chemical imbalances in our brain.
Yet in some ways depression and despair have similar symptoms:
in both there is a feeling of being unworthy, incapable, unloveable,
even evil,
and this can paralyze us;
in both there is a loss of meaning of life.
Depression can engender despair.
Despair is on a more human, spiritual level,
whereas depression is more on the psychological and physical level.
But as I said, they are often interwoven.

Conflict with some Pharisees

Jesus healed this man and told him to rise up and carry his mat
on the sabbath day, the day that God made holy,
the day when the Jewish people were invited to rest from work
and to give time to God, to listen to the word of God.

Some Pharisees during the time of Jesus were like watchdogs,
barking at anyone doing things
that they deemed "illegal" on the sabbath day.
They interpreted "work" in a narrow, rigid way:
a man carrying his sleeping mat was "working"
and thus acting against the things of God.
They said to the man who had been healed:
"It is illegal to carry your mat."
He replied that the person who had healed him
told him to take up his mat and walk,
and that he did not know who this person was.

Later, in the Temple, he met Jesus, who spoke to him.
So he went back to the Jewish authorities and told them
it was Jesus who had healed him.
The group of Pharisees then looked for Jesus
in order to reprimand and even persecute him.

The Pharisees were generally deeply religious men.
They belonged to fraternities
created during the time when the Jews
had been overrun by the Greeks.
They wanted to preserve and deepen their beautiful Jewish faith.
They were concerned that the philosophy, wealth,
way of life and religion
of the Greeks might permeate the people and weaken their faith.
These fraternities had certainly been inspired by God.
Like many fraternities and communities in religious traditions,
some became corrupted, legalistic and rigid.
The members began to feel that they were an elite
and should control others
and tell everybody what to do.
So it was with this particular group of Pharisees.
They were unable to accept that this man who had been paralyzed
for thirty-eight years
had been healed, was now well and fully alive.

Why were they unable to recognize this wondrous event?
Was it because they were paralyzed by fear?
They were not interested in the well-being of their people,
but only in maintaining the law and thus their privileges and power.
Such people accuse and judge.
They do not want to listen to people in pain
or enter into relationship with them.
They do not want to open up to what is new and to change.
Their hope is not in life but in power.
The new freedom of this paralyzed man
must have irritated these Pharisees

and revealed their lack of freedom, their paralyzed hearts,
their fear of all that is new.
They were unable to see how paralyzed they were.
They were convinced that they had been entrusted by God to
enforce the law.

By entering into this asylum,
by going towards the "dregs" of society
and healing this man,
Jesus was creating a social disorder.
He was revealing the value of this paralyzed man
and of each and every person.
Leaders do not generally like disorder.
They frequently want only to maintain the social order.

Jesus responds

Jesus loves these Pharisees
and wants to break through their blindness
and to convince them that he is accomplishing this work of healing
with God and in God.
He tells them,

> *"My Father and I are always working."*   *v. 17*

The work of God is life,
to give, sustain and call forth life
every day and at every moment!
This infuriates these Pharisees even more.
Not only does Jesus do something unlawful on the sabbath,

> *but he called God his own Father,*
> *thus making himself equal to God.*   *v. 18*

This was the supreme blasphemy.
In order to better understand these men and their rigidity,
who were so concerned about obedience to man-made laws,
we must remember that the great treasure of the Jewish people was
their faith

in *one* God, the *unique* God, the *only* God.
They had preserved this treasure
in the face of the beliefs of the Greeks and the Romans
in a multiplicity of gods.
Jesus tries to explain and reveal his oneness with God.
He is not taking the place of God; he is not in opposition to God.
There are not two Gods.
He is in communion with God,
the Beloved Son of God
who does everything the Father wants him to do.
They accomplish everything together; all life flows from them.

> *"Truly, truly, I tell you,*
> *the Son can do nothing on his own,*
> *but only what he sees the Father doing;*
> *for whatever the Father does, the Son does likewise.*
> *The Father loves the Son and*
> *shows him all that he himself is doing."*　　　　*vv. 19-20*

> *"I can do nothing on my own.*
> *As I hear, I judge and my judgment is just*
> *because I seek to do not my own will*
> *but the will of the one who sent me."*　　　　*v. 30*

Jesus has no identity separate from the Father.
His very existence is communion with the Father.
He cannot be separated from the Father
for He is one with the Father.
The Father and the Son are in a unity of love and light.
In this unity, they are source of all life and all creation.
Jesus is revealing that the healing of this paralyzed man
is a sign of the presence and love of God,
who wants to heal the inner paralysis in each one of us.
Jesus wants to help these religious authorities
to believe in the power of God acting in him.
He does not want them to remain closed up
in prejudice and pre-judgments.

Jesus dialogues with them;
he tries to help them to understand and to make an act of faith,
but a faith based on the miracle he has accomplished,
and on the testimony of John the Baptizer.
Jesus is asking them not to jump too quickly to conclusions
and to react from their own prejudice
but to go deeper into themselves,
to listen to the gentle murmurings of God
and to look more closely at Scripture.

But like so many of us, these Pharisees are stuck in their prejudices.
They do not want to be healed of their hardness of heart.
Jesus adds nostalgically:

> *"You do not want to come to me to have life....*
> *I have come in my Father's name and you do not accept me.*
> *If another comes in his own name, you will accept him.*
> *How can you believe when you accept glory from one another*
> *and do not see the glory that comes*
> *from the one who alone is God?"*   *vv. 40, 43-44*

Here Jesus touches our fundamental sin:
we are continually seeking human glory
and admiration from one another;
we refuse to see and accept the signs of God's presence
in the reality of our world, in what we see and hear.
We remain closed up in ourselves
and in our own religious or ethnic group,
seeking our own glory, sure of our own certitudes,
frightened of being opened up to the new.

Jesus came to heal us.
He is calling us
to come out from behind the barriers built up
around our vulnerable hearts
so that we may have life and give life.

9

Food for life

John 6:1-71

*Jesus invites us
to make a difficult
and sometimes stormy passage of faith
from the enthusiasm of discipleship
to the gentleness and humility of friendship.*

*Friendship with Jesus
– the Word made flesh –
becomes the nourishment
for our hearts and lives.*

The need for food

Our lives are a journey
from the weakness of the newborn child we once were
to the weakness of the old person we will become.
Our lives are a journey of growth
from ignorance to wisdom,
from selfishness to self-giving,
from fear to trust,
from guilt feelings to inner liberation,
from lack of self-esteem to self-acceptance.

We human beings do not *possess* life.
We *receive* life in our fragile bodies.
And this life grows, develops and deepens
as long as we are nourished.
Without food, we wither and die.
What is true of our physical life is also true of our life in the Spirit.
We need to be nourished.
We need physical nourishment, intellectual nourishment
 and nourishment for the heart.

Since early childhood we have learned to create defence mechanisms,
walls around our hearts
in order to protect our vulnerability and avoid being hurt.
One of our greatest fears is the fear of failure:
of being lonely, rejected, pushed down,
and made to feel we are no good.
These walls protect us from the dreadful feeling of being no good,
and it is from behind these walls that we try to prove our worth.
We have to be the best. We want power.
We want to be admired, seen as clever and brilliant.
We want to win in some field.
An inmate in a U.S. prison once told a friend of mine,
who was the prison chaplain,
that he was the best car stealer in his city and was proud of it.
He was the best in his field!

Others want to be the best singer, doctor, scientist, Olympic runner.
The best!
Caught up in the world of competition,
we tend to see people in the same field as rivals,
and not as people with whom we can co-operate and grow together.
Competition can certainly help us to develop our potential
but it can also become a source of great conflict.

Jesus came to lead us from this rivalry and competition,
so that we become more human, more compassionate,
more open to others.
He came to liberate us from our personal or collective selfishness,
from the fears and prejudices that enclose us in ourselves.
He came to lead us on the road of love.
We cannot move out from self-centredness to self-giving
unless we receive a new force from God.

This new life or growth in the Spirit needs to be nourished.
Jesus came to give us a special food
so that we may attain fullness of life.

A wonderful picnic

This chapter of the Gospel of John takes place
near the Lake of Galilee.
It is springtime, which is very beautiful.
There are thousands of wildflowers, a gentle and warm sun.
The feast of the Passover is close.
It is also a springtime in the life of Jesus.
People are beginning to flock to him:
"He must be the Messiah. Look how he is healing people!"
Excitement is in the air.

It is springtime as well for the disciples.
They are probably beginning to feel their own importance.
Weren't they the chosen ones of this extraordinary man?

Weren't they going to be the ones who would share power,
spiritual power, in his new government?
They must have been excited and enthusiastic.
They had begun to follow him in faith and trust,
alone or with a few others.
Now they are beginning to see the fruits of their belief.
People are flocking to Jesus; many are being healed.

> *A huge crowd kept following Jesus because they had seen the*
> *miracles that he was doing for the sick.*
> *Jesus went up the mountain and sat down with his disciples.*
> *Now the Passover, the festival of the Jews, was near.*
> *When he looked up and saw a large crowd coming towards him,*
> *Jesus said to Philip:*
> *"Where can we buy bread*
> *so that all these people can eat?"* vv. 2-5

Jesus is concerned about the welfare of all these people.
They have followed him, eating and drinking his words.
Now they must be hungry and exhausted.
Jesus is touched by their needs and their cry.
Philip must have thought that Jesus was crazy.
How could they possibly feed so many families?
How could they find enough food for such a huge crowd?

Andrew intervenes

Andrew has spotted a little boy who has in his bag
five loaves of bread and two fish.
But that is nothing compared with the needs of these people.
It is beautiful to see how Jesus uses little people,
like this boy and the servants in Cana.

Jesus, acting like the host of a big party, says:

> *"Invite everybody to sit down."* v. 10

The evangelist adds a very human touch,
saying that there was lots of grass where they were.
So many families are sitting or lying down on the grass.
Then Jesus took the bread, and after giving thanks to the Father
for all of creation,
he and his disciples distributed the bread and the fish to everybody,
as much as they wanted.
What a wonderful meal! What a wonderful picnic!
It was like a huge party!
All those hungry men and women and children
eating as much bread and fish as they wanted,
resting quietly on the grass and looking at the beautiful lake,
sharing in little groups, chatting joyfully with one another.
A little taste of heaven!
And Jesus with the disciples going around from group to group
or from person to person to see if everybody was well served.
What a glorious day!

Today, some two thousand years after this event,
some of us may smile cynically: miracles!
As if they were wholesome stories intended for children.
We may laugh and say:
"How wonderful if Jesus were present today.
We would not have to go out and buy bread!"
This is what the crowd said when they tried to seize him
and make him king.

Let us go deeper into the significance of this miracle.
Jesus reveals a caring God,
a God who is concerned for our well-being and wants us to be well,
a God who wants us to be concerned about our own welfare.
Do we eat well? Rest well? Nourish ourselves well?
It is not just a miracle of multiplying food
but also of creating and building a caring community
where people are concerned for one another.

An abundant love

When the meal is over,
and everybody is relaxed and happy,
Jesus says to his disciples:

> *"Pick up all that has been left over
> so that nothing may be lost."*   *v. 12*

They fill up twelve baskets full!
At Cana, Jesus transformed an excessive amount of water
into delicious wine.
Here he multiplies five loaves of bread and two fish
into an excessive quantity of food.
That is God.
God gives abundantly, signifying that God loves us abundantly.

What does it mean to love abundantly?
It does not only mean to give *things* but *to give ourselves*.
Jesus gives himself totally to us;
he loves us abundantly so that we may learn to love others abundantly.
But we tend to hold back and seek to protect ourselves.
To love abundantly means also seeking to be well and fit.
It is not love if we burn ourselves out.
We have to look after ourselves
and find enough nourishment and energy
to be open to people and to love them abundantly.

The crowd wanted to make him king

The crowd realized that something extraordinary had happened:
they had not seen cartloads of bread and fish
and yet they had been nourished plentifully.
Some of the elders remembered, perhaps, what God had done for
their ancestors in the desert after they were liberated from slavery,
how God had fed them with the manna.   *cf. Ex 16*
Maybe they realized that something similar

was happening to them there in Galilee.
People were in awe before Jesus.

> *So Jesus, realizing that they were going to seize him*
> *in order to make him their king,*
> *fled all alone into the mountains.*   *v. 15*

They wanted to make Jesus king
so that he would look after them and all their bodily needs.
What a wonderful thing it would be to have a powerful person
like him as leader.
Maybe they wouldn't even have to work anymore!

But Jesus slipped away quietly, up into the mountain.
Jesus does not want to be king with temporal power,
before whom we will be in awe.
He is there to lead people into a gentle relationship with him,
and through him into communion with the Father.

The faith of these people is only at a beginning stage.
They follow Jesus because he has healed some and now
he has fed them all.
Their faith is centred upon themselves and their needs.
They want to use Jesus,
but he runs away.
Jesus performs miracles so that people believe
he has been sent by God
and then trust in his words, even if they appear absurd.
That is what is important.
Let us hope that we can all leave this first stage of faith
and start on the journey to a deeper faith and a greater love.

At the beginning of this gospel,
Jesus brought his disciples to a wedding feast,
to symbolize that he is leading them to love, to intimacy
and to a new form of fecundity, a divine wedding feast.

Here we have something similar.
Jesus is leading people from a wonderful human picnic
and a fulfillment of their human needs
to another form of a wedding feast,
a feast of intimacy and communion with him.
But before he could reveal this new meal of love,
the disciples had to cross the lake.

The disciples are frightened and confused

The disciples were lost when Jesus disappeared
without telling them where he was going.
From the exaltation of success and the taste of spiritual power,
they were now plunged into confusion.
What to do? Where to go? Where was Jesus?
They decided to go back to Capernaum,
where Peter lived with his mother-in-law
and where Jesus and his disciples had made their headquarters.
So they got back into their boats
and started to row across the lake towards Capernaum.

The Lake of Galilee can be quite treacherous.
One moment it is calm and quiet,
then winds rushing down from the mountains
can suddenly stir up the waters into dangerous waves.
This is what happened to these men as they crossed over to
Capernaum; they were caught up in fear.

Suddenly they see Jesus walking towards them on the water.
They are even more frightened! Is it a ghost?
Jesus says to them:

> *"I AM; be not afraid."*   *v. 20*

A passage of faith

Crossing the lake is a passage of faith,
a passage of faith we all have to make.
It takes place between the glorious picnic where Jesus is present,
and the revelation in Capernaum of Jesus as a vulnerable friend
who will feed them with his presence.
Jesus calls his disciples to move from a faith
based on a very visible miracle
that fulfilled their physical needs
to a faith that is total trust in him and in his words,
words that can appear foolish, absurd, impossible, even scandalous.
This can be a difficult passage for us all, like an inner storm.
It can represent the passage from childhood,
where we feel secure with our parents,
to adulthood,
where we become responsible for our lives.
Jesus leads these men from the excitement
and enthusiasm of discipleship
to a mutuality of love and friendship that is more hidden and humble.

The disciples, who were confused and upset in the boat,
are telling us something about ourselves.
How easily they seem to have forgotten the blessedness
of the picnic with Jesus!
How easily *we* forget!
We can live blessed moments of the presence of God in prayer
or through an encounter with someone
where we sense God's presence.
Then something happens
and we are plunged into the depths of sadness and despair.
We forget the moment of blessedness.
Doubt, anger and anguish surge up within us.
We have short memories!

I hear this from married couples:
they can live moments of incredible blessedness,
and then a conflict arises
and all the blessedness seems to evaporate
and become a sort of illusion.
They do not realize that the blessedness was to give them strength
in order to deepen their faith and trust in each other
and thus to help them go through more difficult passages of trust
that would come.

So this crossing of the lake was a physical reality,
but it also symbolizes our growth in faith, our passages of faith.
We all have to go through times of confusion and doubt.
This is all part of the journey of faith.
It is not an easy journey since we have to die to ourselves,
die to the desire to control situations, to control the Spirit of God,
to control Jesus
in order to abandon ourselves to the Spirit of Jesus leading us.

Jesus is the bread of heaven

Many of those who witnessed the miracle
crossed over to Capernaum the next day.
They wanted to be with Jesus again, to learn from him.
They asked him,

> *"Rabbi, when did you arrive here?"*

Jesus answered:

> *"Truly, truly, I say to you, you are looking for me*
> *not because you saw signs [that revealed he was sent by God]*
> *but because you have eaten bread and are filled up.*
> *Do not work for the food that is perishable*
> *but for food that lasts in eternal life*
> *which the Son of Man will give you."*   *vv. 26-27*

What is this food that they have to work for
and which will last forever?
What must they do?
Jesus answers:

> *"The work of God is that you trust [believe in]*
> *the One God has sent."* v. 29

And he adds:

> *"I am the bread of life.*
> *Whoever comes to me will never hunger,*
> *whoever believes in me will never thirst."* v. 35

This was something that these people could understand.
For the Jewish people, the word of God, the Torah,
was an incredible form of nourishment.
It was bread for their hearts and minds.
We read in the book of Ezekiel that the Lord had said to him:

> *"Son of Man, eat what is offered to you;*
> *eat this scroll and go, speak to the house of Israel"*....
> *Then I ate it and in my mouth it was sweet as honey.* Ez 3:1-4

The word of God is the revelation of the love of God
for the Jewish people.
It is also the revelation of what humankind is about,
what our lives are about,
what the whole history of the universe and of salvation is about.
And it is sweet as honey.
Our intelligence needs and yearns for wisdom.
We not only need practical wisdom that shows us how to live,
but also an intelligence that seeks an understanding
of the meaning of the universe.
We need to be nourished by the word of God.

Those who were listening to Jesus could understand
that the bread Jesus was speaking about
was the nourishing bread of the word of God.

The bread of his body

Jesus wants to lead them further.
He is not just the word of God, enlightening their hearts and minds,
he is the Word made flesh, wanting to give himself to them as he is,
in his incarnated person,
and to be present to them as a friend,
a vulnerable friend through his flesh.
He has chosen them, to live with them a communion of hearts.
This implies an important passage of faith for the disciples.
How can they become a friend of the Messiah?
Friendship implies a certain equality and mutual vulnerability.
Jesus no longer appears as the powerful one but as a powerless one
offering his loving person:

> *"I am the living bread which has come down from heaven.*
> *The person who eats this bread will live forever.*
> *And even, the bread that I will give is my flesh*
> *for the life of the world."*   *v. 51*

And he adds:

> *"Whoever eats my flesh and drinks my blood,*
> *dwells in me and I dwell in that person."*   *v. 56*

These words seem incredible. What can they mean?
All of us would have run away upon hearing these words
if we had not seen the miracles Jesus had done
to show that his words were trustworthy
and that they were words of life.
So we need to take time to inquire and understand what Jesus is saying
through and behind these words.

For the Israelites, it is the flesh and blood of a person
that signifies the person with all her or his being.
When Jesus uses the separation of flesh and blood,
he is signifying his death: he has come as the Lamb of God
who will be sacrificed and eaten as the Paschal lamb.

Jesus is offering to us a personal, intimate relationship with him
that will lead us into the very life of God and nourish this life.
It will bring us to dwell in Jesus and to have Jesus dwell in us.

Mutual indwelling

Let us reflect on these words "to dwell in" or "to abide in"
or "mutual indwelling,"
which are a key to this whole passage
and to the whole of this gospel and which I have pointed out
elsewhere in this book.
They reveal a friendship that implies
a certain equality between people,
each one open and vulnerable to the other.
When we become a real friend to another,
we give up a certain personal autonomy or freedom.
In a way we die to ourselves and our needs centred on ourselves,
our need to prove that we are right or are the best.
We listen to friends and try to please them.
We live one in another. That is *mutual indwelling.*
We think of each other and remain in contact even when we are
physically separate.
If Jesus is our beloved friend, we will want to do what he wants
and live for him and for his works and promises,
just as he will want to do what we want; he will listen to our prayer.
What does Jesus want?
That we enter into communion with his Father
and that we love people, even our enemies,
and do not judge or condemn people, but forgive them.

To let Jesus dwell in us means that we have cleaned up
the house of our hearts
in order to give him space so that he can live in us.
We are no longer filled up with ourselves.
We find our joy now in being and living with Jesus, the Beloved,
and in doing what he asks of us.

The promise of a mutual indwelling with Jesus will become clearer, more explicit,
as we continue to delve more deeply into the gospel.
Jesus is opening this door to the mystery of love, of communion, of togetherness.

All of us can understand that the presence of a friend
nourishes us and gives us life.
My mother died at the age of ninety-two.
What gave her joy and energy and life
during those last years of her life
were visits with friends, much more than a meal,
though meals were important for her, too.
Their love and their real presence were food for her.

People with disabilities who have been rejected or abandoned
rise up with new energy and creativity
when they feel loved and respected.
Their lack of self-confidence, poor self-esteem and fears,
which blocked the flow of life, gradually disappear
and they become more alive.
The presence of someone who loves them
reveals to them their value and importance.
Love and relationships and presence
give energy to those crying out for love.
Jesus is not only the bread of life through his words,
nourishing us with his word,
but he gives life in and through his person, his incarnated presence,
his *real presence*.
It is this special nourishment, his very person, blood and flesh, present to us,
giving himself to us, that he refers to.
It is the gift of his total person to each one of us.

These gospel passages about the body and blood of Jesus
shed light on the words of Jesus at the Last Supper
when he took bread, blessed it, broke it and gave it to his disciples,
saying:

> *"Take and eat, this is my body."*   Mt 26:26

And in a similar way he took the cup filled with wine
and invited his disciples to drink from the cup of his blood
shed for us.
Communion at the table of the Lord reveals and nourishes
the friendship Jesus wants to live with us.
It is a gift of his love and a sign of his desire to dwell in us all the time.
The sacrament of his word
and the sacrament of his presence in the poor and the weak
are also signs of his desire to live a heart-to-heart relationship
with each one of us.
The sacraments are like doors
that open us up to this friendship,
reveal it and deepen it.

A union that flows from the unity between Jesus and the Father

Jesus is leading us into a mystery, a secret,
which will become more evident as we continue our pilgrimage
through this marvellous gospel.
Jesus tells us that our relationship with him and the mutual indwelling
will be similar to the relationship he lives with the Father.
In fact, his relationship with the Father will be the source
of our relationship with him.
One flows from the other.

> *"Just as the living Father has sent me*
> *and I live because of him,*
> *so also the person who eats me will live because of me."*   *v. 57*

We are in front of an incredible promise and gift of Jesus,
a mystery that gradually unfolds.
We are called to become like Jesus, to become his beloved friend
and so to become beloved children of the Father.
The nourishment that Jesus is talking about here
is his real presence in our hearts.
He is calling us to hunger and thirst for his presence of love,
his real presence.

No wonder people react to the words of Jesus and say
"this is impossible; it is crazy":

> *"How can he say that he gives his flesh to eat?"*   *v. 52*

And the author of the gospel adds:

> *After having heard him, many of his disciples said:*
> *"His words are too hard. Who can listen to him?"*
> *From then on, many of his disciples left*
> *and no longer walked with him.*   *vv. 60, 66*

The movement from a faith in the all-powerful God
who protects us and whom we admire, obey and fear
to a faith in a God who accepts to be in the flesh,
to become weak, incarnated, to become our friend,
is too great for some people to make.
They turn away.

People want a Jesus who makes things right for the world;
but Jesus wants *us* to make things right for the world.
It is up to us, with the strength of the Spirit of Jesus,
to give food to the hungry,
to struggle for justice and peace,
to be with those who are lonely, oppressed and in pain,
to reveal to them the good news of our friendship
and, through this friendship,
the good news that they are loved by God.

Deeply wounded in his heart
because so many are turning away from him,
refusing the secret of his love,
Jesus, who sees the confusion of the twelve, says:

> *"Do you also want to leave me?"*

We can almost hear the tears in his voice.
Simon Peter responds with loyalty:

> *"Lord, to whom shall we go?*
> *You have the words of eternal life.*
> *We believe and know that you are the Holy One of God."*
>
> *vv. 68-69*

It is the first time that we hear of the twelve who have been chosen
by Jesus to found what we now know as the Church.
Maybe because they lived a special miracle for them alone, on the lake,
they found the strength to make the transition
and believe in the words of Jesus.

In the Gospel of John, this chapter is a turning point.
It begins so beautifully:
many people are following Jesus.
Yet it ends so painfully:
many turn away from him.
They want to follow a powerful Jesus who would make things right,
not a Jesus who wants to love us
and become our friend, dwelling in us.

10

"Come to me," cries Jesus

John 7

Jesus has had enough
of all the theological quibbles
of the religious authorities.
He has come to give life
and wants us to be fully alive.

Jesus cries out:
"You who are thirsty,
come to me to drink!"

It is the lonely and the rejected
who are thirsty
and come to Jesus.

A time of confusion

Dark clouds are gathering in the south.
A big storm is brewing.
After the sunshine and the beautiful picnic
near the Lake of Galilee,
a new phase in the life of Jesus is about to begin.
The miracles in Galilee brought joy and faith,
albeit a rather superficial faith.
Success seemed close at hand.
But the miracles in Jerusalem bring violent opposition
and there is talk of arresting Jesus and putting him to death.
Jesus awakens hope and faith in some,
fear, anger, confusion and hatred in others.

Isn't this what happens when prophets rise up,
calling people to truth and justice?
Oscar Romero was assassinated in El Salvador
because he cried out for justice for the poor and the weak.
Mahatma Gandhi was killed because he sought to bring Muslims
and Hindus together.
It has always been like this, throughout recorded history:
dictatorial powers seek to get rid of those who speak the truth
and call for change.
Do any of us like to hear the truth about ourselves
and be challenged to change and grow?

This chapter of the Gospel of John seems mixed up;
Jesus says he won't go to Jerusalem for the Feast of the Tents,
then later he does go, but in secret.
People seem confused about who Jesus is.
Some say he must be a good person, a prophet,
while others say he is turning the people away from God.
The author of this gospel wants us to understand that
in the lives of each of us there are turning points,
moments when we are called to make a choice,
to leave ways of selfishness, to let go of security and power

and to walk in the ways of love, compassion, faith and insecurity.
As we advance in this story of faith, things become more clear-cut.
There are those who want to follow Jesus
and those who want to get rid of him.
Between these two groups there are many
who are too frightened to take a stand.
It is not easy for them to choose.
Many of the religious authorities, except for people like Nicodemus,
were angry with Jesus and ready to have him arrested and killed.
They saw him as someone who was disturbing the established order
and going against the ways of God.
How could pious Jews, who trusted in their religious leaders,
dare to follow Jesus and take a stand against them?
It was not easy then – just as it is not easy today –
to choose to follow Jesus
with his radical message of peace.
Perhaps that is why it was easier for the poor,
the lame and the lepers –
those who in some way were already excluded from the Temple –
to become followers of Jesus.

The Feast of the Tents

All this takes place during the extraordinary
and beautiful Jewish "Feast of the Tents,"
sometimes translated as the Feast of Booths.
In Jewish tradition, the Feast of the Passover
is a family-focused celebration
where the lamb is shared by the family.
The Feast of the Tents is a community celebration.
Families would leave their homes and live
for eight days under a tent
in remembrance of the forty years the Israelite pilgrims spent
in the desert, sleeping in tents.
The presence of the Lord God was also in a tent,
the "Tent of Meeting" or the "Tent of the Tabernacle."   *cf. Ex 25 and 40*

Those years of exile in the desert were years of poverty
and precariousness,
but the Israelites were together, in community, among themselves,
with all that implies in terms of faith-sharing
but also in terms of interpersonal conflict.
God guided them through all their difficulties,
during the day by a pillar of cloud
and at night by a pillar of fire.   *Ex 13:21*

Once the Israelites were settled in the Promised Land
they were no longer isolated
but living in a mixed, pluralistic society,
living next to Romans and Greeks
and people who worshipped other gods,
with all that implies in terms of compromise and the danger
of losing faith
and being seduced by riches and power.
During the Feast of the Tents,
people celebrate the way God had watched over them
during those forty difficult years.
It is a reminder of the precariousness of human existence
and the need to trust in God's loving providence.
It is also a feast of thanksgiving:
giving thanks to God for water that brings life
and brings forth the harvest.
So those eight days of celebration are very joyful.
There are wonderful processions.
People from different villages dress in their traditional clothes
and march through the streets singing,
waving flowers and palm leaves.
It's a bit like the beginning of the Olympic Games!

Jesus cries out

During those days of celebration of water, light and thanksgiving,
we find Jesus teaching in the Temple.
People are surprised to see him there teaching so openly
because they know that the authorities want to arrest him.
All sorts of theological quibblings come up about whether or not
Jesus is the Messiah
and whether or not it is known where the Messiah will come from.
Jesus cannot stand all these discussions.

> *On the last day of the feast, the great day,*
> *Jesus stood up and cried out:*
> *"You who are thirsty, come to me and drink."*   *Jn 7:37*

Jesus crying out in this way reveals his own thirst to give life.
It is as if his desire to liberate people, to be in communion with them,
is welling up in his heart.
He is thirsty that we thirst for him.
He comes to give life and to give it abundantly,
but people remain closed up in their attitudes of suspicion,
confusion and fear.
They do not dare to trust Jesus.
They are fearful of the consequences,
fearful of the religious leaders,
fearful of change.

In a land where there was so much division and hatred,
where people were locked in despair,
humiliated by the presence of the Roman troops
and in so many cases poor and broken,
it is as if Jesus cannot contain his compassion anymore:
"Come, come to me! And I will give you life."

In Matthew's gospel Jesus cries out in a similar way:

> *"Come to me all you who labour and are heavy burdened*
> *and I will give you rest."*   *Mt 11:28*

Only those who are heavy burdened and thirsty
will discover the immensity of the love of Jesus
and his desire to comfort and fulfill us.

What does it mean to come to Jesus and drink?

We have already spoken of the symbol of water in this gospel.
Arid, dry land thirsts for rain.
Rain means life; no rain means certain death.
To be thirsty in biblical language is to be dried up inside,
to feel totally empty and in anguish.
Those who feel put aside thirst for love, acceptance and affirmation.
They thirst for a personal relationship.

To drink from Jesus is to receive new life through his presence of love
and enter into a personal relationship of trust with him.
We "drink" his words,
which cut through the chains of despair that imprison us.
Jesus reveals to us then who we *are* and who we are called to *become*.
We are loved by God, beloved of God.
We, too, will do beautiful things;
we, too, can give life to others.

We are all called to give the waters of life

After Jesus had promised to give water to those who are thirsty,
he says:

> *"Those who believe in me,*
> *as the Scripture has said, 'Out of their belly*
> *shall flow rivers of living water.'"*　　　　　　Jn 7:37-38

The evangelist adds:

> *He was speaking of the Spirit*
> *who would be given to those who believed in him.*　　　　v. 39

Earlier, Jesus told the Samaritan woman at the well
that the water he would give
would become in the person who drank it
a source welling up in eternal life.
Jesus is calling us to receive him
so that we may give life to those who are thirsty.

Those who believe in Jesus will become like him.
Through their love, their words, their presence
they will transmit the Spirit
that they have received from Jesus.
They will quench the thirst of the poor, the lonely, the needy,
those in pain and in anguish
and will give them life, love and peace of heart.

Jesus comes to teach us all a new way of life.
At the heart of this new "way" are not moral laws or doctrines
but a personal relationship with him
that allows us to live a personal, heart-to-heart relationship
with others.
Jesus, meek and humble of heart, waits patiently
for us to come freely
to drink from him, so that others may drink freely from us.
We are not called to be governed or held back by laws –
however important and necessary they may be –
but to be guided by the Spirit of God
so that we may participate in the
glorious liberty of the children of God.   *cf. Rom 8:21*

11

Forgiveness

John 8:1-11

Feelings of guilt are like roadblocks:
they prevent us from advancing
on the road of faith and love.

Jesus takes away these roadblocks
and tells us: "I do not condemn you."

Forgiven,
we are called to forgive
and to liberate others
from their prisons of guilt.

The woman taken in adultery

L et me tell you the story
found in this chapter of the Gospel of John:
Jesus is teaching in the Temple.
Suddenly there is a commotion
as a group of men burst in to where Jesus is standing.
They are dragging a woman – perhaps half-naked –
towards him and they say to him:

> *"Teacher, this woman was caught*
> *in the very act of committing adultery.*
> *Now in the Law, Moses commanded us to stone such women.*
> *What do you say?"*   *vv. 4-5*

They are doing this not because they are concerned about the law
but because they want to put Jesus to the test,
to discredit him and destroy his reputation.
How better to do this than to have him contradict himself?
Jesus had preached a lot about forgiveness.
He was frequently with those who were considered sinners,
because, as he said, he had come for the sick
and not for those who are well.
If he says now that this woman should be forgiven,
then he is going against the law of Moses.
If, on the other hand, he says that the law should be followed,
then the woman will be stoned,
and all his teaching about forgiveness will be contradicted.
If Jesus contradicts himself or he goes against the law,
he cannot be the Messiah.

Jesus is silent.
Bending down, he starts writing on the ground.
The group of Pharisees and scribes demand a reply:

> *"What do you say?"*

Jesus stands up and says to them:

> *"Let he who is without sin throw the first stone."*   *v. 7*

Then he bends down again and writes with his finger on the ground.
The men start to leave one by one, beginning with the eldest.
By tradition, it was the eldest who threw the first stone.

Three trials

In this scene we can see three trials taking place:
the trial of the woman: should she be stoned?
the trial of Jesus: can these men discredit Jesus?
the trial of these men: maybe they are acting out of guilt?
Behind these trials is fear.

There is fear in these men;
they are frightened of Jesus and want to get rid of him.
But what are they frightened of?
He is announcing a message of love, of closeness to the poor
and of a relationship with his Father.
Jesus is attracting more and more people who are beginning to believe
that he is the Messiah.
Are they frightened that he might instigate a revolt
and that the Romans might then clamp down on them?
Could it be that they are frightened of the light and the truth in Jesus,
fearful that the evil in their hearts will be disclosed?
Are they frightened because Jesus is close to the poor
and the little people of Israel
whom they have under their control?
In many ways these men reflect a fear of the new that is in all of us.
We are all frightened of change,
of losing control and of losing our power.
We may be frightened of prophetic figures
such as Nelson Mandela, Mahatma Gandhi or Martin Luther King.
Look at the fear, not that long ago, in the white people
in South Africa or in the United States,
when black people began to assert their rights.
Look at the fear of those who are rich and possess much land
in the face of the prophetic cry of those who have no land.

We can become hard and frightened when prophetic figures reveal
the selfishness and evil in our hearts.
They call for justice for people who are oppressed.
Some, such as Dorothy Day and other peace activists,
find themselves in prison after crying for peace in a time of war.

Here, in this gospel story, there is fear and panic in this woman,
caught in adultery.
They are talking of stoning her, killing her!
She is filled with guilt, shame and fear of death.
Did her husband and children know about this relationship?

And then there is Jesus.
There is no fear in Jesus.
He is quiet, but perhaps deeply wounded by the attitude of these men
and their attack on this woman.
Why is Jesus silent?

The silence of Jesus

A trial implies a judgment.
A judgment implies *a separation*.
When we judge someone, we are "the good one,"
the other is the "bad one";
we are superior, the other inferior;
we *know* and the other *does not*.
We build a barrier between us.
Don't we all tend to judge others,
seeing what is negative in them instead of the positive?
But the Word became flesh *to be close* to people.
He calls his disciples to love as he loves:

> *"Be compassionate as my Father is compassionate;*
> *do not judge and you shall not be judged;*
> *do not condemn and you shall not be condemned.*
> *Forgive and it will be forgiven to you."*   *Lk 6:36-37*

> *"Why do you see the speck in your neighbour's eye*
> *but do not see the log in your own?...*
> *You hypocrite, first take the log out of your own eye*
> *and then you will see clearly*
> *to take out the speck of your neighbour's eye."*   *Mt 7:3, 5*

These men want Jesus to judge this woman,
but he cannot.
His very identity as the Word made flesh is to love people – all people –
to be close to them, and to reveal to them their value and beauty.
He came not to condemn people
but to save them, liberate them and lead them to love.
Jesus is silent.
He loves this woman filled with fear;
he also loves these men filled with fear,
a fear that is covering up their real beauty as human beings
and as children of the Father.

The mystery of the love of Jesus

We are touching on the very heart of the mystery
of the love of God and the God of Love.
In the parable of the prodigal son, the Father lovingly awaits his son,
who had left his Father's house and misused
his part of his Father's fortune
on drink and on women.   *cf. Lk 15:11*
When the Father sees his son returning home,
bedraggled and hungry,
he rushes to him and embraces him.
No criticism. No judgment. Not even a word of reproach.
Just a hug, a warm embrace.
The Father rejoices because his son has come back.
He reveals to the son who he is, his deepest identity: he is beloved.
He loves his son and yearns to live in communion with him.
He cannot bear the separation.
That is why he decides to give a huge party
to celebrate his son's return.

God did not create us in order to push us away
into a place of punishment.
God knows our weakness and hardness of heart.
God knows that we are born with much emptiness
and darkness in our hearts.
He knows our capacity to separate ourselves from him.
What God wants is for us to open our hearts
to his healing love and friendship.
Our God is a God of life, love and communion,
who wants us to stand up and become a people
of compassion and justice.

God does not say: "If you change, I will love you."
We discover that God loves us
and then we change and want to respond to God's love.

Jesus and the woman

When the men had left, Jesus was alone with the woman.
He stood up and asked her
(and we can almost hear a change in the tone of his voice):

> *"Woman, where are they? Has anyone condemned you?"*
> *"No one," she replied. "Neither do I condemn you," said Jesus.*
> *"Go and sin no more."*   Jn 8:10-11

Words filled with kindness and understanding.
He begins with a humble question
in order to enter into relationship with her
and call her to communicate with him.
Then Jesus affirms that he does not condemn her either.

Does that mean that Jesus does not see adultery as wrong?
No, what Jesus wants is to liberate people
so that they change their ways
and discover their real value as human beings and as children of God.

Jesus does not want this woman to grovel in guilt,
but to admit that she has done something wrong,
and to discover that she is forgiven,
that she can be free of guilt.
Then she can go free knowing she is a precious person
called to love God, her husband, her children and her neighbours
and to give life to others.
Changed, she can stand up and be herself,
for she has discovered that Jesus loves her.

To be relieved of guilt

Many people today are struggling with a sense of guilt,
as this woman probably was.
I can see in myself this fear of being seen as bad
or as having done something wrong,
the fear of being rejected,
pushed down into the depths of loneliness.
Our greatest need is to feel that we have value, are worthy
and can do beautiful things.

A few years ago we welcomed Daniel into our community.
He had had a very painful life when he was a baby.
His parents did not want him.
He went to live with his grandparents
but they could not cope with him.
He was put into two different family placements,
which did not work out.
He was finally sent to a psychiatric hospital.
He had always been seen as a nuisance.
Nobody wanted him.
Now and again in our community he would flip out of reality,
hiding his anguish and himself behind hallucinations.
He had constructed thick walls around his heart
that prevented him from being who he was.
He felt guilty for existing, because nobody wanted him as he was.

Daniel's situation was an extreme one,
but most of us have experienced, at one moment or another,
the feeling of not being wanted
when we were children;
we felt rejected.
Perhaps when a younger brother or sister arrived in the family,
we lost our place.
Perhaps when our parents were unwell, under stress,
they shouted at us unjustly.
The heart of a child is so easily hurt.
This hurt can become a wound:
"If I am not loved it is because I am not loveable.
And if I am not loveable I must be no good."
So children build walls around their hearts
to protect themselves from this painful feeling.
This feeling of guilt, or shame, as psychologists frequently call it,
is induced in children by people around them
who want them to correspond more to their own desires.
This form of guilt affects our very being.

Normally the word "guilt" is used when we consciously
do something wrong;
We can be guilty of stealing or cheating or hurting someone.
There is the feeling of guilt
but there is also an objective reality: we have stolen something.
This is what we call moral guilt.
These two forms of guilt – shame and moral guilt –
are of course intertwined.
We all feel guilty because we do not love people as we should.
There is so much fear and anger and selfishness in us all
and we do not always know what comes from an inner hurt
and brokenness,
from the feeling of being no good,
and what is really our own fault.
People who have been made to feel that they are no good
will tend to do bad acts.

They do not know how good they really are.
How can we be relieved of these two forms of guilt,
which can paralyze us
and prevent us from seeing our fundamental beauty,
our capacity to give life and do beautiful things?

What is sin?

Sin is an act that we do consciously.
It is disobeying a commandment of love given to us by God.
In the Gospel of John, however, sin is above all
the refusal to welcome Jesus and to trust him.
It is remaining obstinately blind
in the face of the signs and miracles he did
to show that he was sent by God.
It is turning our back on him.
It is refusing to change and to open our hearts to those in need.
Sin, then, is the wall constructed around our minds and hearts
that prevents us from being open
to Jesus, to others and to our deepest self.
This wall of sin is strengthened
as we consciously refuse to be healed
and even try to get rid of Jesus.
Sin, then, is being closed up in oneself and in one's group.
It leads to conflict, oppression and all forms of abuse of power.
Sin leads to death.

We are *all* this woman and these men

The woman taken in adultery in this gospel story
symbolizes each one of us
when we turn away from God and refuse God's gift of life and love,
when we hurt others and ourselves.
In biblical language, adultery symbolizes all sin
when we turn away from the One who loves us
and calls us to a new inner freedom.

Jesus says to each one of us, as he said to this woman:

> *"Neither do I condemn you.*
> *Go and sin no more."*

Forgiveness at the heart of the message of Jesus

The Word became flesh not to reward or even compensate people
for all the good things they have done during their lives,
but to lead people from darkness to light, from death to life.

> *"God so loved the world*
> *that he gave his only Son*
> *so that whoever believes in him*
> *is not lost*
> *but has eternal life.*
> *For God did not send his Son into the world*
> *to judge the world,*
> *but so that the world might be saved by him."*   *Jn 3:16-17*

The names of God revealed by Jesus are Compassion,
Mercy, Forgiveness, Goodness, Kindness and Tenderness,
Light and Truth.
He did not come to judge or condemn,
but to reveal to each one how beautiful they are and can become.
The Greek word for "to forgive" also means to liberate,
to bring people out of danger and into life.
This liberation implies an acceptance on our part.
God is Love and yearns to give himself in love.
Love is never imposed; love is offered.
Jesus invites; he does not violate our freedom.
We are called to open the door of our hearts.

Why do we refuse love?

How is it that we can choose death rather than life,
depression rather than healing,
prison rather than freedom?

There is no easy answer.
This touches on the secret freedom of each person.
For some it seems just not possible.
They do not know Jesus as a healer and liberator.
Those who have known only a possessive love
cannot believe that there is such a thing as a liberating love.
Some want to remain in the depression
they have learned to live with.
Some have been taught that success is the only value:
in order to *be* they must win; they must be strong like God.
For them, to be weak means to be bad.
For others, it is better not to think personally,
but just to do what they are told, to obey the culture, and so on.
The way Christian life has been taught and lived over the centuries,
and even today,
has often blurred the healing, liberating message of Jesus.

Inner struggles also prevent us from opening our hearts
to the forgiving, healing love of Jesus:
struggles between the desire and need to prove our worth
and the humble acceptance of our need for Jesus, for his love,
for his help.
We can be frightened of losing something,
some wealth or pleasure or power,
if we welcome Jesus.
In each of us there is a desire to show that we are God
rather than that we need God.
We can also be frightened of admitting
all the mess and evil within us,
so we hide it behind the walls of our hearts and memories.
We try to show our own worth
rather than to accept that we are loved in spite of all the mess.
Each one of us has our own struggle
to allow the healing love of Jesus
to penetrate the darkness of our hearts and to liberate us.

Forgiven, we are called to forgive

We are also like these men who judge and condemn
this woman taken in adultery.
It is significant that Jesus does not condemn them, either.
Instead, he calls them not just to be spectators and accusers,
but to discover their own sinfulness, to grow in truthfulness
and to become more conscious of what they are doing
and who they are.

Jesus says to them:

"Let he who is without sin throw the first stone."

These are words of truth, light, unity and peace.
Only truth can confront power when one is in a place of weakness.
There must have been a deep silence after these words of Jesus,
a moment of grace and truth.
Maybe some light had penetrated into the men's hearts;
a change had begun to take place.
Now, conscious of their own sin and need for forgiveness,
some of them may have begun to walk the road to inner freedom.
Instead of insisting that the woman be stoned or that Jesus be
discredited,
the men leave, one by one.
The trial is over, the woman is free.

When we judge or accuse people,
is it not because we are unable to accept the truth
of our own brokenness
and to forgive ourselves?
We project onto others what we refuse to see in ourselves.
We accuse, judge and condemn others
because unconsciously we are judging ourselves.
When we condemn others, we are also placing ourselves on trial.

We all have difficulty accepting that we are guilty of hurting others
and of being selfish,
so we reject the law and claim that we can do what we like,
as long as we do not get caught.
We justify ourselves and our actions.

However, Jesus calls us to face the truth, not to judge or condemn,
but to accept that we are selfish, turned in upon ourselves,
unable to share and love as truly as we might.
He calls us to forgive ourselves and to ask forgiveness
for all the hurts we have committed towards others,
for all the acts of love and justice that we have not done;
for all our indifference to those who are weak and broken.

As we become conscious of God's forgiveness,
we learn to forgive others.
As we enter into a new and deeper communion with God,
we find once more our deepest self, our deepest identity,
and our real self begins to emerge.
We begin to love others as God loves them.
If God forgives us with all the dirt and mess inside of us,
then we can forgive others with all the dirt and mess
inside of them.
The walls that separate us from others begin to fall.
But it is a real struggle to forgive.
Feelings of anger and vengeance may remain within us.
We need a new force from God
to give us the strength to forgive
and thus become men and women of peace.

The whole gospel of Jesus is contained
within the words of the "Our Father":

> *Forgive us our sins,*
> *as we forgive those who sin against us.*

Forgiveness is not, however, just a one-time event
where we go up to the person who has hurt us
and give them a big hug.
Forgiveness is a process.
To move from hate to acceptance and love is a long journey.
Even when we have been deeply hurt,
we can grow into forgiveness.

Some years ago I spoke with a woman in Rwanda.
Seventy-five members of her family had been killed.
"I have so much hate in my heart," she said,
"and everyone is talking about reconciliation!"
I asked her if she wanted to kill those who had killed her family.
"No," she answered. "Too many people have been killed already!"
I said to her: "Do you know that the first movement
in the process of forgiveness
is not to seek revenge? You are on the road to forgiveness."

I heard about a woman who had been put in prison
because of a man's false testimony.
She did not know about Jesus
but met regularly for support with a religious sister.
One day she met Jesus and discovered the gospel message.
It was a revelation for her.
The Sister asked her if she could look at forgiving the man
who had given the false testimony.
"No," she replied. "He has hurt me too much."
"But," she added, "I pray for him each day,
that he may be liberated from all the evil in him."
The second step in the process of forgiveness is to pray
for those who consciously or unconsciously have hurt us.

Another step is to become conscious of who the person is
who has hurt us,
how he or she came to be as they are.
What are the fears in them? How did these fears come about?

They, too, have been deeply hurt somewhere.
Little by little, we begin to understand them.

Jesus came to liberate us by the power of his Holy Spirit
so that we can gradually enter into this process of forgiveness.
He reveals a whole vision of humanity
where the chains of violence
and the walls of separation
are broken
and where we are liberated
in order to love as God loves.

Victor Hugo, the novelist, describes forgiveness this way:

> God is the huge urn of perfume
> which continually washes the feet of creatures;
> he pours the perfume through all the pores of his being
> and empties himself through love.
> His work is to forgive.

Forgiveness is at the heart of every relationship.
It is the essence of love.
Forgiveness is loving people as they are
and revealing to them their beauty,
which is hidden behind the walls they have built around their hearts.
Forgiveness is a new force that comes from God.
Forgiveness is the road to peace.
"There is no peace," wrote Pope John Paul II, "without justice;
and no justice without forgiveness."

12

The truth will set you free

John 8:12-59

With Jesus
we are called
to bear witness
to the truth
and to be liberated
by the truth.

No longer slaves
to fear and illusions
or to what others think
or want of us,
each one of us can stand up
and say with Jesus,
"I AM."

Opposition grows

Up until the beautiful picnic near the Lake of Galilee
Jesus seems to be going from success to success.
Many are following him.
However, after Jesus speaks about his body and blood
as food and drink,
a rift appears.
Opposition grows and people start to leave him.
This chapter of the Gospel of John is austere.
It does not begin with an event or a story.
It is what we might call a tough discussion
with some of the religious authorities of the times.
It is about truth
and the light of truth,
which we can seek and love or reject and hate.

Jesus begins by saying:

> *"I am the light of the world;*
> *whoever follows me will not walk in darkness*
> *but will have the light of life."*　　　　　　　　　v. 12

Jesus is echoing and fulfilling the prophecy of Isaiah:

> *"The people who walked in darkness*
> *have seen a great light;*
> *those who dwelt in a land of deep darkness,*
> *in them has light shone."*　　　　　　　　　Is 9:2

To be enveloped in darkness is a difficult experience.
When we are lost at night, fear can overwhelm us.
Unable to see where we are going, we can fall and hurt ourselves.

In biblical language, "darkness" is not only the night
but also the forces of evil that can seduce us
and turn us away from walking in the right direction,
from walking towards the light of life
that flows from love and communion.

When we are lost or confused we lose our inner unity,
our deepest self.
We become divided within ourselves,
pulled in a multiplicity of directions.
So many of us today have lost our way
and do not know what direction to take.
We tend to follow whatever everybody else in our culture is doing.
We become enslaved by fear.

Scientists have discovered amazing new things in the universe:
new technologies, the mysteries of the atom and of matter,
the secrets concerning life and the conception of life.
But the question remains:
With all our knowledge and power,
do we know where we are going?
What do we want for ourselves and for humanity?
Do we want to use our technology for our own power and glory
and to dominate others,
or do we want to use it for life, for relationships,
for peace, for the common good,
so that each person –
whatever their race, culture, religion, abilities or disabilities –
may find their place and dignity?
Do we want to be governed by fear or by love?

Jesus, Light of the world, came to give meaning and direction
to our lives
and to the whole of humanity, with all its history.
He came to reveal the evolution of humanity
through love and the acceptance of others,
through a new and deeper communion with God.
This evolution of humanity is different from a vision of history
that sees history as the growth of power through force,
and the history of knowledge as a means to serve power.
Jesus came to show a new way
and to lead us out of darkness, conflict and death

into the light of life and compassion
where we commit ourselves to people, especially to people in pain,
in order to give life and to work for peace.

Jesus came to reveal to each one of us who we are,
with all that is in us.
It is the revelation of our deepest identity.
He came to reveal that we are precious and important,
and that each of us is called not to be frightened,
but to grow in love and truth.
He came to reveal that we are to take our place in the world
as messengers of peace.

People react

Some of the Pharisees react to the words of Jesus:

> *"I am the light of the world."*

It is as if they are saying, "How dare you say such a thing!
With what authority do you speak?
Nobody can say such a thing about himself!"

Jesus answers:

> *"Even though I give witness to myself,*
> *my witness is true because I know where I am from*
> *and where I am going.*   v. 14
> *...and the Father who sent me gives witness to me."*   v. 18

They continue aggressively: *"Who are you?"*
And Jesus replies:

> *"When you have lifted up the Son of Man*
> *then you will realize that 'I AM.'"*   v. 28

Here we have again a direct reference to the book of Exodus,
where Moses asked God:

> *"What is your name?"*

God replied:

> *"I AM who AM...*
> *Say to the people of Israel,*
> *'I AM has sent me to you.'"*   Ex 3:13-14

Jesus is the light of the world because in and by his very being, he *IS*.
We, by our very being, do not possess existence.
We are born and we die.
We *receive* our existence. Jesus *is* Existence.
All things came into being through the *Logos*, the Word,
and without him nothing was made.
Jesus, Light of the world, is truth:
he is the Way, the Truth and the Life,
because he is at the source of all reality.
When we welcome Jesus, we welcome reality.
Little by little, we become free.

The truth will set you free

Jesus continues:

> *"If you abide by my word, you are truly my disciple*
> *and you will know the truth*
> *and the truth will set you free."*   vv. 31-32

Dictators like Hitler, Stalin or Idi Amin do not want people to be free
to say what they think, or to value their own experience.
They enslave people in fear, silence and an ideology,
and oblige them to speak and live according to the party line.
Dictators use lies, propaganda and secret police
to maintain their power and control over people
and to prevent them from thinking and speaking the truth.

Throughout history, however,
men and women have stood up
to abusive power without fear of the consequences.

They spoke the truth to those in power who did not want to hear it.
These men and women were not slaves, they were free.
Many of them were imprisoned or put to death
because they spoke out.

All those men and women who give their lives for truth
are not frightened to be themselves
and to say what they believe,
to name what they have seen
and proclaim what they have experienced.

In one of her letters from Westerbork, Etty Hillesum tells how one day
she watched hundreds of Jews going into the train cars
that would cart them off to the gas chambers of Auschwitz.
They were singing psalms.
Then she looked at the hard, immobile faces of the Nazi guards:
which of these two groups was free, free to be themselves?

Nelson Mandela spoke about the guard who had said to him,
"Do you not know that I have the power to have you killed?"
Mandela responded:
"Do you not know that I have the power to go to my death freely?"

This freedom is found not only in well-known people
who have given their lives.
Many others have withstood pressures that take people from the truth,
by following their own personal conscience.
I see it in those young people who refuse to succumb
to the temptation of using others for their own sexual pleasure,
or to be dragged into using hard drugs.
I see it in those people who, whatever the consequences,
have chosen not to give in to the temptation of making money
by illegal means and by impoverishing others.
I see the same courage in those who have chosen
not to get rid of an unborn child
even when the pressure to abort is great.

Such people announce the truth by their lives.
They are witnesses to the truth.
No longer fearful of being who they are,
they are free to follow their conscience.

Free to be ourselves

When we discover that we are all part of a larger family,
united in a common humanity,
and that over and above us and within us
there is a universal truth and justice,
where the God of Compassion and Goodness is present,
then we find ourselves on the journey to freedom.
When we have an experience of the love of God
and the God of Love,
we begin to discover how precious each person
is in God's plan for humanity.

With all our beauty and brokenness, each one of us is important.
We can be ourselves and let the beauty in us grow.
We are not the centre of the world – and we do not have to be!
We are part of a broken humanity, and in the company of others,
we can stand up and continue the quest for freedom, truth and peace.

Jesus says to Pilate:

> *"I was born and came into the world
> in order to give witness to the truth."*

Pilate replies:

> *"What is truth?"*   *Jn 19:37-38*

That is the question.

Truth is reality

Truth is what we see and touch and experience.
It is not something we invent,

but something we humbly receive and welcome,
something that is bigger, greater than ourselves.

But truth is often hidden from us,
which is why it takes time and the help of others to discern the truth.
We often find truth only after we choose to let go of
some of the illusions of life that we may still have.
It takes time to find inner freedom –
this is the ongoing work of a lifetime.
I do not have this freedom yet,
but my hope is to continue to keep my heart open to receive it.

Even though truth makes us free, we never *possess* it.
We are called humbly to contemplate the truth that is given to us,
to search unceasingly in order to be drawn into truth,
to let ourselves be led, in the company of others,
into the unfolding mystery of truth,
to be possessed by truth and to serve truth.
To live in truth is to live a relationship of love
with the Word of God made flesh,
who is truth, compassion and forgiveness.
To be true is to let oneself be challenged by others
and to accept all the brokenness in us.
The truth, then, is not something to make us feel superior.
On the contrary, it calls us into humility, to littleness
and to the light of love.
All the light in us comes from the light of the Word of God.
The light of truth, then, is the gentle marriage
of what we see and experience,
with what we have received from above and the Word of God,
each one enlightening the other, each one calling us to live in God
and to see things through the loving eyes and loving heart of God.

Our fear of truth

Human sciences, psychotherapy and psychoanalysis have shown us
that there is a part of our being to which we do not have ready access.

This is a world of unnameable fears and hidden motivations.
All that has happened to us in our early childhood
is inscribed in our body and has formed our being.
We cannot easily remember –
nor do we necessarily want to remember –
all that has happened.
This is what some call the "shadow side" of our lives,
the darkness or chaos within us.

Even the most loving parents can hurt their children at times
by being too possessive and controlling,
or by refusing to honour the truth in their children.
All parents have their difficult moments when they are upset
or empty inside, under stress or so depressed
they cannot listen to their children.
It is never easy to be a parent.

Children, vulnerable as they are, must somehow learn
to deal with all the contradictions, conflicts, violence,
abuse, hypocrisy, rejections,
injustices and double messages that they live.
These can make them hide away inside their shell
and flee from all the pain and from reality
as well as from adults.
They find a welcome escape in illusions and imaginary worlds,
where there is no need for them
to name their anger, their confusion, and all these contradictions,
or what has caused them.
They cannot or do not want to name the truth.

Children need their parents.
How can they be angry with the parents who have given them life
and are their unique source of nourishment?
How can they live in truth if their parents have hurt them,
even unwittingly,
or have said contradictory things, *speaking* one set of words
while *living* another?

Truth and reality can be too dangerous, too terrible for some people –
and not only to children.
No wonder they do not want truth.
What can truth be for them?
Is the truth just finding a way to survive?
Is it hurting and diminishing others in order to feel superior?

The need for security

Perhaps the greatest fear of us all is the fear of being pushed down
into depths of confusion and loneliness and so not to exist.
There we are confronted by the demons of anguish and violence.
We crave admiration and depend so much
on the affirmation of others
that we do not see the truth and the loving eyes of God.
Children can struggle
between their need for truth and justice and their fear of rejection,
between their need for their parents
and their anger against their parents.

We all experience the same struggle living in a society,
culture or group that imposes certain values
where we find security and a sense of belonging.
Our need for this group can crush our deepest sense of freedom,
our need to be ourselves.
We can be frightened of saying something that we know to be true
but that does not fit in with what our group
or our friends might affirm.
We can be frightened of being banned from the group,
of losing face in front of our friends.
We can become dependent on what others think of us
 and want us to do or be.

How easily, then, we can live an illusion about ourselves,
our group, our country, our religion
by refusing to see the failings and chaos within ourselves and in them.

We can be frightened of uncovering certain truths about ourselves
and our group,
frightened of the consequences,
frightened that we might have to change,
frightened of being left alone.
We pretend to be the elite
and hide behind walls we have created for ourselves
to prevent us from looking directly at the facts,
from listening to others, outsiders, who are different
and who may reveal to us other truths about life
and what it means to be human.

Institutions of all sorts, churches and communities,
can be so frightened of losing their reputation and power
that they start to hide the truth
or distort the facts by interpreting them in a subjective way
in order to uphold their "truth," their reputation, their certitudes,
and continue to affirm that they are right, "the best" –
and have been all along.
We just have to look at how "facts" are distorted
and passed on in the history books of different countries and eras.

Today, the dividing lines between the imaginary – *the virtual* –
and *reality* can become blurred.
We have become so accustomed to a proliferation of images,
we begin to wonder if there is such a thing as reality!
The world of the imagination appears to be
more beautiful than the real world.
Faced by such imagery, it is so easy to hide and to refuse to speak
about what we know and what we believe to be true.

If little children are truly respected, loved, listened to
and seen as unique,
they begin to trust themselves and the light that is within them.
If they are helped to discover
that, over and above themselves and their parents,
there is a universal truth, justice, a law, a bond with God

or faith in God
that we are called to accept, to welcome and to love,
they will grow to inner freedom and will develop
their personal conscience.
They will realize that their parents are not all-powerful, are not God –
that they, too, are called to submit to a higher truth.
If parents commit an injustice, they should admit their fault
and ask forgiveness.
As people develop their sense of truth and justice,
their personal conscience and identity grows.
People discover who they are.
They discover that they are someone and that they are called to be free.
They are no longer slaves to what others want them to be,
no longer slaves to the consumerism and the media
that surround them.
We grow in a sense of truth as we meet people
who not only *speak* the truth but *live* it.
These people become like Jesus, a light of the world.
They are witnesses to the truth that leads to the light.

Slavery to what others want of us

Some of the Pharisees react to the words of Jesus
when he says that those who become his disciples will know the truth
and become free:

> *"We are descendants of Abraham*
> *and we have never been slaves of anyone.*
> *How can you say: 'you will become free?'"*
> *Jesus answers:*
> *"Truly, truly, anyone who sins is a slave,*
> *and the slave does not always remain in the home."*   *vv. 33-35*

To sin is to be a slave to our compulsions
and to our need for power and admiration,
a slave to what others think of us,
a slave to our fear of others.

To sin is to think that we are God
and thus refuse the reality of our mortality.

Slaves are never free. They cannot be at peace
in the "home" of their own body,
in the "home" of reality, or in the "home" of God.
They are always on the run, consumed by anguish,
running from reality, from what *is*
into a world of illusion.
Only the Son can liberate us from slavery
and bring us into our real home: the home of God.

Jesus says to these men locked up in their ideology of power:

> *"I know you are descendant of Abraham*
> *but you seek to kill me*
> *because you do not accept my word."*   *v. 37*

They are frightened of Jesus, frightened of reality and truth.
They want to get rid of the one who announces the truth
and who offers to bring them into reality.
They cannot hear the words of Jesus or recognize who he is.
They are cemented in fear and in hate.
They refuse to see and accept the facts of the miracles of Jesus
because if they did see and believe,
then they would have to change their ways
and lose some power over others.

Who are those *we* refuse to look at, listen to and accept
because they make us see our own brokenness
in such a way that we would be forced to change our ways?

The force of evil

In this chapter of the Gospel of John,
we discover that the antagonism that Jesus faces,
the powers of hate that encircle him,
have some deeper origin.

This is not just a conflict between faith and doubt,
between what is reasonable and what is not.
It is the sign of the struggle between God
and evil forces that seek to rule the world.

Unwittingly, these men are caught up in this struggle,
letting themselves be seduced by the illusions of power
and the fear of reality.
Jesus says to them:

> *"You are of the devil, your father,*
> *and you want to do what your father desires.*
> *He was a murderer from the beginning*
> *and has nothing to do with the truth....*
> *He is the father of lies."*   *v. 44*

These religious authorities get more and more angry with him.
They insult and provoke him:

> *"You are a Samaritan*
> *and you have a devil in you!"*   *v. 48*

Jesus answers serenely:

> *"I do not seek my own glory,*
> *there is one who seeks it and he is the judge.*
> *Truly, truly, I tell you whoever keeps my word*
> *will never see death."*   *vv. 50-51*

Before the incredulity and anger of these men,
Jesus reaffirms who he is, his pre-existence before all things.

> *"Your father, Abraham*
> *rejoiced that he could see my day.*
> *He saw it and was glad...."*   *v. 56*
> *"Truly, truly, I tell you before Abraham was I AM."*   *v. 58*

The men are even more furious.
They pick up stones and start throwing them at Jesus,
but he slips away, out of the Temple.

"I AM" is the truth and the light of the world,
and those who follow "I AM"
are also in the light and live in the truth.
They, too, can then say, "I am," and "I am free
because I have discovered I am loved by God,
with all that is broken and mortal in me – all that is beautiful, too.
I have a mission with others to be a sign of peace and love."
In front of "I AM" are those who are beside themselves with anger.
They want to kill Jesus, kill truth, kill love and reality.

Thus, Jesus shows us two paths that are open to us.
We can follow "I AM," seeking to live in the truth,
be fully alive and give life to others.
Or we can follow our anguish, hide in ourselves
and in the darkness of our being and of our group.
We can sow life or death.
This is the meaning of the text in Deuteronomy
that has it echoes in this chapter:

> *"I have set before you life and death, blessing and curse;*
> *therefore choose life,*
> *that you and your descendants may live."*   Deut 30:19

13

Do you want to see?

John 9

*Jesus
the excluded one
is close to a blind
and excluded beggar.
Jesus heals him.*

*Some of the Pharisees
are blind to the miracle.*

*We too can be blinded
by an ideology.*

Eyes open to the truth?

There is a beautiful hymn in the Presbyterian church taken from a prayer written by Richard of Chichester in the Middle Ages:

> Dear Lord, three things I pray,
> to see thee more clearly,
> love thee more dearly,
> follow thee more nearly,
> day by day.

This chapter of the Gospel of John,
which includes the healing of a blind beggar,
is not just about a miracle Jesus did many years ago.
It is about seeing reality and seeing Jesus more clearly today.

Do we want our eyes opened to the truth?
So often we do not want to look at the truth of our world as it is,
with its injustices, violence and hatred,
the oppression of the weak and of minorities,
the divisions between rich and poor.

We do not want to see our own inner reality, our brokenness and fear.
We pretend that everything is all right and that we are all right.
Why are we frightened of the truth?
Is it because everything seems so terrible,
that if we see reality too clearly we will fall into despair?

Yet if we seek deeper, we will find underneath our brokenness
the beauty in our own hearts and in the heart of each person:
our capacity to love, to give life and to take our place in the world –
with others –
to become a source of life and hope.
If we saw more clearly, if our eyes of faith were opened,
we would discover an immense hope coming from Jesus.

This hope would imply change.
Let us look then into what happened near the Temple of Jerusalem.

Jesus and his disciples have left the Temple,
where there had been a painful discussion.
They meet a beggar who had been born blind.
Jesus is moved by this unwanted beggar
who has been excluded from society,
especially at this moment
when Jesus himself feels unwanted
and excluded by the Jewish authorities.

The poor seek and find refuge with other poor,
the excluded with the excluded.

The disciples ask Jesus a question that every culture asks:
"Why is someone born with a disability?
Whose fault is it?"
I have heard this question time and again
from parents of people with disabilities: "Why us?"

> "Rabbi, who sinned, this man or his parents,
> that he was born blind?"   v. 2

Here we see people talking *about* a person with a disability;
they are not entering into a conversation or a relationship *with* him.
It is as if he is a nobody, without a voice, hopes or needs of his own.
People with disabilities are often treated as nobodies.
Why are they pushed aside like that?
Why are we so full of prejudices concerning them?
Can a handicap be a punishment from God for some secret sin?
Such an idea can only come if we think that God acts like us:
"You hurt me, so now I will hurt you. Eye for eye and tooth for tooth."

We often feel that if people have success, wealth,
good work, good families,
it is a sign that they are blessed by God,
while failure, broken relationships and bad health
are a sign of something wrong, something bad, in their lives.

A Christian doctor told me once that he was present
at the birth of his daughter,
and when he saw that she had a disability,
his immediate reaction was, "What have I done to God
that he should send me a catastrophe like this?"
Is that the vision of Jesus? No.
That is why he answers the disciples' question:

> *"Neither this man nor his parents sinned;*
> *he was born blind so that God's works*
> *might be revealed in him."*   v. 3

People with disabilities are like everybody else.
Each person is unique and important,
whatever their culture, religion, abilities or disabilities.
Each one has been created by God and for God.
Each of us has a vulnerable heart
and yearns to love and be loved and valued.
Each one has a mission.
Each of us is born so that God's work may be accomplished in us.

People with disabilities may have many disadvantages
when it comes to capacities of knowledge and power,
but in respect to the heart and the things of love,
many have an advantage.
They need help and cry out for presence and friendship.
In a mysterious way,
they seem to open up to the God of Love and the love of God.
By contrast, those who are seeking influence, acclaim and wealth
for themselves
often seem closed to God in their self-sufficiency.

Jesus reveals that this man born blind was made for love.
Paul, in his letter to the Corinthians, was deeply conscious
that people with disabilities were *chosen by God:*

> *God has chosen the foolish of the world*
> *to shame the so-called wise;*
> *God has chosen what is weak in the world to shame the strong;*
> *God has chosen what is low and despised,*
> *people who are nobodies,*
> *in order to reduce to "nobodies" those who are "somebody,"*
> *so that no one might boast in the presence of God. 1 Cor 1:27-29*

That does not mean that those who are strong, clever,
or well adapted to society are not precious and chosen by God!
However, they must discover –
and maybe the weak and the "foolish" can help them to do this –
how weakness can draw us to God.
Frequently it is only when those who are powerful experience failure,
sickness, weakness or loneliness that they discover
they are not self-sufficient and all-powerful,
and that they need God and others.
Out of their weakness and poverty they can then cry out to God
and discover God in a new way
as the God of love and tenderness, full of compassion and goodness.

I must say that for myself it has been a transformation to be in l'Arche.
When I founded l'Arche it was to "be good" and to "do good"
to people with disabilities.
I had no idea how these people were going to do good to me!
A bishop once told me:
"You in l'Arche are responsible for a Copernican revolution:
up until now we used to say that we should do good to the poor.
You are saying that the poor are doing good to you!"
The people we are healing are in fact healing us,
even if they do not realize it.
They call us to love and awaken within us
what is most precious: compassion.

Jesus heals the blind man

I am touched by the personal involvement of Jesus
as he heals this blind man.

> *Jesus spat on the ground and made clay out of the spittle*
> *and put the clay on the man's eyes.*
> *He then said to him: "Go and wash in the pool of Siloam."*
> *The man went and washed and came back seeing.*   *vv. 6-7*

Jesus, the Compassionate One, touches the man.
He heals not only through the word but through his touch.
Voice and touch are extremely important for blind people.
Touch is the first and foremost of our five senses.
It is the sense of love, for it implies presence, proximity and tenderness.
Tenderness, which is the opposite of hardness,
does not mean possession or seduction,
but the giving of life.
We defend ourselves in the face of hardness;
we open up in the face of tenderness.
A baby needs tenderness in order to live and grow in wholeness.
A sick person needs tenderness in order to trust.
Tenderness never hurts or destroys the weak and the vulnerable,
but reveals to them their value and beauty.
It implies respect.
Jesus touches this blind beggar with deep love and respect.

This miracle of course causes much excitement.
Neighbours and others who knew this blind beggar
begin to discuss the matter:

> *"Is it really he who was blind?"*   *v. 9*

He keeps telling them, "Yes, it is me, it's really me!"
So they all troop off to see a group of Pharisees.
Such a miracle had to be verified by the religious authorities.
These Pharisees, like the neighbours,
ask him how he received his sight.

He tells them exactly what Jesus had done.
Some of the Pharisees respond:

> *"This man is not from God*
> *for he does not observe the sabbath."*   *v. 16*

Jesus had healed this man on the sabbath day.
Other Pharisees think that a sinner could never do such a miracle.
They are divided among themselves, so they ask the man
who is now able to see:

> *"What do you say about him?"*

The man replies:

> *"He is a prophet."*   *v. 17*

The Pharisees do not want to believe that this man had been born
blind, so they call his parents and ask them:

> *"Is this your son who you say was born blind?*
> *How then does he see now?"*   *v. 19*

The parents answer:

> *"We know that this is our son and that he was born blind,*
> *but we do not know how it is that now he sees,*
> *nor do we know who opened his eyes.*
> *Ask him; he is of age, he will speak for himself."*   *vv. 20-21*

The parents are afraid.
They realize that the religious authorities had already agreed
that anyone who recognized Jesus as the Messiah
would be excluded from the synagogue.
Fear of their own exclusion
overshadows their joy at their son's healing.

The Pharisees then call back the man born blind and say to him:

> *"Give glory to God. We know that this man is a sinner."*   *v. 24*

He answers with a lot of common sense:

> *"I do not know whether he is a sinner.*
> *All I know is that I was blind and now I see."*

They ask him again:

> *"What did he do to you? How did he open your eyes?"*

He answers, perhaps with a touch of mischief:

> *"I have told you already and you would not listen.*
> *Why do you want to hear it again?*
> *Do you also want to become his disciples?"*   *vv. 25-27*

Then they revile him, saying:

> *"You are his disciple. We are disciples of Moses.*
> *We know that God has spoken to Moses,*
> *but as for this man, we do not know where he comes from."*

The man replies:

> *"What an astonishing thing!*
> *You do not know where he comes from*
> *and yet he opened my eyes.*
> *We know that God does not listen to sinners,*
> *but he does listen to the one who worships him*
> *and obeys his will.*
> *Never has it been heard*
> *that anyone has opened the eyes of a person born blind.*
> *If this man was not from God, he could do nothing."*

They reply:

> *"You were born totally in sin and you are trying to teach us!"*
> *and they cast him out of the synagogue.*   *vv. 28-34*

Jesus hears that they have excluded this man from the synagogue, and goes to find him, saying:

> *"Do you believe in the Son of Man?"*

The man answers,

> *"Who is he, Lord? Tell me so that I may believe in him."*

Jesus replies:

> *"You have seen him, it is he who speaks to you."*
> *"Lord, I believe," he said,*
> *and he bowed down and worshipped Jesus.*   *vv. 35-38*

This beggar is the first person in the gospel to be rejected
and persecuted because of Jesus.
He bears witness to Jesus and in this way he is the first martyr.
The Greek word for "witness" and "martyr" is the same.
Having found his sight, he could have become
well integrated into Jewish society.
He would no longer have to be marginalized
and seen as a punishment of God,
unworthy to worship in the Temple.
Instead, he chose the truth,
and gave witness to the healing he had just experienced.

It is interesting to compare what this group of Pharisees knows
and what the ex-beggar knows.
The ex-beggar says:

> *"All I know is that I was blind and now I see."*

The Pharisees say:

> *"We know this man [Jesus] is a sinner."*

Blocked by their own limited, rigid interpretation of the word of God,
they refuse to be open to experience and to reality.
They are frightened of the truth that flows from experience
and refuse to discern whether Jesus is of God or not.

Ideology and experience

We are touching here upon a delicate question:
the relationship between tradition and revelation
and the way we interpret this in light of personal experience.

Some people can turn the word of God and revelation
into an ideology.
They judge only from the written word of God as they interpret it
and refuse to listen to reality and experience
and to see the presence of God there.
Others completely reject Scripture.
For them, only their experience matters.
They cut themselves off from the word of God,
which reveals the meaning of reality.

Scripture is the story of God's encounter with the world,
with people and with the history of humanity.
Revelation flows from events that are given meaning
through the prophets and holy people
who see God's presence in these events.

Some of these Pharisees deny the truth of this healing
and refuse to discern whether God is present in it or not.
They have a pre-judgment concerning Jesus,
whom they have already determined cannot be from God.

It is not only the Pharisees in this story
who are closed up in an ideology refusing to listen to reality.
Aren't we all?
We cling to our own ideas, laws, doctrines or religion,
refusing to recognize the manifestation of God in reality,
in those inside or outside our group.
It is said that Aristotle was passionately interested in all that existed,
in all that was human.
Shouldn't seekers of God be open and passionately interested
in all that speaks of God and manifests God in creation,
in all that we are discovering about this creation through science
and in the hearts of people in different churches, traditions,
religions and other groups?
We all need to belong to a community
and to be well rooted in a faith, a church,

a vision of God and of reality.
But we need to deepen our understanding of the word of God.
We are left impoverished
if we are not passionate for the truth in all its manifestations
and if we no longer see how God is being revealed
outside of our group.

Why are we blinded to these manifestations of God?
Is it because we are comfortable and secure
in our way of life, our certitudes and our feeling of elitism
and do not want to change?
Are we frightened of anything that might disturb us?
The God of Love and the love of God are calling us to go forth
on this journey to union with God.
That means deepening our interior life –
which is our only real security –
in order to walk more confidently into the things
God may be calling us to.

To grow in truth

The contrast is striking between
these men imprisoned in their ideology
and this man living in reality, saying simply how things are.
These Pharisees close up more and more;
they become more and more blind,
while the ex-beggar opens up more and more to the truth.
He sees Jesus more clearly.
As his eyes are opened,
so too are his heart and his intelligence.
He begins by knowing *"this man called Jesus."*
Then he sees him as *"a prophet"* and someone who *"comes from God."*
Finally, he believes he is *"the Son of Man."*
The story ends with the man saying, *"Lord, I believe,"* and
worshipping Jesus.

Aren't we all called to the same growth,
to let our consciousness expand towards new truths and new
revelations?

My own intelligence and understanding were gradually opened up
over the years.
I have lived an expanding consciousness.
While in the navy, I assumed that everything in our Western
societies was beautiful,
that we were on the "right side"
and that we were the best!

During the 1960s and '70s, when I first came into contact
with men and women with disabilities in big institutions,
I discovered the injustices of our societies.
My eyes became more open to the pain of oppression.
When I went to India for the first time in 1969,
my mind was expanded.
I encountered the poverty of slum areas,
a stark contrast to the West, where we were living comfortably.
I met disciples of Mahatma Gandhi
and was touched by the vision and holiness of this man:
his prayerfulness,
his compassion for the weak and the poor,
and his thirst to bring people of different religions together in peace.

I had been closed up in my own church, where I have my roots.
I love my church.
I have received much in and through it,
and I believe it can be prophetic for the world.
However, through my experience in India,
I discovered that India and Asia could be prophetic for the church.

I realized that in my church as well as in myself
there was a lot of beauty and also much brokenness;
much faithfulness, but also much infidelity.
The history of Christian churches is painful.

The message of Jesus and of the gospel have been given to me
through my church,
and I am grateful for that.
I am grateful for the Gospel of John,
grateful for baptism and the sacraments,
for holy men and women throughout the ages in the church
who have touched and nourished me.
I have found other holy men and women
in the Orthodox, Anglican and various Protestant traditions.
I have been nourished not only by my own church
but by other churches,
and also by people of other religions,
as well as those of no specific religious tradition.

My expanding consciousness has come about little by little,
and not without tension and pain.
It was not easy for me to let go of simple certitudes in theology.
And I know these tensions between revelation and experience
are not over.
I still have much to discover.
I need to be called more deeply into the mystery of God and of life.

My desire is to love Jesus more dearly,
to see him more clearly,
to follow him more nearly,
day by day.
That is my desire,
but I realize that I still have fears and blocks in me.
I need help on this journey to be faithful.
This journey will end on the day of my death
when I will truly see, love and be with him more clearly.
I give thanks for the journey!

Jesus must have been deeply touched by this trusting beggar,
who had been excluded from society,
and who was excluded again because he believed and trusted in Jesus.

Maybe it is precisely because this man had been excluded
and pushed aside
that he was able to distinguish in Jesus a *real* person,
someone sent by God, profoundly human.
People with disabilities are sometimes more realistic
than those caught up in a competitive society,
who so often have little or no time for the things that are essential.
The gospel chapter ends with Jesus saying:

> *"I came into this world for judgment*
> *so that those who do not see may see*
> *and those who do see become blind."*   *v. 39*

This story calls us to admit that we are sick and blind
– or at least very short-sighted –
and that we need the Light of Truth: the Light of Jesus.

14

The good shepherd

John 10

Jesus is the
"Good Shepherd"
leading us all into oneness
with God.

He is also calling
each one of us
to grow in responsibility
to care for others
and to become
good shepherds:
servant-leaders.
This is a sign
of spiritual maturity.

We need help

I n order to grow in inner freedom, we need others,
and we need a spiritual father or mother who shows us the way.
Such people instil trust in ourselves
because they trust us and see in us gifts and capacities
that we do not always see.
Shepherds care deeply for those entrusted to them.
But caring is not coddling or protecting;
it implies firmness,
helping people to make clear choices.
What is important is that people be helped to grow to fulfillment.

Jesus reveals that he is the Good Shepherd.
Although the word "good" is used in most translations,
it does not capture the nuances of the original.
In Greek, the word is *kalos*,
which can be translated as "noble," "beautiful," "perfect,"
"precious" or even "wonderful."
So every time I use the familiar phrase "good shepherd,"
please translate this as
"wonderful shepherd" – "*the*" shepherd.

Jesus, and those listening to him,
were well aware of the importance of shepherds in their rural setting,
and what shepherding meant in the history of the Israelites.
The Lord was the Shepherd who had led the Israelites to freedom
through the Red Sea,
nourished them in the desert,
and guided and led them through the desert to the promised land.
He indicated to them a way of life in the ten commandments
that they needed to live in order to reach fulfillment.
The Lord had given them shepherds
throughout their history to lead them:
Moses, Joshua, David, Solomon, the prophets Isaiah, Ezekiel,
and many others.

Isaiah reveals that the Lord

> *will feed the flock like a shepherd;*
> *He will gather the lambs in his arms*
> *and carry them on his bosom*
> *and gently lead those that are with young.* Is 40:11

Shepherding is about caring for those who are weak, lost and in need.
It is about presence, love and support.
Shepherds are needed as much today as they were in the time of Jesus,
to love people and guide them to greater life.

Children know that they need their parents to feed them,
care for them, love them, look after them, protect them,
guide them and help them grow up.
Those who are not totally self-sufficient need kind, compassionate
and competent people, as well as good teachers, to help them develop.
Young adults need role models who will help them
grow up and make good choices.
All of us who want to deepen spiritually and grow
in a life of love and prayer
need a spiritual father or mother who will help us on this road.
Many people who feel lonely and a bit lost in our rather rich,
materialistic societies
are looking for people who will guide them in a good and healthy life
and help them to find meaning to their lives.
Aren't we all looking for people who really care for us,
understand us, respect us?

I feel personally blessed.
Not only did I have loving parents who cared for me,
trusted me and encouraged me to be myself
and to make my own choices,
but I was also shepherded by a holy and wise priest,
Père Thomas Philippe.

When I left the navy to follow Jesus,
Père Thomas guided me towards the essential,
never telling me what to do,
but always calling me to ask Jesus what to do.
Now, years later, I see what a gift that was
to have been shepherded by him for so long.

Jesus, the Word made flesh,
knows how much we all need good, loving and wise shepherds
so that we may grow to a fuller human and spiritual maturity.
Not only does Jesus reveal himself
as the Good and Wonderful Shepherd,
but each one of us, as we grow to maturity,
is called to be a good shepherd, a servant-leader for others.

To become a shepherd like Jesus

In order to be real shepherds who lead others,
we have to learn first of all to be good followers.
Jesus is revealed as the "Lamb of God"
before he reveals that he is the Good Shepherd.
He listens to the Father and obeys the Father
before revealing to us what to do.
To be good parents, don't we first of all have to be
good sons and daughters?
Can we teach others if we have not learned from others?
How can we love if we have not been loved?

Some people, however, have not experienced the care of others.
Their parents hurt them, abused them,
and did not help them to grow to freedom.
What about these people?
Will they find substitute parents,
people in later life who will understand and appreciate them
and reveal to them the person they are
and the person they are called to be,
who is hidden under a lot of inner pain, guilt or violence?

Jesus, Light of the world,
calls his disciples to become light for the world.
Jesus, the Good Shepherd, calls us to become good shepherds,
to mature spiritually,
to help others in need
and to seek out those who are lost, crushed or oppressed,
who have been pushed to the margins of society.

The qualities of a shepherd

Jesus reveals to us the qualities of good shepherds:

> *"The shepherd calls his own sheep by name*
> *and leads them out [of the sheepfold].*
> *When he has brought out all of his own, he goes before them*
> *and the sheep follow him for they know his voice.*
> *A stranger they will not follow."*   *vv. 3-5*

Shepherds are the ones
who lead those who have been entrusted to them
to inner freedom –
the freedom to make good choices, to take initiative,
and to grow to greater maturity and love.

In biblical language, to know someone by name
implies a growing understanding of a person,
of his or her unique gifts and weaknesses,
needs and mission in life.
That means taking time with that person, listening,
and above all creating a mutual relationship of communion,
revealing to that person that he or she is loved,
has value and is precious.
One can only guide someone
if there is no desire to possess, control or manipulate the other,
if mutual trust, respect and love have been born between the two.

Trust is the basis for all shepherding and all education.
A man working with street kids told me
that he is unable to help any of them until trust is born,

trust that he is there because he cares for them
more than for his salary.
Trust can only come if the shepherds are good models,
living what they teach,
showing the way by the way they live, act and love.
Double messages, whereby a person does not live what they say,
break trust.

Real shepherds give of themselves freely;
their love and caring communicate life to those who are weaker
and immature.
That is why Jesus says:

> *"I came so that the sheep may have life and have it abundantly.*
> *I am the good shepherd.*
> *The good shepherd lays down his life for the sheep...."* vv. 10-11

Jesus loves us abundantly and wants to give us
all we need to grow in wisdom
and greater human and spiritual maturity.

Being a good shepherd does not mean being perfect,
for no one is perfect.
Instead, it is being humble and open,
recognizing one's faults and compulsions
and asking for forgiveness when one has not acted justly.
In l'Arche we need to ask forgiveness of people with disabilities
with whom we have been too harsh.
Parents need to ask forgiveness of their children
if they have been too angry or unjust towards them.
All those in a role of leadership are called to be a model of forgiveness.
We cannot help others to grow to greater maturity
if we ourselves are not seeking to grow in greater maturity,
compassion and acceptance of self and of others.

In contrast to the good shepherd,
Jesus talks about thieves and bandits,
who flee in the face of difficulties or danger.

These *false* shepherds
are more concerned about their salary, their reputation,
about structures, administration and the success of the group
than about people and their inner growth and freedom.
They *use* people because of their need to have power and control
over them,
and to prove that they are superior.
They seem frightened of personal contact
and hide behind rules and regulations.
They prevent others from growing to freedom
and from taking initiatives.
They are hard on weaker people
and lack compassion.
They do not seek to understand people
but tend to judge and condemn others.
In the face of conflict they leave people lost and alone,
not knowing what to do.
They are closed up in their own needs.

Productivity and fecundity

To become a good shepherd is to come out of the shell of selfishness
in order to be attentive to those for whom we are responsible
so as to reveal to them their fundamental beauty and value
and help them to grow and become fully alive.

Here we touch the fundamental difference
between *productivity* and *fecundity*,
between *making an inanimate object*, such as a car or a piece of furniture,
and *transmitting life*.
When we make an object, it is ours.
We can discard it or do with it what we like.
This is not so with people;
if we are bonded to a weak person
or to someone whom God has given to us in friendship,
in responsibility,
in accompaniment or in community,

we cannot discard them or do what we like with them.
They have been confided to us
and we carry some responsibility for them.
It is not easy to be a good shepherd, to really listen,
to accept another's reality and conflicts.
It is not easy to touch our own fears and blocks in relation to people,
or to love people to life.
It is a challenge to help another gradually to accept responsibility
for their own life,
to trust themselves, to become less and less dependent on us
and more dependent on Jesus, the Good or the Wonderful Shepherd.

At different stages in our lives
we need people to be more or less close to us.
When people are totally weak or lost,
they need a shepherd who is close to them
and who looks after them.
Little by little, however, as people discover who they are
and become more mature,
the shepherd becomes more of a friend and companion
rather than a father or mother figure.
A parent acts differently towards an adolescent
than towards a child of five.

Becoming fully human does not just mean becoming autonomous,
in the sense of doing everything on our own.
This can make us close up in our own selves.
Rather, we are called to be open: needing each other,
doing things together,
in wonderment of the beauty of others.
Shepherding has its source and goal in communion.
It involves serving each other, washing each other's feet,
giving our lives.

Jesus wants to give life to us all:

> *"I am the good shepherd.*
> *I know my own and my own know me,*
> *as the Father knows me and I know the Father,*
> *and I lay down my life for the sheep."*   *v. 14*

To give one's life can have three meanings:
It can mean *communicating to another* all that is precious
and that gives us life so that others may live this treasure as well.

It can mean *giving oneself to another* in total trust and love.
It can also mean *risking my life*
by throwing myself into the raging waters
to save someone who is drowning.

Jesus came to give life and to give his life,
the life of love and light that he was living with the Father.
He came to give his life on the cross,
to take away all the blocks that prevent us from being
in communion with God
and with our fellow human beings.
Jesus is the Gift of God
and calls us to let go of certain things in order to give ourselves.

> *"I lay down my life for the sheep.*
> *I have other sheep that do not belong to this fold.*
> *I must bring them also*
> *and they will listen to my voice.*
> *So there will be one flock and one shepherd.*
> *For this reason my Father loves me*
> *because I lay down my life*
> *in order to take it up again.*
> *No one takes it from me*
> *but I lay it down of my own accord.*
> *I have the power to lay it down*
> *and I have the power to take it up again."*   *vv. 15-18*

To give one's life

Jesus yearns for unity between all people.
He came to break down the barriers that separate people
and to bring them together.
This unity has its source in the unity he lives with God,
for the Son and the Father are one.
This unity between people will flow from the gift of life,
the gift of *his* life.
Death no longer has the last word.

As we pray and reflect our way through this gospel,
we now see that the dark clouds of death are looming.
The religious authorities want to kill Jesus.
We are approaching a terrifying conflict.
Here Jesus is revealing a deeper meaning to death.
He came to give life and to give his life freely,
so that people might live and find freedom.
His death is not the end of life but the culmination of life;
it is the greatest act of love that gives life
and becomes a gateway to a fullness of life.
The sting of death has been conquered.
Are we not all programmed to die?
Is death such a tragedy?

Rabindranath Tagore says:

> Death is not extinguishing the light
> but merely putting out the lamp
> because the dawn has come.

There are, of course, tragic deaths through wars and accidents.
There are sicknesses that bring death at an early age.
The death of those whose lives have come to an end after a full life
can be painful for those who are left behind,
but it is a passage to God and into eternal peace for those who die.
Their time has come.

As children they received life;
they lived life as young people,
they gave life as parents
or as people who communicate life to others
through their commitment and love;
as old people they gave life to others through their presence and love.
The joy of human beings is to leave this earth
having given life to others
who in turn are called to give life to another generation.
Isn't this the cycle of life on our earth?
Spring brings leaves and flowers.
Summer brings maturity.
Then comes autumn,
when the harvest of grain and fruits is picked and eaten to give life.
The leaves fall, and nourish the earth, also to give new life.
Then there is the silence of winter,
a time of waiting for new life to rise up.
The Good, the Wonderful, "the" Shepherd
leads us into this cycle of life
where we are called to receive and give life.

15

Rise up in love!

John 11:1–12:11

Jesus raises Lazarus from the dead.
He calls each one of us
to rise up
in love.

Lazarus, loved by Jesus

This is one of the simplest and most beautiful
chapters in the Gospel of John.
It reveals how *profoundly human and totally divine* Jesus is.
It is about Jesus loving people and raising from the dead
a man who had already been in a tomb for four days,
whose body was starting to decompose.
It is about Lazarus, who was sickly (*asthenés*).
In the language of today, we would probably say
"who was disabled."
The Greek word *asthenés* can be translated as
"sick," "without strength," "feeble" or "insignificant."
Lazarus is deeply loved by his two sisters
and Jesus has a special relationship with him.
At one moment his life is in danger,
so the two sisters send word to Jesus:

> *"Lord, the one you love is sick."*　　　　　　　　　*v. 3*

And the evangelist tells us:

> *Jesus loved Martha and her sister and Lazarus.*　　　　*v. 5*

Later Jesus says:

> *"Our friend Lazarus,"*　　　　　　　　　　　　*v. 11*

and further on in the chapter,
when people see how Jesus is deeply moved
by the death of Lazarus, they say:

> *"See how he loved him."*　　　　　　　　　　*v. 36*

This is the first time in the Gospel of John
that we hear of Jesus' love
for individual people,
the first time that John, speaking of Jesus,
uses the Greek words *agape* and *philia*.
Agape is a preferential love for someone;
a love whereby we seek his or her welfare.

Philia implies the same reality
but with a connotation of mutuality and friendship.
In later chapters, we will hear a lot
about the preferential love of Jesus
for his Father and for his disciples.
Up until now, however, the men whom Jesus chose to follow him
are called disciples, not friends.
There is an inequality between them,
an inequality which Jesus came to level into the mutuality
and equality of genuine friendship.
It is only later in this gospel that Jesus call them "friends."   *Jn 15:15*

In this gospel, Lazarus is present but he never speaks
and is never described.
In Luke's gospel, when Jesus visits this family in Bethany,
the home is described as the "home of Martha,"
not the home of Lazarus.   *cf. Lk 10:38*
In the home, we find Martha and Mary, but Lazarus is not present.
Lazarus seems to be a "nobody,"
except to his sisters and Jesus, who love him deeply.
He seems to be at the centre of the family,
living with his two unmarried sisters.
As I read all this I cannot help but come to the conclusion,
which of course comes from my experience in l'Arche
with people with disabilities,
that Lazarus has a handicap and probably a serious one.
The word *asthenés* can imply this.
Were the two sisters unmarried in order to look after him?
The words of his sister, "the one you love is sick,"
seems to me significant.
To me, these words imply
"the one that you visit and bathe,
the one you love with tenderness and affection,
is in danger of death."
This is of course only a supposition and is in no way central
to what John seeks to reveal here about the love of Jesus
for each one in this family.

Martha comes to Jesus

When Jesus learns that Lazarus is sick,
instead of leaving immediately for Bethany, he waits another two days.

He then says to his disciples:

> *"Lazarus is dead,*
> *and I rejoice for you that I was not there*
> *so that you may believe.*
> *Let us now go to be with him."* vv. 14-15

When Jesus arrives in the village of Bethany,
Martha, having heard that Jesus was there,
goes out to meet him
while Mary stays in the house.
Martha says to him:

> *"Lord, if you had been here, my brother would not have died.*
> *But even now I know that all you ask of God, God will give you."*

Jesus replies:

> *"Your brother will rise up."*

> *"I know that he will rise up in the resurrection," she says,*
> *"on the last day."*

Jesus says:

> *"I am the Resurrection and the life.*
> *Those who believe in me, if they die, will live.*
> *Whosoever lives and believes in me will never die.*
> *Do you believe that?"*

> *"Yes, Lord," she says, "I believe you are the Messiah,*
> *the Son of God who comes into the world."* vv. 21-27

Martha is a woman of faith,
similar to that of Peter, who in other circumstances said:
"You are the Messiah, the Son of the living God." Mt 16:16
Mary, her sister, is quite different.

197

Luke's gospel tells us that when Jesus stopped
at Martha's house in Bethany,
Mary, her younger sister, who had a more affectionate temperament,
sits at his feet, drinking in his words.
Martha, more organized and efficient than Mary, a bit bossy,
complains to Jesus:

> *"Lord, doesn't it matter to you,*
> *that my sister leaves me all alone to do the work?*
> *Tell her to help me!"*   *Lk 10:40*

The one who is more organized can sometimes get exasperated
by the more affective, younger sibling who just sits
and listens lovingly to Jesus.
Jesus responds:

> *"Martha, Martha,*
> *you are worried and distracted by many things.*
> *There is need of only one thing.*
> *Mary has chosen the better part,*
> *which will not be taken from her."*   *Lk 10:41-42*

Here we have an insight into the different characters
of these two women,
which might help us to understand why Martha,
after her conversation with Jesus,
goes back into the house and tells Mary secretly:

> *"The master is here and is calling for you."*   *Jn 11:28*

Mary rushes to Jesus

When Mary hears this, she gets up quickly and rushes to Jesus.

When she sees Jesus, she falls at his feet and says,
as Martha had said earlier,

> *"Lord, if you had been here,*
> *my brother would not have died."*   *v. 32*

This could have been a slight reproach, as if she was saying:
"Why didn't you come quickly and save him?"

> *When Jesus saw Mary, with all her friends and neighbours,*
> *weeping, he shuddered in his spirit and was agitated.*
> *"Where have you put him?" he asked.*
> *"Lord, come and see," they answered.*
> *Jesus wept.*   *vv. 33-35*

Earlier, Jesus had spoken serenely of death, his own death,
as the culmination of life and the ultimate gift of life.
Here he weeps in front of death; he touches the horror of death,
the void created in hearts when someone who is loved dies.
Jesus loves Mary and is moved by her pain;
he weeps with Mary.
He lives a moment of intense emotion with her.
This is the only place in the gospel where Jesus reveals his deep,
human emotions.
When he met the Samaritan women he was tired,
but here something is broken in him.

The deep emotion of Jesus

It is difficult to translate the Greek verbs *embrimáomai* and *tarássō*;
I have translated them as "shuddered" and "agitated."
Embrimáomai is a word filled with emotion;
it can mean "groaning" and can even be used for a horse snorting!
Tarássō can mean agitated, anguished, troubled.
Jesus shudders, he is in anguish, he gives out a cry of pain.
It is clear that Jesus is living something hard to describe.
Jesus is generally serene and peaceful.

We have seen him passionately angry with those who were turning
the Temple into a marketplace.
Here we see something else: Jesus in emotional pain.
Something seems broken in him.
Never have we seen Jesus so profoundly human.

What has happened?
Is it because he is confronted in a new way with human pain,
the pain of weakness and death,
the pain of ultimate separation?
Is he being confronted by the pain that his own death will cause
to his mother, friends and disciples?

The rest of the story shows how the miracle of raising Lazarus
from the dead
is the last straw for the Jewish authorities.
It is because of this miracle that they decide Jesus must die.
So here, in front of Mary, he is torn between
his love for her, his desire to respond to her call,
and the inner certitude that if he does respond,
he will be condemned to death.
It is this inner tension that seems to provoke his shuddering,
this deep disturbance within him, and his tears.
Jesus is so profoundly human, vulnerable and loving.

"Lazarus, rise up!"

Jesus is brought to the tomb of Lazarus,
which is like a cave in front of which has been placed a huge stone.
The evangelist says once more that Jesus

> *shuddered with emotion*   *v. 38*

then says,

> *"Take away the stone!"*

Martha intervenes with her practical temperament:

> *"Lord, already there is a stench;*
> *he has been dead for four days!"*
> *"Did I not tell you," says Jesus, "that if you believed,*
> *you would see the glory of God?"*

So they take away the stone.
Jesus looks towards the heavens and says:

> *"Father, I thank you for having heard me.*
> *I know that you always hear me,*
> *but I have said this for the sake of the crowd standing here*
> *so that they may believe that you have sent me."*
> *Then he cried out in a loud voice: "Lazarus, come out!"*
> *The dead man came out,*
> *his hands and feet bound with strips of cloths*
> *and his face wrapped in a cloth.*
> *Jesus said, "Unbind him and let him go!"*　　　　　*vv. 38-44*

I can imagine Mary, the tears running down her cheeks,
her heart overflowing with joy,
not knowing whether to embrace her brother
or to embrace the feet of Jesus in love and adoration.
She is enveloped in awe and peace. She must have said to herself:
"I never imagined that he loved us like that!"
Is she aware that this act of love will bring his death?

Jesus must die

Many of the people present at the miracle
are obviously moved to faith and trust.
Others go to tell the Pharisees what Jesus has done.
So the High Priests and the Pharisees summon the Council
to decide what to do.

> *"This man is performing so many miracles," they said.*
> *"If we let him go on like that everyone will believe in him*

and the Romans will come and destroy
both our holy places and the nation."
Caiaphas, the High Priest for the year, got up and said:
"You know nothing at all!
You do not understand that it is better for you to have one man
die for the people than to have the whole nation destroyed."

He does not realize that he is prophesying that Jesus
was going to die not just for the nation, but

to gather into one all the dispersed children of God.   *vv. 47-52*

The pain Jesus confronts is that
while some are brought to faith by miracles,
others harden their hearts in the face of such a challenge
to their sense of reality.
They do not want to see; they are blind to reality;
they cannot believe that if Jesus is really from God,
then God will look after them
as God has done so often in the past.
Their refusal to believe in Jesus
makes them refuse to believe in God's love for the Jewish people.

Why do they refuse to trust Jesus?
Is it their fear of an uprising and the retaliation of the Romans?
Is it their fear of change?
Is it their fear of losing power and control of the situation?
Is it their fear of trusting and surrendering to God?
Is it jealousy of Jesus, because so many are going to him?
It is probably a mixture of all these things,
which find a home in the dark areas of our own hearts.
We, too, can refuse to look at and listen humbly to reality,
to read the signs of the Holy Spirit
in what is going on in the world and in the church around us.
We can also refuse to trust the power of God within us and in others.

Jesus calls each one of us to rise up

There are different levels of understanding in the Gospel of John.
There is the *historical* level:
the fact that a man who had been dead for four days
comes back to life,
a miracle that proclaims the glory, majesty and power of God,
Lord of life and death.
The crowd sees this glory and many believe.

There is also a *symbolic* level.
Aren't we all Lazarus?
Are there not parts in each one of us that are dead,
caught up in a culture of death?
All that is dead in us, more or less hidden in our unconscious self,
in the shadow areas or the "tomb" of our being,
provokes a kind of death around us.
We judge and condemn and push people down,
wanting to show that we are better than they.
We refuse to listen to those who are different and so we hurt them.
All these destructive acts have their origin in all that is dead within us,
all that creates a stench in the hidden parts of our being,
which we do not want to look at or admit.

Jesus wants us to rise up and to become fully alive.
He calls us out of the tomb we carry within us,
just as God called Ezekiel to raise up from the dead
all those people of Israel who were lying in the tomb of despair:

> *Thus says the Lord God,*
> *"I am going to open your tombs*
> *and raise you up from your tombs, O my people....*
> *I will put my spirit in you and you shall live."*   *Ez 37:12, 14*

This is what Jesus wants for each one of us today.
To each of us he says:

> *"Take away the stone!"*

Maybe we, like Martha, cry out,
"No, it is too dirty, it smells too bad!"
At his command maybe the stone is removed
and Jesus can call us by name
and cry out:

> *"Come out!"*

We can then rise up, a bit more whole and holy,
with the Spirit of Jesus in us.
We are being put together again.
We can let the light of Jesus penetrate all the darkness within us.
As we find greater unity inside us,
we bring greater unity around us.
The story of Lazarus is the story of each one of us.
It is the revelation that Jesus came to call us to rise up
and to become fully alive in order to give life.

This resurrection is a process that begins every morning,
every night, every day.
We are called on a journey of resurrection
to do the work of God,
to bring love into our families, our communities and the world.

Mary anoints the feet of Jesus

A few days later – in fact it was six days before the feast of the Passover –
Jesus comes back to Bethany
for a celebration meal in the home of Simon the leper.
Just as there was a marvellous feast at Cana
at the beginning of the mission of Jesus,
so, too, there is a joyful feast during the last week of his mission.
Lazarus is there, of course, reclining with Jesus.

Martha serves the meal.
In the middle of the meal, Mary,
in an audacious act of love and gratitude,
takes a large measure of costly perfume made of pure nard,
anoints the feet of Jesus and wipes his feet with her hair.
The house is filled with the fragrance of the perfume,
reminding us of the contrast with the stench of Lazarus' dead body.
It is an excessive, extravagant gesture, an act of love,
similar to the excessive amount of water turned into wine at Cana.
There is obviously a close relationship
between Jesus and Mary of Bethany.
Judas reacts quite violently to her attitude and gesture:
"What a waste of money!"

> *"Why," he asks, "was this perfume not sold for 300 denarii*
> *[which corresponded to a year's salary for a labourer]*
> *and the money given to the poor?"*   Jn 12:4-5

I wonder if there isn't something else
in this opposition of the disciples to Mary.
Why are they so upset?
Where does this anger come from?
Why do these men want to control Jesus
and those who have a relationship with him?
Could they be jealous of Mary's relationship to Jesus?
Maybe they cannot believe that women are important for Jesus
and could be true disciples?
After all, hadn't Jesus chosen *them* as his disciples?
Weren't *they* the chosen ones?
What is this woman doing here, anyway?
Jesus rebukes them, saying:

> *"Leave her alone.*
> *She keeps it [the perfume] for the day of my burial.*
> *You have always the poor with you*
> *but you will not always have me with you."*   vv. 7-8

Jesus silences Judas and the disciples with strong words:
he proclaims his love for her!
In a corresponding passage in the Gospel of Matthew, he says
that what Mary has done
will be proclaimed throughout the world.   *Mt 26:13*

Can you imagine any greater defence of Mary?
He is confirming her in her passion and in her dignity as a woman.
He is liberating her love.
By defending Mary,
he is also revealing his need for her love and trust
at a time when people have rejected him
and are preparing to kill him.

Mary is aware that because Jesus brought her dead brother
back to life at her request,
he is going to be arrested and killed.
He has given his all for her.
She responds to his self-giving love by giving her all,
giving herself in a beautiful, foolish and scandalous way.

16

The path of peace

John 12:12-50

Jesus invites us to leave the security
of certain aspects
of our culture and ways
in order to accept
the beauty in others
who are different
and to reach out to them.

Unity and peace
can only come between
people and culture
as we disarm ourselves,
die to our own plans,
and let God's plans and ways
take hold of us.

Our divided, broken world

We are living in an incredibly beautiful and exciting time.
So many discoveries have been made
and continue to be made.

More people have access to education and medical care,
to new technologies and new forms of communication
than at any time in the history of our world.
Yet we are also living in a terribly painful time.
It is as if we are on the verge of universal peace
or universal destruction.

In the hearts of many people
there is a growing sense of the value and importance of each person,
whatever their culture, religion, abilities or disabilities.
Yet, huge divisions and fear remain
as new chemical and biological weapons are being developed,
and wars and genocides take their ever more horrible tolls.

A global economy is emerging
where competition and rivalry are encouraged,
where the gap between rich and poor countries,
or the rich and poor within each country,
increases at an alarming rate.

These are the seeds of new conflicts.
Yet at the same time, there are also precious seeds of peace.
In this passage from the Gospel of John,
the beloved disciple is going to lead us
to the ultimate desire of Jesus: to bring peace.
It is a peace that will flow from his death
but also from and through death to cultural success and power.

In order for peace to come in our world,
don't we all have to come out from behind the walls we have created
around our hearts
and around the group we belong to,
to discover the beauty and gifts of those who are different
and, together, discover our common humanity?

Jesus, king of peace

Jesus enters Jerusalem
just a few days after raising Lazarus from the dead
in Bethany, a few miles from Jerusalem.
This caused a great stir.
Many people were beginning to believe that Jesus was the Messiah.
When word got around that he was approaching Jerusalem,
a crowd gathered and, waving branches of palm trees,
they welcomed and acclaimed him:

> *"Hosanna! Blessed is the one who comes*
> *in the name of the Lord –*
> *the King of Israel!"*   v. 13

Excitement is in the air.
Maybe some people feel that they are on the verge of a liberation
from the power of the Romans.
Jesus finds a young donkey.
He does not enter Jerusalem triumphantly,
powerfully, in a chariot or on a horse,
but on a baby donkey.
The crowd calls him king
but he is not a worldly king;
he is king of another world, the inner world of love;
he is a humble king with no desire to exercise temporal power.
He has come to lead us into an era of peace.

A prophet of peace

John explains that Jesus is fulfilling a prophecy of Zechariah:

> *"Do not be afraid, daughter of Zion.*
> *Look, your king is coming,*
> *sitting on a donkey's colt."*

Jn 12:13-15;
Zech 9:9

And the prophet adds that
this king will banish all the instruments and armaments of war;

> *"He shall command peace to the nations,*
> *his dominion will be from sea to sea*
> *and from the river to the ends of the earth."*

Zech 9:9-10

Jesus is the humble king of peace sitting on a donkey
Who will bring peace to the whole world.

At this point a few people from Greece ask "to see" Jesus,
which in the language of John means "to believe" in Jesus.
This is the sign for Jesus that his hour has come,
and for his message of peace and love
to cross over the frontiers of Israel
into the whole world.
At that time, conflict and war filled the world.
Each culture, each linguistic group, each with its own religious beliefs,
was struggling to survive against enemies
or to conquer more and better land.
Each one was convinced of its superiority,
believing that its people alone were blessed by God or by the gods.

Jesus came to break down the barriers
that separated people and groups from one another.
He did not come just for his brothers and sisters in Israel
but also for people all over the world.
He realizes that the hour has come
for the ultimate manifestation of his self-giving love,
which will give new life and bring people together.

"The hour has come for the Son of Man to be glorified.
Truly, truly, I tell you, unless a grain of wheat
falls into the earth and dies, it remains just a single grain.
But if it dies it bears much fruit."   *vv. 23-24*

Jesus is announcing his death,
and from this death new life will flow into people's hearts,
uniting them directly to God and gradually to one another.

The grain of wheat must die in order to bear much fruit:
fruits of unity and universal peace.
Jesus is speaking of his own death,
and he is also speaking for each one of us.
We, too, are called to die to selfishness
in order to bear fruit and be messengers of peace:
we are called to die to some things that may be good in themselves
but that hinder us on our path towards unity, peace
and greater openness in the Spirit of Jesus.

Dying to selfishness

Jesus adds,

> *"Those who love their life [psyche, psychological life], lose it;*
> *and those who hate their life [psychological life] in this world*
> *will keep it for eternal life [zoé, life]."*   *v. 25*

What is this "life" that Jesus is referring to,
that we hold onto so desperately
and that we must lose?
It is not just *physical* life but *life according to the values of the world,*
a world as empty of God as it is filled with idols:
greed for wealth and greed for power.
This "life" refers also to our *psychological tendencies:*
our desires or compulsions for success,
to be loved, to be held in esteem,
to be acclaimed by those in our group,

to have power and control over others.
These passions of life are found in each of us
and they appear in different ways at various stages of our lives.
We can feel a desire to be admired by the group,
to become the best spiritual person and to control others,
or to become the best theologian in our own church or group.
We can seek self-glory and self-satisfaction in doing good things,
even by being in l'Arche!
We can create an intellectual or religious or "good" personage or mask.
These passions for life and the need for recognition can be oriented
towards good and holy goals:
they may be necessary at the beginning of our journey to God.
But if we want to go further on our spiritual journey
and grow in humility, love and openness,
we must separate ourselves from them.
If we want to live eternal life now and follow the Spirit of God,
we must die to our need for recognition, admiration and power.

For many of us, it is through an illness, an accident, loss of work
or some form of failure
that we are called to "die" to our own ways of doing things.
Our lives are suddenly changed.
A friend of mine who had just finished a doctorate in philosophy
had been offered a good job when he was diagnosed
with a brain tumour.
The operation left him unable to read.
At first he was upset and angry with God.
All his plans had collapsed.
It took him a few years to discover that he had a new gift:
counselling people.
Instead of books and ideas, he began to discover the beauty of people.
His life was transformed as he entered into a new life
of openness to others.

Someone told me about a successful man.
He was happily married with healthy children,
but was closed up in his own private and fulfilled world.
Then one of his children developed a severe psychotic disorder.
The father felt completely lost, angry and powerless.
Nothing seemed to help his son.
Then he met other parents living similar situations;
he discovered a world of pain he had previously ignored.
His son's illness helped him
to become committed to others in difficulty.
He, too, was led into a new life of openness to others.

These two men "died" to their successful careers
in order to discover another part of their being
and to grow and develop in a more human way.

Dying to elements of our culture and ways of living

In this chapter of the Gospel of John,
we are being led further and deeper
into the gift of God for humanity.
The hour has come for the reign of Jesus, the reign of love,
to be announced to all people from all cultures.
The seeds of universal peace are going to be sown
in the hearts of people through the death of Jesus.
This openness to those who are different implies a deeper purification,
a death to aspects of one's own culture and ways of doing things,
even the ways we think or use words,
that close people up in themselves or in their own culture.

We are all part of a culture and live certain values –
we have rituals that we follow
that give a cohesion to our communities,
that strengthen our identity.
However, some of these are not necessarily in harmony with the
message of Jesus and the fulfillment of the gospel message.

As Christians, we may want to follow Jesus
while also holding on to certain rituals and external signs
of our own culture.
Religion, culture and national pride
can become so bound up in one another
that they prevent growth in universal love
and in the life of the Spirit.
We can be unable to understand the way people in other cultures
express themselves.

Many countries in Europe imposed their culture and language
as well as their religious beliefs on aboriginal peoples,
whose culture was destroyed as a result.
How difficult it is to leave behind elements of our culture,
and even of our churches, that forge so much of our identity.
How difficult it is to accept the brokenness
of our societies, cultures and religious traditions,
to be open and to learn from the culture of other people
and to live according to the urgings of the Spirit of God.

This openness to and respect for others implies a belief
in our common humanity,
in the beauty of other cultures, and in God's love for each person.
We are one human race.
We human beings are all fundamentally the same.
We are all people with vulnerable hearts,
yearning to love and be loved and valued.

This openness, which brings together people who are different,
is inspired by love,
a love that sees the value in others through and in their differences
and the difficulties they might have,
a love that is humble, vulnerable and welcoming.
Jesus does not enter Jerusalem triumphantly,
but humbly, gently, sitting on a baby donkey.

Peace comes as we approach others humbly, disarmed,
from a place of truth,
not from a place of superiority.

Isn't that the vision at the heart of all interdenominational
and interfaith dialogue?

I am profoundly touched by Pope John Paul II,
who went to the Jewish synagogue in Rome,
who spoke to young Muslims when he was in Morocco,
and who travelled to Jerusalem in order to ask for forgiveness
for the ways Catholics have treated Jewish people
over the centuries.
I am touched by his meeting with religious leaders in Assisi in 1986
and again in January 2002:

> We commit ourselves to educating people
> to mutual respect and esteem,
> in order to help bring about a peaceful and fraternal coexistence
> between people of different ethnic groups,
> cultures and religions.

As he gets older and weaker,
Pope John Paul II continues to bring people together,
to share together and to enter into dialogue together.

This openness means that we need to be clear
about what is essential or
non-essential to our faith in Jesus, our love for Jesus,
and our desire to live in the Spirit of truth.
The more we are called to be open to others,
and encourage the gift of God in them,
the more we must be rooted in our own faith,
growing in a personal relationship with Jesus.
And the more we become one with Jesus,
the more we open up to others and begin to see and love them
as Jesus loves them.

People from our own group may not always encourage us
to walk this new path of openness towards those who are different.
They may even criticize us as being unfaithful to our tradition,
as some people have criticized Pope John Paul II
for his openness to other faiths.
We will live times of grief and the pain of loss,
feeling alone and in anguish.
We need a new strength, love and wisdom
given to us by the Spirit of truth.
Our inner sanctuary, where God resides,
needs to be strengthened by the power of the Spirit.

At times, my own journey to openness was quite difficult.
We in l'Arche were not always understood
as we welcomed people from different traditions,
into our communities.
Some people could not see or understand
that we were not losing faith in our tradition,
but were being called to go deeper into it,
to be more firmly rooted in it.

Others criticized us in l'Arche and in Faith and Light
because we were not able to share totally together
with people from different churches
at the moment of eucharistic communion.
We felt that each church tradition has its gifts,
that we should respect differences in theology, liturgy and worship,
and the rules and disciplines of our respective churches.
It is never easy to remain firmly rooted in one's own traditions
and at the same time to be open to people of other traditions,
to receive from them the gift of their tradition
and all that they are living.

Cardinal Walter Kasper, president of the Vatican Council for
Christian Unity, says:

> We need a new spirituality of communion
> which Pope John Paul II described as
> "the ability to see what is positive in others,
> to welcome it and prize it as a gift from God;
> not only as a gift for the brother or sister
> who has received it directly,
> but also as a gift for me."
> A spirituality of communion means,
> Pope John Paul went on, "to know how to 'make room'
> for our brothers and sisters bearing each other's burdens."   *Gal 6:2*

Serve those who are broken

To die in order to bear much fruit,
to separate ourselves from our psychological tendencies
and some very human needs for recognition,
which seem to be so much part of our make-up,
to live loss and grief, to no longer be held
in the security of the group,
is only possible if the eternal life of love and light springs up
from within our hearts, from that deepest place
where we know we are loved and held by Jesus.
It also becomes possible as we serve Jesus in the weak and the poor.

> *"Whoever serves me, must follow me,*
> *and where I am, there will my servant be also.*
> *Whoever serves me, the Father will honour."*   *v. 26*

To die to self and rise up in love will come gently
as we touch and care for wounded, weak bodies;
as we enter into a person-to-person,
heart-to-heart relationship with them,
as we let them touch and transform our hearts.
We know through Matthew's gospel that whatever we do
to the least of our brothers and sisters, we do to Jesus.

As we serve the hungry and the thirsty,
as we visit the sick and those in prison,
as we welcome strangers and clothe the naked,
we become close to Jesus
and let Jesus touch and awaken our hearts.
We become their friends and the friends of the God of compassion.
The Father blesses and honours us
and leads us on the path to unity and universal peace.
In l'Arche and in Faith and Light,
our brothers and sisters with disabilities
belonging to different churches and different religious traditions
are showing us a way to mutual love and understanding.
Some of our communities have become interdenominational and
interreligious because God has called us to welcome people with
disabilities who belong to different churches and religions
and who are alone, lost, in pain and in need.
They cry out for relationship and for community.

They call us to leave certain ideas and certitudes,
and to listen to their need to deepen their own humanity and faith;
they call us to deepen our own humanity and faith.

The anguish of Jesus

Having spoken of his own death
and the death we are all called to live,
Jesus then becomes conscious of what it means for him.

Death implies a terrible separation from his body,
but also from the body of his Jewish people, with all its traditions.
His body bonded him to our world, to the beauty of our world,
to people, to those he loved:
to Mary his mother,
to the little family in Bethany,
to his disciples
and to his race.
His body had been the expression of his love.

His tenderness, his goodness,
his healing powers flowed through his body.
He lived a moment of emptiness and anguish,
a moment of loss and grief similar to what is described
in Luke's gospel.
In the Garden of Gethsemane, when Jesus is in anguish,

> *his sweat became like great drops of blood*
> *falling down on the ground,*
> *and he said,*
> *"Father if you are willing, remove this cup from me;*
> *Yet not my will, but yours, be done."*   *Lk 22:42-44*

Here Jesus says:

> *"Now my soul is in anguish [troubled].*
> *And what shall I say – Father, save me from this hour?*
> *No, it is for this reason that I have come to this hour.*
> *Father, glorify your name."*   *Jn 12:27-28*

It is a moment of deep inner pain,
but Jesus quickly offers all to the Father,
and a voice is heard coming from heaven:

> *"I have glorified it and will glorify again."*   *v. 28*

All that Jesus is and does is for the glory of the Father.
All he does reveals who God is: an incredible Lover.

The *fruit of death*, the fruit of this inner breakage in Jesus,
the fruit of his total, loving submission to the Father, will be *unity*:
he will bring together, into one body,
people from different races, languages and cultures.
He will draw them all to God in love:

> *"Now is the judgment of this world.*
> *Now shall the ruler of this world be cast out*
> *and I, when I am lifted from the earth,*
> *will draw all people to myself."*   *vv. 31-32*

We, too, will be called to live this anguish
as we walk with Jesus,
as we leave behind some of our human and religious securities
to bring others to God,
and we feel alone.

The need to conform

Who could believe in this impossible reality
at that time or at any time?
Who can believe that people could find a unity
that transcends culture,
and that there would be no more wars?
That is why the evangelist repeats the words of Isaiah:

> *"Lord, who has believed our message*
> *and to whom has the arm of the Lord been revealed?"*　　*Is 53:1*

Not everyone refused to believe, but

> *Many, even among the authorities, believed in him,*
> *and because of the Pharisees they did not confess it*
> *for fear that they would be put out of the synagogue;*
> *for they loved human glory more*
> *than the glory that comes from God.*　　*vv. 42-43*

Such people are stuck in their group. They refuse the new.
They are unable to cross over the frontiers
that close them up in themselves
and to venture into the truth,
which transcends their own habits, vision and culture.

I notice in many people, as well as in myself,
the fear of breaking out from a group or of being rejected by it.
This fear can bring anguish.
We fear speaking the truth.
A group, a community, friends, offer a place of security;

it is like a family where we have our particular place,
where we receive love and esteem
and we give love and esteem to others.
We are challenged to avoid getting stuck in such a group,
where we can get caught up in a certain mediocrity.

A community, whatever form it takes,
can be a wonderful place of intellectual and spiritual formation,
a place where we learn forgiveness and grow in the ways of God.
It can also become closed up,
a place of conformity and respectability
where everyone must adhere to the same rules
and have the same attitudes and certitudes,
where enthusiasm of mission has given way
to the need for comfort and security.
The community becomes an end in itself,
instead of being there for the growth of each of its members
to freedom.
It can be frightened of anyone who "rocks the boat,"
reveals the closedness of the group,
and calls for renewal and a deepening of the mission.
Such a person risks being seen as a nuisance, and even being rejected,
condemned as a rebel.
As Martin Luther King writes:

> We are called to be people of conviction, not conformity;
> of moral nobility, not social respectability.
> We are commanded to live differently
> and according to a higher loyalty.

There can, of course,
be some real rebels who cannot submit to a group,
and who are constantly fighting authority.
They are seeking their own power and glory,
not the glory of God.
That is why we need to discern
whether a person who appears different
is seeking his own power and glory,

or truly seeking the truth and the glory of God
and the renewal of the group.
In this passage of the Gospel of John, leaders who believed in Jesus
are afraid to manifest this belief for fear of being rejected.
They seek to conform.
They love human glory more than the glory that comes from God.
Finally, we hear Jesus crying out in the Temple:

> *"Whoever believes in me believes not in me*
> *but in the one who sent me.*
> *And whoever sees me, sees him who sent me.*
> *I have come as light into the world*
> *so that everyone who believes in me*
> *should not remain in darkness.*
>
> *"I do not judge anyone who hears my words*
> *and does not keep them,*
> *for I came not to judge the world*
> *but to save the world."*

vv. 44-47

Jesus, through his love and humility,
came to break down the barriers of security
that have been built around our hearts and our cultures
so that we may reach out to others who are different
and so bring unity and peace to our broken world.
The disciples of Jesus must have been surprised and shocked
to discover, little by little,
that Jesus did not come to bring freedom and dignity
only to the Jewish people
but to each person,
whatever his or her culture, origins or religious traditions –
even to the Greeks and the Romans!

We, too, can be surprised and shocked
as we discover the Holy Spirit
working in the hearts of people of different Christian traditions,
or of different faiths
or of no particular faith.

17

Jesus and vulnerability

John 13:1-17

*Jesus kneels
at the feet of his disciples;
as a slave,
he washes their feet.*

*In this simple gesture
he reveals the face of God
and a new way for us
to exercise authority
to bring people to unity
and to work for peace.*

*This is the way of humility
and service.*

The work of a slave

This chapter of the Gospel of John,
which marks the start of the second part of the gospel,
begins in a solemn way:

Now before the feast of the Passover, Jesus,
knowing that his hour had come to depart from this world to
the Father,
having loved his own who were in the world,
he loved them to the utter most.   *v. 1*

Up until now Jesus has been the shepherd leading the flock.
He has been strong and has performed miracles,
standing his ground and defending himself
in difficult discussions with religious leaders.
He has spoken with the power of truth.
The last and greatest of his miracles, raising Lazarus from death to life,
brought many to believe in him.
He entered Jerusalem with the people crying out:

"Hosanna!
Blessed is he who comes in the name of the Lord –
the King of Israel!"   *Jn 12:13*

But Jesus has read the signs; his hour has come.
He has announced his message of love
and now he is going to offer himself up
in humility, in weakness and in silence even to death.
He will no longer defend himself.
He will go to the very end of love,
he will love totally and unconditionally,
giving life, giving *his* life.
He will reveal in a new way
who he is
and who God is.

The Prologue shows us a descending God who becomes flesh
to lead us into the womb of the Father.
Now, we see Jesus descending to his knees
to wash the feet of his disciples.

> *The devil had already put into the heart of Judas to betray him.*
> *During the supper, Jesus,*
> *knowing that the Father had given all things into his hands*
> *and that he had come from God*
> *and was going to God,*
> *got up from table, laid aside his outer garment,*
> *tied a towel around his waist, poured water in a basin*
> *and began to wash the disciples' feet*
> *and to wipe them with the towel*
> *that was tied around him.*   *Jn 13:2-5*

In the Jewish culture, it was a slave's job to wash the feet of others:
an inferior would wash the feet of a superior,
a disciple the feet of the master, a lowly person the feet of a king.
Never would a king kneel down in front of one of his subjects,
nor a teacher before his disciples.
Peter and the other disciples cannot understand what is going on.
They are unable at that moment to understand that Jesus is revealing
a totally new vision –
not only about the relationship between God and human beings,
but also between people of different backgrounds, cultures and races.

We admire and obey those who do great, brilliant things;
we put them on a pedestal.
But admiration is not love.
Admirable people do not need us.
Love implies proximity, mutuality.
When people love, they need each other
and are vulnerable one to another.
With the incarnation,
the all-powerful One becomes the little, powerless one.

He needed his mother to feed him, love him
and be in communion with him.
He needed the Samaritan woman and asked her for water.
And we will discover that he needs each one of us.
He wants to dwell in each of us as a friend.
He is knocking at the door of our hearts,
begging to enter and to become our friend:

> *"Behold I stand at the door and knock [says the Lord];*
> *if anyone hears my voice and opens the door,*
> *I will come in and eat with them*
> *and they with me."*   *Rev 3:20*

The history of humanity has changed
since God has knelt humbly at our feet, begging our love.
We can accept or refuse.
Jesus is chained to our freedom.

Peter refuses

When Jesus came to wash Peter's feet, Peter reacted:

> *"Lord, you are going to wash my feet?"*
> *Jesus answered:*
> *"You do not know now what I am doing, but later you will*
> *understand."*
> *Peter retorted: "You shall never wash my feet!"*   *vv.6-8*

Peter is so human, like us all.
He has his culture and his own ways of doing things.
Jesus is superior, the Lord and Master.
He should never wash the feet of his lowly disciples.
It is they who should wash the feet of Jesus,
while those inferior to the disciples should wash their feet,
and so on down the hierarchy of importance.

Peter cannot understand the meaning of this gesture.
He needs Jesus above him, not below him.
Jesus gives him security.
Jesus obviously has authority and power.
Isn't he the Messiah, the Son of God, the Holy One?
But Jesus wants to enter into a new relationship with Peter,
to call him to rise up and discover
that he is called to love others as Jesus loves him.

The model of the pyramid

All groups, all societies, are built on the model of a pyramid:
at the top are the powerful, the rich, the intelligent.
They are called to govern and guide.
At the bottom are the immigrants, the slaves, the servants,
people who are out of work, or who have a mental illness
or different forms of disabilities.
They are excluded, marginalized.
Here, Jesus is taking the place of a person at the bottom,
the last place,
the place of a slave.
For Peter this is impossible.
Little does he realize that Jesus came to transform
the model of society
from a pyramid to a body,
where each and every person has a place,
whatever their abilities or disabilities,
where each one is dependent upon the other.
Each is called to fulfill a mission in the body of humanity
and of the Church.
There is no "last place."

Jesus, revealing himself as the least one in society,
the one who does the dirty jobs,
the one who is in the last place,
calls his followers to be attentive to the least in society.

God is not out of reach, in the skies.
God is hidden in the "heavens" of the hearts
of all those who are in the last place.
The gospel message is the world upside down.

Paul compares the Church to the human body.
In the body, each member is important and precious.
Each is needed for the good of the whole.
And Paul adds that those who are the weakest
and the least presentable –
those who are hidden away –
are necessary to the body of Christ
and should be so honoured.   *cf. 1 Cor 12*

Peter's attitude is natural and normal.
It reveals the distance that exists
between the gospel message and our human attitudes
and the ways of all our cultures,
between the real Jesus and the image we have of him as a leader
and a king,
between the vision of God in the gospel
and our human way of seeing God.
We all have in our heads the model of a pyramid,
where authority has power and is on top.
Don't we all seek to become friends
with the important people on top,
not with those on the bottom?

If it is easy to understand Peter's attitude,
it is more difficult to understand Jesus' response:

"Unless I wash your feet, you have no part with me."   *v. 8*

In clear language this means "you are no longer one of my disciples.
We can no longer share together."

Peter's heart is loyal, good and generous;
he does not want to offend Jesus.
He just thought that to be a good and generous disciple
he should wash Jesus' feet.
He reacts in a panic to Jesus' threat and says:

> *"Not only my feet but my hands and my head."*   v. 9

He does not understand that Jesus' answer
shows that the washing of the feet
is not a new ritual that we can follow or not
or that we should accomplish at certain moments.
It is an essential part of his message of love.
It is the revelation that in order to enter into the kingdom
we have to become like little children;
we need to be "born" from on high
to discover who God is
and who we are called to be.
It is only if we receive the Spirit of God
that we can understand and live
this message of littleness, humility and service to others.

You must do to others what I have done to you

Once Jesus has washed their feet,
he puts on his outer garment and sits down.
He then entreats them to do for each other
what he has just done for them.

> *"You call me Lord and Master –*
> *and you are right for that is what I am.*
> *So if I, your Lord and Master, have washed your feet,*
> *you also must wash one another's feet.*
> *I have set you an example,*
> *that you also do as I have done to you."*   vv. 13-15

When Jesus calls us to wash one another's feet,
he is calling us to love, to serve and to forgive each other.
It does not mean we have to actually wash everybody's feet!
The washing of the feet is a powerful symbol.
And symbols are important: they signify something crucial.
The bread in the Eucharist is symbolic.
So, too, are the water in baptism and the oils in confirmation.
Symbols can and do become a sign.
Sharing the consecrated bread at the Eucharist
becomes a source of grace.
We are body, soul and spirit.
All three are important.
To actually wash each other's feet
can and does become a source of grace, a presence of Jesus
which gives us the grace, strength and love
to be truly servant-leaders.

At special moments in l'Arche and in Faith and Light,
we wash each other's feet as an expression of our love.

It is always very moving for me when someone with disabilities
washes my feet
or when I see a person wash the feet of their mother or father.
It is the world turned upside down.
In 1998 the Central Committee of the World Council of Churches
in Geneva asked me to animate a day on spirituality.
I suggested that after my talk, all the members of this Central
Committee, representing some 230 different Christian churches,
be invited to wash each other's feet during a special liturgy.
It was particularly moving to witness an Orthodox bishop
kneeling down and washing the feet of an American woman
who was a Baptist minister.
Gestures sometimes speak louder and more lastingly than words.
It was a moment of both grace and unity.

Jesus gives his body to eat and washes his disciples' feet

In the gospels of Matthew, Mark and Luke,
we read of the "Last Supper"
where we see Jesus breaking bread, passing the cup,
giving his body to eat and his blood to drink.
It is a moment of intense communion through his body.
To *receive* communion is to be *in* communion with Jesus,
and Jesus tells the group:

> *"Do this in memory of me."*   Lk 22:15

John does not speak of the institution of the Eucharist in his gospel,
but only of the washing of the feet that took place at the same event.
There is a deep link between these two realities.
The washing of the feet, too, is an intense moment of communion
through the body.
Jesus tells the disciples that he is giving them an example;
they are called to do for each other what he has done for them.
In the mind of John,
communion at the table of the Lord cannot be separated
from the communion lived in washing each other's feet.

Love at the heart of l'Arche

To wash a person's feet
is a gesture that creates and expresses a communion of hearts.
I became more aware of the importance of this gesture
when I left the leadership of my community
and lived a sabbatical year in one of our homes
that welcomes people with severe handicaps.
Among them was Eric.
We had met him at the local psychiatric hospital.
When he arrived he was a young lad of sixteen:
he was blind, deaf and could not walk or speak.
He was not toilet trained.
I have never seen so much anguish in a young person as I saw in Eric.

There was a desire in him to die;
he just would not keep down food in his stomach.

Many of those with disabilities
who are welcomed in our l'Arche communities
have a broken self-image.
They have been seen as a disappointment for their parents;
they are not wanted as they are,
so they feel that they are no good.
If people are not loved,
they can feel that they are in fact not loveable,
that they are somehow bad or evil.
Our hope in welcoming such people
is to help them transform their broken or negative self-image
into a positive one and find self-esteem.
The vision of l'Arche is to help people rediscover their value,
their beauty, their importance.
Only then can they begin to grow and do beautiful things;
they respond to love with love.
Someone who has a negative self-image will only want to do
negative things to themselves or to others.

But how could we help Eric make this transformation
when he could neither see nor hear nor understand?
The only way to communicate with him was through touch.
Through the way we touched, held and washed his body
with respect and love,
we were able to communicate and reveal to him
that he was precious.

Revelation of the love of Jesus

I can imagine with what tenderness
Jesus touches the feet of his disciples,
looks into their eyes,
calls each one by name and says a special word to each one.

When he speaks at the meal, he speaks to them all;
he does not have a personal contact with each one individually.
But as he kneels humbly before each one and washes their feet,
he has a *personal* contact with each one.
He reveals to each one his love,
which is both comforting and challenging.
He sees in each one a presence of his Father,
whom he loves and serves.
The love of Jesus reveals that we are important,
that we are a presence of God
and are called to stand up and do the work of God:
to love others as God loves them,
to serve others and to wash their feet.

By washing his disciples' feet, Jesus does not diminish his authority.
He affirms that he has authority, that he is "Lord and Master."
But he wants to reveal a new way of exercising authority
through humility, service and love, through a communion of hearts,
in a manner that implies closeness, friendliness, openness and humility,
a desire to bridge the gap that so often exists
between those "in" leadership
and those "under" their leadership.
Some leaders feel insecure,
and that can make them pompous, self-satisfied, aloof.
They tend to lord it over others and control them.
They hide their insecurity,
their weakness and their difficulties in dealing with relationships
behind symbols:
big desks, big cars, magnificent clothes,
all of which keep people at a distance.

Mahatma Gandhi was deeply influenced
by the life and message of Jesus,
especially by the Sermon on the Mount and the washing of the feet.
Even when he had great power as a leader of his country,
he took the humblest place in the ashram where he lived.

His role each day was to clean the toilets:
a sign that he wanted to serve others.

Model of forgiveness

To wash is *to cleanse.*
Jesus washes his disciples' feet as a sign of cleansing their hearts,
a sign of forgiveness.

It is never easy to exercise authority.
Those who routinely do exercise it –
parents, teachers, ministers, priests –
can either be too controlling
or too frightened of intervening,
frightened of conflict and other people's freedom.
Leaders can easily make mistakes.
When one is in a leadership position
it is not easy to be wise, compassionate and yet firm.
The Holy Spirit teaches us to be *servant-leaders* in truth.
Some people always seem to be in opposition to authority;
not everyone can be happy with all decisions.
That is why leaders are frequently criticized
and attacked verbally.
They are called to be models of forgiveness.
But how difficult it is to accept those who criticize or reject us!
We easily build walls to protect ourselves from those who oppose us.
We feel insecure and frightened of conflict.
We do not always want to wash their feet
as Jesus washed the feet of Judas.

Through the washing of the feet,
Jesus reveals a new way of exercising authority,
not from above but from below.

As the Good Shepherd, Jesus exercises his authority *standing upright*:
he calls each one by their name
and leads them in the right direction, correcting them when necessary.

Here, Jesus *kneels* at their feet,
wanting to help them to rise up.
He is their servant.

Later he will exercise authority by *lying down*,
on the cross,
offering his life for those he loves,
giving life through the offering of his very being.

The difficulty of having power

Jesus, by washing the disciples' feet,
is saying something about the distinction so common in humanity
and throughout the history of humanity
between master and slave,
between those in power and the powerless,
between superiors and inferiors.
In many cultures, slaves did all the really difficult, strenuous,
hard manual labour,
and were forced to work horribly long hours.
They were the ones who built the pyramids
and the palaces of the emperors.
They were the ones on whose shoulders
industrial societies depended,
as they worked in inhuman conditions and for a pittance.
Then, as now, immigrants in Europe did the work that others refused,
just as factory workers in the South
provide designer-label products for consumers in the North.

Aristotle justifies it this way, saying that those with good heads,
the thinkers, should govern,
while those who are essentially "hand"-driven
should do manual labour.
For him, this was a natural distinction:
those with good heads were superior and closer to the gods.
Even so, Aristotle affirmed that superiors should treat slaves with justice
at a time when slaves were usually treated with disdain.

Very quickly, this distinction between the thinker and the doer,
the intellectual and the labourer,
the superior and the inferior,
those who govern and those who are governed,
became the basis of all forms of racism and sexism.

Jesus came to make things new.
For Jesus, each person is precious,
each one is loved by God,
each is called to become the "home" of God;
each has a gift to bring to others,
each one should be deeply respected.

Unfortunately, Christian communities often reflect
the model of a pyramid
rather than the one of a body.
After the conversion of Constantine in the year 313,
Church and State became intertwined.
Kings and princes exerted a huge influence on the Church
and on church affairs.
Many bishops and abbots acted like princes and lords,
wielding a lot of power.
Building huge palaces and beautiful buildings
became more important than being attentive to the poor
and seeing them at the heart of the Church.

Christianity became magnified and projected
through architecture and the arts,
through philosophy, theology and all forms of creative expression.
Beauty and creativity certainly have their place.
Yet power can quickly corrupt, as the people who crave it
seek influence and honour.

The dominant cultures of society
slowly penetrated the life of the Church.

Those with power became the "important ones" and were magnified.
Francis, the "Poverello of Assisi," reacted in a strong yet simple way –
as many other holy people have done
throughout the history of the Church.
He did not attack the institution,
which included many good and loyal people
caught up in the structures of the institutional church.
Instead, he took seriously the call to poverty
found in the message of Jesus
and his commitment to the poor.
He chose another way.
Men and women flocked to him and embraced his way of life.
The institutional church, despite being caught up in its own culture,
still encouraged him and his followers to walk the way of poverty.

Francis managed to bring back to life
the gospel message *within* the Church:
a message of humility and service,
a message of peace and unity,
a message of washing each other's feet,
a message of non-violence, poverty and commitment to the poor,
a message of prayer and of Providence.
In his Admonitions, Francis writes about the heads of his fraternities,
whom he calls the servers:

> And blessed is that servant
> who does not place himself in a high position of his own will
> and always desires to be under the feet of others.

Followers of Jesus will continually be caught up in the paradox.
Shepherds, teachers and leaders are necessary.
They have power, but how should they exercise that power
in the spirit of the gospels?
How should they give a clear message
about the truth of Jesus' message?
How should they speak out against the powers of wealth?
How should they be servant-leaders who humbly give their lives?

The need for power, acclaim and honours
can undermine the message of Jesus
and lead to a road of compromise with the values of society.
We all imagine that if we had more money, more influence
and more power,
we would be able to set things right.
I am very familiar with this need to compromise,
for it is something I sense in myself
as well as in my own communities.
It is sometimes easier for me to accept
the experience of being acclaimed
for a book I have written or a talk I have given
than just to sit down, poorly and humbly,
and share my life lovingly
with my brothers and sisters in l'Arche.
How quickly at times I feel the urge to set things right,
to control or dominate situations,
rather than to wait humbly and find the right way of doing things.
We all have to avoid getting caught up in the power game.
In order to exercise authority humbly, in a spirit of service, as Jesus did
we need the humble, loving force of the Holy Spirit.

The message of Jesus is clear:
stay close to people, especially to those who are lonely,
weak and in need;
become their friend, their brother, their sister.
Maybe we cannot all live with the disadvantaged of our city
or be with the most oppressed,
but each one of us can befriend a weak person,
an elderly lady who has Alzheimer's or a young man with HIV/AIDS.

When the poor and the weak are present,
they prevent us from falling into the trap of power –
even the power to do good –
of thinking that it is we who are the good ones, the spiritual ones,
who must save the Saviour and his church.
As we get close to the poor and the weak

we begin to accept our own poverty and weakness;
we learn how to become vulnerable to others, not to control them,
and how to cry out to others and to Jesus:
"I cannot do this on my own!
I need your help."

As we get closer to the poor,
we begin to live the beatitude of the poor.
When St. Lawrence, a deacon in the church in Rome,
was commanded at the point of the sword
to give up the riches of the church,
he arrived in front of the Roman authorities
with all the poor and the lame of Rome.
He said, "Here are the riches of the Church!"

St. Lawrence was burned alive, martyred for that action,
in the year 258.
His voice continues to speak throughout the centuries:
the poor and the lame are the riches of the Church
because they are a presence of Jesus.
In their vulnerability they, like Jesus, are begging
for our hearts, our love and our friendship.

After telling the disciples
that they are called to wash each other's feet, Jesus says:

> *"If you know this, blessed are you if you do it."*

The Greek word for "blessed" implies being "blessed by God."
It also implies an abundance of joy, a beatitude,
a participation in the joy of God.
If we choose to take the last place,
if we wash each other's feet and humbly serve one another,
we receive a blessing from God.
We are close to God and live in God's presence.
We become like God and, our hearts overflowing with love,
we transmit the love of God.

18

How do we react to love?

John 13:18-30

Peter, Judas and the "beloved disciple":
three men who react in different ways
to Jesus' love.

Judas rejects and fears love. He pushes Jesus away.

Peter cannot understand Jesus. He loves Jesus
but wants to do things his own way.

The beloved disciple surrenders to Jesus' love
and becomes his intimate friend.

These three attitudes are in each one of us
at different moments of our lives.

The betrayal

Having washed his disciples' feet,
revealing to them his yearning for love,
unity and communion, Jesus is troubled.
He recalls the words of Psalm 41,
which speak of a bosom and trusted friend,

> *who ate of my bread*
> *and lifted the heel against me.*   *v. 18*

He is referring to Judas.
Judas, his disciple, his bosom friend.
Judas, whom he had trusted.
Judas, whose feet he had washed.
Judas, who had already betrayed him.
Is there anything more horrible than betrayal?

Betrayal is more than separation or rejection.
To betray is to use the secrets of a person's personal life,
thoughts confided to a "friend,"
and to turn against that person,
to use their confided thoughts or words
in order to hurt and defile them,
to destroy a reputation.

Jesus can no longer contain his emotion and anguish.

> *Having said these things, Jesus, in anguish*
> *[or troubled in his spirit] testified:*
> *"Truly, truly, I tell you,*
> *one of you is going to betray me."*   *Jn 13:21*

The disciples are shattered by this statement
but probably even more so by the emotion revealed in Jesus:
his face, his eyes, his body.
His hands must have quivered,
his voice faltering and tear-filled.

What is happening?
Is it possible that one of the chosen ones is going to betray Jesus?
Who can it be?
We read in the Gospel of John:

> *There was a disciple, the one whom Jesus loved,*
> *who was reclining on the heart of Jesus;*
> *Peter motioned to him, asking him to ask Jesus*
> *of whom he was speaking.*
> *He then, reclining on the heart of Jesus, said: "Lord, who is it?*
> *Jesus answered: "It is the one to whom I will give this piece of*
> *bread dipped [in the wine]."*
> *Then, Jesus took a piece of bread, dipped it*
> *and gave it to Judas, son of the Iscariot.*
> *After Judas had received it, Satan entered into him.*
> *Jesus said: "Do quickly what you are going to do."*
> *Judas, having eaten the bread, went out.*
> *It was night.*   *vv. 23-27, 30*

To put into someone's mouth a piece of bread dipped in wine
is an act of intimacy and friendship.
Jesus continued to reveal his love for Judas.
But Judas is blocked, too broken and anguished
to continue this two-faced play.

He gets up and quickly goes out.
As the text says:
"It was night."
Yes, it was night, the time of darkness and evil.

There, in the midst of this scene filled with emotion,
are *Judas*,
the unnamed *beloved disciple*,
and *Peter*.
three men who have radically different relationships with Jesus.

Judas refuses the love of Jesus, is in opposition to him.
He has begun to hate Jesus.
The beloved disciple totally trusts and loves Jesus
and knows that Jesus loves him in return.
Peter? He is confused.
He refused to let Jesus wash his feet
because he did not understand Jesus.
He feels awkward in front of him
and does not dare speak directly to him.

These three men represent each one of us
at different moments of our lives.
Like Judas, at times we can be in revolt towards Jesus,
and want to be left alone, autonomous, not dependent on love.
Like the beloved disciple,
we may have moments of intimacy with Jesus,
surrendered in love, *"resting on his heart."*
Like Peter, we can have moments where we are confused by Jesus
and by the way he lives and loves.
We may want to do things that are acceptable
on the social or political level,
or change things in an urgent and highly visible way.
In pursuing tangible, visible, instant results
we may turn away from a communion of love with Jesus.

Let us look more closely at these three men.

The "beloved disciple"

The beloved disciple is reclining on the heart of Jesus.
The Greek word *kolpos,* which is translated as *"heart,"*
really signifies "womb," the inner part of our being,
which is the source of life and fecundity in each woman.
In the Prologue of this gospel,
it is said that Jesus is in the "womb" of the Father.   *Jn 1:18*
It is because he is at the source of all life in the Father
that he alone can make the Father known.

By saying that the beloved disciple is reclining
"in the 'womb' of Jesus"
the author of this gospel is signifying that
the beloved is *dwelling in* Jesus;
he is an intimate friend of Jesus
so he can reveal to others the secrets of Jesus' heart.

With his head resting on the heart of Jesus,
the beloved disciple must have sensed
the wounded, anguished heartbeat of Jesus,
his vulnerability, his littleness, his pain in the face of Judas' betrayal.
Jesus is terribly hurt,
wounded by the rejection of his love.
The closedness and hardness of Judas,
the hate emanating from him, must have awoken deep anguish
within Jesus.

The beloved disciple must have wanted to comfort and console
the wounded heart of Jesus
by showing him his love and trust.

Can we, too, sense the pain in the heart of God –
the pain caused by all the hatred that exists in our world,
by people who do not want to receive God's healing love?
Can we, too, remain close to the heart of God
to console our loving God?
The beloved disciple reveals to us that we are called
to be in communion with Jesus,
to be still, to be present to Jesus
and to receive in our hearts all that is in his heart,
the love and the pain:
to remain in him and he in us,
one in love.

Peter

Peter, on the other hand, is unable to understand the weakness,
vulnerability and humility in Jesus and in his message.

In Matthew's gospel, when Jesus tells the disciples
that he is going to suffer greatly and be killed,
Peter takes him aside and rebukes him:

> *"God forbid it, Lord. This must never happen to you!"*

Jesus retorts:

> *"Get behind me, Satan! You are a stumbling block to me.
> Your vision is not of God but of human beings."*   Mt 16:22-23

These words apply to many of us,
especially when we are unable to understand Jesus
and what he is saying,
influenced as we are by the preoccupations of our culture and society.
Peter is very human and generous
and has a very human vision of Jesus and of his mission.
Later on in the chapter, Peter says to Jesus:

> *"I will lay down my life for you."*   v. 37

He wants to save the Saviour!
Jesus tells him then that a little later on, *"before the cock crows,"*
Peter is going to deny Jesus three times.
Peter is a complex personality, both strong and weak at the same time,
divided in himself.
He will deny Jesus
but he will weep bitterly over that and ask for forgiveness.
He has to become more humble and to trust
even when he does not understand.
He needs to learn
to no longer count only on his own strength and resources
but to accept his own weakness,
and to depend upon the Holy Spirit.

Isn't Peter a sign of hope for all of us
who want to follow and serve Jesus,
yet who at the same time end up denying him again and again?
Even worse, we pretend not to know him.
We are sometimes frightened of love
and of the responsibility of an intimate relationship with Jesus.
We can say "yes" to a powerful Jesus who calls us to do big things –
as long as we remain in control.
On the other hand, to say "no" to a Jesus who is weak and calls for love
and a communion of hearts is much harder.
It is difficult to become like a child
and to trust unconditionally in love.
Like so many others, I like to hold onto
what I can exert power over and control.
Peter is indeed in me.
And in each one of us.

The relationship between Peter and John
is similar to the relationship between Martha and Mary.
Mary is clearly the loved one, the "beloved."
Martha, the elder sister, is a woman of faith whose declaration of faith
in Bethany is similar to Peter's in Matthew's gospel.
Martha, after having spoken to Jesus, goes and gets Mary,
probably feeling that Mary can influence him
to bring Lazarus back to life.
In this chapter of the Gospel of John,
Peter, the *"elder brother,"* asks the *"beloved disciple"* to ask Jesus
who is going to betray him.
Peter has made such a fool of himself at the washing of the feet
that he doesn't dare ask himself.
Martha and Peter are obviously loved by Jesus but both of them,
good organizers and people of strong faith, act in a very human way.
They have their gifts and, as different as they may be,
they are both important disciples of Jesus.
They will eventually learn that what is most important
is to let themselves be loved by Jesus.

Judas

Then there is Judas.
Who is this bosom friend of Jesus,
chosen by Jesus,
who turns to hate him
and finally agrees to help get rid of him?
Who is this strange, complicated person
who appears three times in the gospel,
 each time in opposition to Jesus?

Judas loses his trust in Jesus and starts to oppose him
when Jesus speaks of giving his body to be eaten
and his blood to be drunk
as a sign of friendship and intimacy.

> *"Wasn't it I who chose you, the twelve?*
> *However, one of you is a devil," said Jesus.*
> *He was referring to Judas, son of Simon Iscariot,*
> *because he was going to betray him:*
> *Judas, one of the twelve.*   Jn 6:70-71

In Bethany, Judas becomes angry with Mary
when she covers Jesus' feet
with precious ointment and wipes them with her hair.
Is Judas angry because he steals money from the community purse?
Or is he angry with Mary because of the special relationship of love
that bonds her so closely to Jesus?

Is he angry at love and closeness,
a love and a closeness he craves
but can never find or knows he can never trust?

In this chapter we see that even before Jesus washes the disciples' feet,
the devil has already put into the heart of Judas the idea to betray Jesus.

Now the idea becomes a reality, a choice,
even after Jesus has knelt down at Judas' feet
in a gesture of humility and love,
after Jesus has put into Judas' mouth the piece of bread dipped in wine,
a gesture of love.
Satan enters into him and Judas leaves the table.
Judas, imprisoned in darkness,
filled with an anguish of self-hate,
cannot remain still.
He is unable to open up to Jesus;
he has to leave.
It is a night of inner darkness and hatred.

How can we explain this hatred in Judas?
Some people hate love or are angry with love.
They want power, efficiency and affirmation
of their personal power, capacities, authority and identity.
Love appears to them as weakness, a horrible emptiness.
In love we submit to the one we love.
We even share our weakness with the friend.
We lose a certain freedom.
We offer ourselves and give ourselves to the beloved.
Some forms of love can distort themselves
into an unhealthy dependence
because we do not know who we are.
Our real self disappears in a form of fusion.
This is not love.
Love is an affirmation of our personhood.
Each person freely gives himself or herself and receives the other,
not out of fear or from a place of emptiness,
but out of love.
True love is a communion of hearts joined together in a fullness of joy.
It is the completeness of our humanity,
the fullness of a person.
Far from suppressing freedom and creativity, it enhances them.
We accomplish activities not from a place of fear or the need to prove,

but out of love.
This is essentially true when we become one in Jesus
and God dwells in us and we in God.
Our creativity flows from this oneness.

Judas seems to have hated love

To hate an unhealthy love that creates fusion, dependency
and the suppression of our inner person is normal and good.
We must separate ourselves from such attitudes.
But to hate a true, healthy love is dangerous.
This hate comes when a child has never been treated with respect,
has never been seen as unique and important,
has never tasted any real love but only indifference,
violence and abuse.
Such children have had to build thick barriers around their hearts
in order to protect themselves.
It is very difficult for them to recognize and accept real love.
This hate can also come when a person
has locked himself or herself up in pride,
when the person has decided not to submit to anyone
and to pretend that he or she is God.
It is a conscious refusal of love because love implies openness,
sharing and humility
and that he or she is not God.

What is the source of this hate in Judas?
We do not know.
We do know, however, that Jesus wants to liberate Judas,
and each one of us, from fear.
Judas wants to be part of Jesus' group of chosen disciples
and enjoy power,
but he cannot accept to humbly open himself to Jesus
in a communion of hearts.
He wants spiritual power but not love.
His betrayal of Jesus leads him to take his own life.   *cf Mt 27:5*

Perhaps, just before he actually loses consciousness and dies,
he remembers the loving and forgiving face of Jesus
as Jesus washed his feet,
and his heart opens to the love and mercy of Jesus.

The glory of God

Once Judas leaves the room, it is as if Jesus makes a cry of victory.
He is no longer troubled by the vibrations of hatred
coming from Judas.
He can speak from his heart:

> *"Now the Son of Man has been glorified*
> *and God has been glorified in him.*
> *If God has been glorified in him,*
> *God will also glorify him in himself,*
> *and at once will glorify him."*   *vv. 1-32*

We will see later in the Gospel of John that Jesus is the glory of God;
the glory of God is the manifestation of who God is:
it is God's almightiness and love,
it is God's littleness and humility,
it is God's love and deep respect for each one of us.
The glory of God is Jesus walking serenely
towards the total gift of himself in love:

> *"Little children, I am with you only for a little longer.*
> *You will look for me, and as I said to the Jews now I say to you,*
> *where I am going you cannot come."*   *v. 33*

Jesus calls the disciples *"little children,"*
because in a sense they really are little children still.
They have been barely born in discipleship,
they have known Jesus for only three years.
They are still very immature.
They will be asked to grow quickly
in order to assure their mission to the world.
These chapters are about growth in love.

From little children they will become friends of Jesus;
more than that, they will become Jesus
and the Temple of God.
Jesus is going to show these rather immature, generous men
the road to wholeness and holiness,
a road that will pass through wondrous joys and terrible pain,
and end in a union with Jesus in glory.

Love one another as I have loved you

Then he leaves them his last instruction,
his spiritual will and testament,
the heart and soul of his whole message:

> *"I give you a new commandment, that you love one another.*
> *Just as I have loved you, you should love one another.*
> *All will recognize that you are my disciples.*
> *by the love you have one for another."*   vv. 34-35

In the Law of Moses, the Hebrews were called to love God
with all their soul, heart, mind and strength
and to love their neighbours as themselves.
Here Jesus is calling his disciples not only to love others as they love
themselves
but to love as he – Jesus – loves them.
That is what is new.
He is creating a holy, sacred covenant between them.

They are called to live in communion with each other,
to share with one another,
to serve one another in simple acts of love and caring,
never judging or condemning but forgiving.
They are called to love as Jesus loves.
Jesus surprised and shocked these men
by kneeling down and washing their feet.
And now he shocks them even more by announcing
that he is about to leave them.

19

God comes to dwell in us

John 14

Jesus, after having knelt down at his disciples' feet,
is going to reveal to them
the plan of God: he will be leaving them
but he and his Father
will send them the "Paraclete,"
the Spirit of Truth,
who will always be with them
and guide them.
They together, as the first
assembly of believers –
the church Jesus is founding –
will continue his mission:
to reveal the compassionate
face of God to people,
giving them new life,
liberating them from fear
and leading them on the road to peace.

Absence and presence

T oday, many people, young and old alike,
are seeking a spirituality
that will give meaning to their lives
and bring them to inner wholeness and a new communion
with the universe, particularly with God.

Some do not find this experience within their own tradition;
they may be attracted to gurus and spiritualities
from other parts of the world that seem to offer them
inner silence and even an experience of God.

Other seekers, frustrated with the drudgery of life,
the despair of the world,
the hypocrisy of competitive, well-ordered societies
where work and signs of wealth have become all-important,
look for ways to break through all that is limited,
to live exciting experiences,
and to touch and feel the freedom of the infinite within them.
They yearn to experience the thrills of life in all its forms.
It is sad to see that our Christian churches have so often covered up
the mystical life with morality, dogmatic statements and rituals.
The Gospel of John reveals to us a spirituality
that is not a flight from drudgery and pain,
but a road to fullness of life and joy
where we receive the love of God so that we can love others.
It leads us to an experience of the love of God
through a deepening love and friendship with Jesus.

After kneeling down and washing the disciples' feet
during the Last Supper, Jesus says goodbye,
and at the same time promises to see them again soon.

Announcing his departure and proclaiming his return
seems to have another meaning, too:
about the growth of each one of us in love.

This growth takes a lifetime
and implies times of presence and absence, encounters and departures.
What is true in regards to human friendship
is particularly true in the friendship that bonds us to God.
The presence of someone we love brings joy.
We savour their presence.
But their absence requires trust, hope and fidelity;
it deepens the "well" of our being.
Absence hurts
but as the pain increases, the desire is strengthened,
so that the presence that will come will be even fuller and more total.
In order to live more deeply this friendship with God,
other desires that have taken up too much room
in our hearts and lives may have to be pruned or cut away.
But their loss can also be the prelude
to being filled in a new and deeper way with God.

Jesus' farewell discourse after the Last Supper
tells us about this *journey towards oneness with God*,
of its immense joys and pains.
Jesus is conscious of the disciples' pain and anguish
at his impending departure:

> *"Do not let your hearts be troubled [or in anguish];*
> *place your trust in God and in me.*
> *In the home of my Father there are many dwelling places,*
> *otherwise I would have told you.*
> *I go to prepare a place for you.*
> *And if I go and prepare a place for you,*
> *I will come again and will take you to myself*
> *so that where I am, there you may be also."*   *vv. 1-3*

What delicacy, gentleness and thoughtfulness! What kindness!
These words of Jesus imply that when he comes back
he will draw us into a long, loving embrace.

Jesus: the way to God

Jesus then provokes a question by saying:

> *"And where I go, you know the way."*

Thomas reacts and asks:

> *"Lord, we do not know where you are going;*
> *how can we know the way?"*

Jesus answers:

> *"I am the Way, the Truth and the Life.*
> *No one comes to the Father except through me.*
> *If you know me, you will know my Father.*
> *From now on you do know him and have seen him."*   *v. 4-7*

The disciples still do not understand who Jesus is.
All they want is to *really* see the Father.
So Philip says:

> *"Show us the Father and that will be sufficient for us."*

Jesus answers in a plaintive way,
saddened by the lack of Philip's understanding of who he is:

> *"Have I been with you all this time, Philip,*
> *and you still do not know me?*
> *Whoever has seen me, has seen the Father.*
> *How can you say 'show me the Father'?*
> *Do you not believe that I am in the Father*
> *and the Father is in me?"*   *vv. 8-10*

The heart of the gospel message is contained in these six words:
Jesus and the Father are one.
Those who see, hear and touch Jesus
see, hear and touch the Father!
Jesus is the Word-made-flesh. He is God.
There can be no other way to God except through
the Word of God, who is God.

Before the Word became flesh, many people sought God,
living their lives according to the laws of God as revealed
through creation, through holy people, through prophets.
Some even talked with God and heard God's voice;
others received messages from God through dreams;
still others received the light of God through
and in their own conscience.
In all cultures, and at all times, people heard in some way the voice
and word of God:
Noah, Abraham, the Hebrew prophets and holy people in Israel,
but also such people as Socrates
and holy people in India, China,
the Americas and other cultures.
God never forgot God's people, never left them on their own.
The darkness never overcame the light of God that continued to
burn in people's hearts and minds.   *Jn 1:5*

Maybe some could not name God, but they sought
the light of truth and the origin of all things.
The word of God was the light for many people.

When the Word became flesh, Jesus brought to fulfillment
all these different paths to God.
He does not destroy them: the Word is in each of these paths.
But the Word-made-flesh becomes a new path for human beings
precisely because Jesus has become one of us, the first born,
and thus the treasure of creation.
He is the beloved brother of every man and every woman
of all times.
His body is the body of God and gives meaning to the body
of each person;
all who see and touch his body,
or are in communion with him through his body,
see and touch God.

This new way to God is not through a separation from our bodies,
a struggle to become a pure spirit;
it is in and through our bodies
and in all that is weak and broken in us
that we meet God.
Jesus is showing a simple way to union with God,
a way of compassion, love, service and humility that is for all people:
not just for the strong, the clever, the capable and the virtuous,
but also for the weak and the humble.
All Jesus asks is that we come to him with humble
and trusting hearts.
He will lead us little by little to a greater union with the Father,
who is compassion and forgiveness.
This is the journey that we followers of Jesus are called to make.

You will do the works Jesus does

Then Jesus tells something to his disciples that must have surprised
and shocked them:

> *"Truly, truly, I tell you,*
> *the one who trusts me will also do the works that I do,*
> *in fact, will do greater works than these,*
> *because I go to the Father."*　　　　　　　　　*v. 12*

This is what Jesus is leading up to:
his disciples will continue his mission and his works.
But what is this mission?
It is to give life, eternal life,
and to reveal the face and heart of God to people.
It is to be a presence of God in the world
where there is an absence of God.
God's works are not big miracles,
which some heroic disciples may be called to do,
but all those works of simple kindness and goodness
which give people life and lead them to trust
in themselves and in God.

That is why disciples of Jesus must be audacious
and ask to accomplish these works of God:

> *"I will do whatever you ask in my name*
> *so that the Father may be glorified in the Son.*
> *If in my name you ask me for anything, I will do it."*   vv. 13-14

If we trust God and ask to accomplish his works of love,
we will give life, the very life of God.
But how is this going to be?
These disciples are very human men.
They do not really understand Jesus.
Sometimes, like Peter, they tell him off:

> *"No, you shall never wash my feet!"*

Something will have to happen to change and transform them,
so that they will be able to do the works of Jesus,
and even greater ones!
Jesus tells them how this will be:

> *"If you love me, you will keep my commandments.*
> *And I will ask the Father*
> *and he will give you another Paraclete to be with you forever.*
> *This is the Spirit of truth whom the world*
> *cannot receive because it neither sees him nor knows him.*
> *You know him because he abides with you*
> *and he will be in you."*   vv. 15-17

That is the answer:
the disciples are going to receive another Paraclete,
the Spirit of truth, who will live in them and transform them.
They will no longer be caught up
in a lot of very human queries and needs
flowing from their fears, culture and education;
they will be separated from the emptiness of the world
and brought into the place of God.

Jesus reveals to them that they are not first of all going to do things,
but God is going to live in them.
Later we will see that because the Spirit is in them,
they will do the works of God.

Jesus is going to fulfill the prophecies of the great Hebrew prophets
who had announced that the Lord God would send his Spirit
upon his servant, the Messiah,
but also upon a few chosen prophets and kings,
and later upon all the people, as announced by Joel: *Jl 3:1*

> *"I will sprinkle clean water upon you*
> *and you shall be cleansed from uncleanliness*
> *and from all your idols I will cleanse you.*
> *A new heart I will give you and a new spirit I will put within you.*
> *I will remove from your body the heart of stone*
> *and give you a heart of flesh.*
> *I will put my spirit within you...."*   *Ez 36:25-27*

Jesus is the one who will instill the reign of the Holy Spirit
in the hearts of *all* his disciples.
He has already told Nicodemus – and, through him, all of us –
that in order to enter the kingdom of God
we must be born of water and the Spirit, born from "on high,"
and thus become in a special way children of God, inspired by God.
Those born of the Spirit are compared to the wind;
they do not know where the wind is coming from
or where it is leading.
So, too, with the Spirit:
we do not know where it is coming from or where it is leading us.

Spiritus and Paracletus

Clearly, what is of the world is separated from what is from the Spirit.
Jesus had already said to the Pharisees and Scribes:

> *"You are of below, I am from above.*
> *You are of the world. I am not of the world."*   *Jn 8:23*

Those "of the world" are closed to the ways and things of God.
They do not know God.
The disciples will receive the Spirit, a new life, which will give them
a new inner force, a new heart, a new vision,
a new freedom that will separate them from the ways and influences
of the world
so that they will no longer be enslaved in fear and greed,
craving money and power – even spiritual power.

The word "paraclete" is one of those rich Greek words
that are difficult to translate completely.
A paraclete is someone who defends and comforts,
and speaks up for and helps a weak person.
So the word "paraclete" can be translated as "advocate," as well as
"comforter," "consoler" or "helper."
Etymologically, the word "paraclete" means
"the one who answers the call."
What a beautiful name!
God is the one who answers the cry of the weak and those in need.
A mother is a "paraclete" for her child
when she answers the cry of her little one,
holds and loves him or her.
Every time we look after a person in need and answer their cry,
we become paracletes.
Jesus was a paraclete for his disciples.

The Paraclete is given
to those who are lonely and need the presence of a friend,
to those who are lost and poor in spirit
and who cry out to God.

"Paracletus" is different from *"Spiritus."*
"Spiritus" implies movement; it is "wind" or "breath";
it is an inner enthusiasm,
the enthusiasm of the prophets who speak and do wonderful things.
The Paraclete takes away the anguish of loneliness;
she brings presence, security, peace and communion.

Spiritus and Paracletus are two aspects of God who lives and acts in us,
who inspires us and urges us forward,
but who also holds us, loves us, carries us
and dwells in us as we dwell in God.

The Spirit "Paracletus" gives us a new strength and a new love
to do the works of God,
to do all those things that we seem unable to do by ourselves,
by the strength of our own willpower:
to love certain people, to forgive enemies,
to become the friends of those who are different,
to be open to those who have a different vision
and way of doing things.

Jesus and the Father will come

It is not only the Paraclete who will come
and be with and in the disciples,
Jesus himself will come and be with them:

> *"I will not leave you orphans.*
> *I am coming to you.*
> *In a little while the world will no longer see me,*
> *but you will see me;*
> *because I live, you also will live.*
> *On that day you will know that I am in my Father*
> *and you in me and I in you."*   *vv. 18-20*

This provokes Judas (not Iscariot) to ask the question:

> *"Lord, how is it you will manifest yourself to us*
> *and not to the world?"*

Jesus is not going to do wondrous acts
to convince everyone in the world
that he is the Messiah, the Son of God.
His plan is to live in his disciples – to begin with just a few:

"If anyone loves me, he or she will keep my word
and my Father will love that person
and we will come and make our dwelling place
in him or her."   *v. 23*

It is they, the Church, the community of believers
who will continue his mission.
It is they who will manifest Jesus to the world.

But the Paraclete, Jesus and the Father will only come if…
This is not a threat but a promise,
a promise that if we keep his commandments or his words,
the Paraclete will be given to us.
The "if" is a condition
and implies that we are called to struggle
against all those forces of egoism
that prevent us from keeping God's commandments.

And these commandments, what are they?
Essentially they are all the commandments of love:
to serve each other,
to be compassionate,
to live in communion with one another,
not to judge or condemn but to forgive,
to love enemies,
to live the beatitudes,
to wash each other's feet.
The commandment of Jesus is that we love one another as he loves us.
This is his *way*, the *way* to God.
We are called to leave behind all the selfish attitudes of the world,
to no longer put all our energies into the pursuit of power,
wealth, honour and superficial friendships.
It implies struggles, moments of grief, purifications.
We cannot be moved by the Spirit for the things of God
if we are seeking only the things of the world.

Our inner "home" has to be emptied, cleansed of all the mess and dirt,
freed of all forms of selfishness and certain human needs
in order for it to become the dwelling place of God.
This takes time –
a whole lifetime!

In these passages, sometimes Jesus uses the plural "you,"
meaning *all of you, together,*
and sometimes the singular "you," *an individual person.*
The Holy Spirit will be in the group, will live in the Church,
but the Spirit will make her home in each person "*if*"...
each one of us keeps God's word and commandments.

God dwells in us

We have already seen that the body of Jesus is the new Temple
or dwelling place of God.
But as Jesus and the Father are coming to dwell in us,
we, too, become the Temple of God, the place where God lives.
We as church – that is, the assembly of believers –
but also we as individuals.
That is why Paul says to his disciples in Corinth:

> *"Do you not know that your body*
> *is the Temple of the Holy Spirit?"*   *1 Cor 6:19*

Jesus and the Father are with the Church,
guiding it through the upheavals of history.
They are with each one of us,
guiding us through the upheavals of our lives.
In other words, Jesus is telling his disciples:
"Do not be afraid. I am with you and I will be with you.
Listen to me.
Do not have your own agendas, which will prevent me from
living and acting in and through you.
Let yourselves be guided by the Holy Spirit living in you.
And I will be with you *if* you love one another."

Jesus gives us peace

Before this chapter of the Gospel of John closes,
Jesus tells the disciples that the Holy Spirit, the Paraclete,
will not only be with them and in them,
but will teach them all things and will bring back to the memory
of their hearts and minds all that he has taught them.
This is true for all of us.
That does not excuse us from the need to study,
to spend time with the word of God
as it has been understood over the centuries.
That does not mean we shouldn't study theology,
each one according to our call, needs and possibilities.
But it means that everything we learn must be viewed, reviewed
and tested
in the silent light of the Spirit
and in a prayerful attitude.
It means that each of us has direct access to God,
who is the centre and light of all things.
It is those who are poor enough, humble enough, crying out enough,
who will receive the Paraclete and will be able to see the light
and presence of God
in the word of God and in all things.
If Jesus and the Father are dwelling in us
we will live a new and deeper peace,
because peace comes from the presence of God.

> *"I leave you my peace.*
> *I give you my peace.*
> *I do not give it as the world gives it.*
> *Let your hearts not be anguished nor afraid."*   *v. 27*

The peace Jesus promises is not just a balance of forces
or an absence of war.
It is not just a good feeling inside of us,
a feeling of centredness, wholeness, quietness, stillness or inner silence.
It is not merely an absence of inner conflicts or of desire,
as early Greek philosophers taught.
No, this peace is more than all of these things combined.
It is the trust that Jesus is there
with us and in us.
For Jesus *is* our peace.
Peace is resting in the Beloved,
having total trust in him.
It is the peace of a child resting in the tender arms of her mother.

20

Giving life to others

John 15

Jesus came not only to dwell in us
but also to give life to others
through us.

The "home" of our hearts
needs to be emptied and cleaned up
so that we can be filled with God
and so become
a fountain of life
for others.

Jesus is the real Vine

The Word became flesh
    in order to lead us into communion with God.
    He came to bridge the gap
that separates weak and vulnerable human beings from God.
He came to live in Mary's womb
and to dwell in each one of us.
But he came not only to dwell in us
but also to act in and through us,
to give life to others, in and through us.
We are called to participate in the creative and loving activity of God.
We will bear much fruit if we dwell in God.
This mutual indwelling implies a friendship.
It is a process of growing towards greater oneness with Jesus.
To help us understand how this is to be, Jesus speaks of the vine:

> *"I am the true vine and my Father the vinedresser.*
> *He removes every branch in me that bears no fruit.*
> *Every branch that bears fruit,*
> *he prunes so that it bears more fruit."*   *vv. 1-2*

Jesus tells us that he *is* the Vine;
he is not separate from the Vine.
He is not separated from the people of God, but is part of them,
one with them.
Now that the Word has become flesh,
he is one of us and we are one with him.
We are of the same human race.
He is the first-born of creation.
All life flows from him and through him
and then through us, the little branches, to bear fruit,
just as the sap runs through the vine,
through the branches to produce grapes.

> *"Those who abide in me and I in them*
> *bear much fruit, because cut from me you can do nothing."*   *v. 5*

The fruit is the life we are all called to give to others.
But it is not just we who give life, nor is it just Jesus,
it is we and Jesus,
Jesus in us and us in Jesus.
We cannot distinguish what is of God and what is of us.
It is the life of the Spirit flowing through each one of us,
coloured by our own particular gifts,
by who we are and our particular mission.
The magnificence of God is giving life in and through us.
God does not want to act only directly on the hearts of individual people:
God uses each of us as mediators and instruments for grace,
through our words, gestures, presence and prayer.
In this way we take part in the creativity of God giving life.
We give the life of God to each other
and we receive this life from one another.

When Jesus and the Father come and live
or make their dwelling place within us,
this is not something static.
They are living and acting within us.
We receive and give life in and with them.
This is another way of saying
what Jesus said to the Samaritan woman: *Jn 4:14*
that whoever drinks from the waters of life that Jesus gives
will become a source, a spring of living water,
of divine life, for others.
The life-giving Spirit we receive will flow from us.
The life-giving words and gestures we give to others
will flow from the life of Jesus within us,
changing, opening and deepening the hearts and minds of others.

The need to be cleansed

To be this fountain or spring of life that transmits the Holy Spirit,
we need to be cleansed or pruned.
Our words and our gestures no longer
come from our compulsions and needs

to prove we are someone
or from our fears, brokenness and inner wounds.
Instead, they flow from the Trinity dwelling in us.
This cleansing takes time.
Jesus comes to dwell in us little by little.
We have already seen that in order to receive the Paraclete
we need to keep the commandments of Jesus;
this can imply a struggle.
Now Jesus tells us of another, deeper purification:
the Father will prune all the branches that bear fruit
so that they bear even more fruit.
To prune means to cut off some of the branches
and that can hurt.
This new purification comes directly from the vinedresser,
the Father, cutting the branches.

Accidents, sickness, failures, the loss of a job,
the death of someone we love – various unexpected events –
can hurt and wound life in us
and leave us in a state of grief and desolation.
We feel empty.
Life no longer flows through us;
we have lost our enthusiasm
and sometimes even all desires.
We are wounded in our energies of life.
Like the wounded vine whose branches have been cut off,
we have to wait for new life to flow in us.
We are pruned for something new,
for a life more centred in God and the things of God.
Before the pruning, we were perhaps too taken up with "things to do,"
maybe even good things, and had no time for God.
We were like the people in the parable
who were invited to the wedding feast of love
but did not accept because they were too busy.   *Lk 14; Mt 22*
When life is cut or pruned in this way,

we may have feelings of emptiness and anguish.
This emptiness can bring forth anger and depression,
but it can also prepare us for something new.
Our emptiness can become a cry to God.
We must wait patiently, sometimes in pain and anguish,
for this new gift of God.

Some pruning comes unexpectedly and violently.
Some comes gradually, as we grow older
and are less taken up by things to do
and the need for success, reputation and power.
We have more time for God and the things of God,
and can give more attention to the sacred space within us.
Some pruning comes because we want it,
ask for it, wait for it;
we yearn to have more time with and for God.
That is what Jesus means when he says to his disciples:

> *"You have already been cleansed
> by the word I have spoken to you."*　　　　　　　*v. 3*

All growth in love implies pain and loss

Choice implies loss.
To marry is to accept the loss of countless other potential partners.
Fidelity in love can cost a lot.
To grow in love we have to pass through pain and anguish.
It is the same in our relationship with God.
In order to be more present to God,
we have to be less present to other things.
This is a form of pruning that will take place.

There can be an even more violent cutting or pruning.
It will be to those parts of our being
that have led us to refuse to follow Jesus' commandments of love
and to remain locked up in selfishness.
These parts will be purified by a fire

that will burn away all the self-centredness that has grown in us.
This burning takes place after death, before we are totally
transformed into God:

> *"Whoever does not abide in me," says Jesus,*
> *"is thrown away like a branch and withers;*
> *such branches are gathered,*
> *thrown into the fire and burnt."*   *v. 6*

The important thing is not to wait until our death
but to walk with God today,
to accept loss, grief and all the pruning
so that we can begin to abide in God.

> *"If you abide in me*
> *and my words abide in you,*
> *ask whatever you wish*
> *and it will be done for you.*
> *By this my Father is glorified*
> *that you bear much fruit*
> *and so prove to be my disciples."*   *vv. 7, 8*

It is the joy of the Father that we give life to others –
through our prayers, our words,
giving the gift of ourselves –
we give it abundantly.
The glory of human beings is not first and foremost
to do or produce things
or to build beautiful monuments or churches,
to write wonderful books
or to create new technology.
All these will pass.
The glory of human beings is to communicate life,
pouring the oils of compassion on suffering people.
It is with Jesus and in him to transform others,
to help them move from inner death, sadness and aggression
to inner peace, joy and fullness of life.

To abide in Jesus and become his friend

What does it mean to abide in Jesus?
Here we have again the key word "abide" or "dwell."
The first two disciples asked Jesus: *"Where do you dwell?"*
And they went to dwell with him.
Jesus had told the disciples that if they eat his body
and drink his blood, they will dwell in him and he in them.
In this chapter of the Gospel of John, Jesus reveals to us:

> *"As the Father loved me, so I have loved you.*
> *Abide in my love.*
> *If you keep my commandments, you will abide in my love,*
> *just as I have kept my Father's commandments*
> *and abide in his love."*   *vv. 9-10*

To abide or dwell in Jesus is to *make our home* in him
and *to let* Jesus make his home in us.
We feel at home with him and in him.
It is a place of rest for one another and presence to one another.
It is a place of mutual indwelling and friendship.
This rest is also a source of life and creativity.
Abiding in him, we bear fruit, we give life to others.
We live a mutual indwelling.
This indwelling is friendship.

At one moment, Etty Hillesum found herself crying out to God
to help her and the many others in distress.
Then she realized that
"It is not I who need God but God needs me...."

God was waiting for her to open the door of her heart to let him in.
Jesus waits patiently for us to accept his friendship.

Even though we may be separated from a friend by distance,
we are held together by love,
we are one in love.
Love is a uniting force.

In human friendships, the other person abides in us
virtually, intentionally, spiritually, not with a real presence.
In friendship with Jesus, he abides in us, in a *real presence*.

We are with him and dwell in him.
Keeping the commandments of Jesus, then,
is not like obeying in a military sense:
it is rather following the desire of the one we love;
it is being pleasing to him, sensing what he desires for us.
Together we have one heart, one mind, one spirit;
there is no discord or conflict or barrier between us.
This indwelling with Jesus can be on the level of a simple friendship,
but it can also become a burning love as in the *Song of Songs,*
which is often seen as a love poem between God and each one of us.
Mystics like John of the Cross lived this burning love,
seeing Jesus as the bridegroom of the soul.

The source of our friendship with Jesus
is the oneness between him and the Father.
As the Father loves Jesus and gives himself to the Son,
Jesus loves us and gives himself to us.
This love between the Father, Son and Holy Spirit is like a fire;
it is total unity.
That is why it is so difficult to describe the friendship, love and unity
we live with Jesus.
It is deeper than anything we can imagine
because it flows from the communion that is God.

Jesus then says:

> *"I have said these things to you
> so that my joy may be in you
> and that your joy may be full."*   *v. 11*

Jesus wants us to be filled with joy and fully alive.
His joy is our joy, our joy is his joy.
His joy is to be totally one with the Father,

and that is our joy.
There can be no greater joy than to know that we are valued,
precious and loved by God;
that we have at last found the place of total rest for our hearts.
There is no greater joy than to be with the Beloved of our heart,
transformed in God.
There is no greater joy than to love people abundantly
and to participate in the creative, life-giving activity of God
with a sense of divine life flowing through us.
The joy and excitement of giving life on a human level
is but a pale reflection
of the joy of giving eternal life to others in and with Jesus.

To love one another is to give our life

Abiding in Jesus and bearing abundant fruit
implies that we love with the love of Jesus
all those who are given to us:

> *"This is my commandment,*
> *that you love one another as I have loved you."*

And Jesus adds:

> *"There is no greater love than this –*
> *to lay down one's life for one's friends."*   *vv. 12, 13*

To love people as Jesus loves them
is to wash their feet, to serve them in humility;
it is to help them rise up in truth and love.
Here Jesus is revealing something more:
to love is to lay down one's life for others,
to place their interests before our own.
It is to give them life.
That can mean accepting difficulties, danger and even death
so that they may live and grow in love.
To love is to live in communion with others,
to transmit to them the life and love of Jesus.

It is to reveal to them that they are loved,
loved by Jesus.
In this way we become their friend
because we are a friend of Jesus.

> *"You are my friends if you do what I command you.*
> *I do not call you servants any longer*
> *because the servant does not know what the Master is doing;*
> *but I have called you my friends*
> *because I have made known to you*
> *everything I have heard from my Father."*　　　*vv. 14-15*

In this friendship nothing is hidden or secret.
Jesus has shared everything he has heard from the Father; all is given.
And Jesus recalls:

> *"You did not choose me, but I chose you*
> *and I appointed you to go and bear fruit, fruit that will last,*
> *so that the Father will give you*
> *whatever you ask for in my name.*
> *This I command you, to love one another."*　　　*vv. 16-17*

The barriers that separated the finite from the Infinite,
the temporal from the eternal,
the human from the divine,
have disappeared.
At times it is necessary for us to live an austere life,
like John the Baptizer,
and to seek a certain separation from our bodies,
to strain to reach God through our efforts.
But God has appeared in the flesh, has become vulnerable in the flesh.
He has come to offer us his friendship,
to invite us to become his beloved.
He has become little and vulnerable,
to live a communion of hearts with us
and to join him in giving life to others.

It is not a question, then, of striving towards God
but of humbly opening the door of our hearts to God,
who is knocking there.
This friendship with Jesus is something deep but simple,
like other friendships.
It is not a big, mystical experience or impressive apparitions;
it involves living day by day with Jesus,
walking with him, listening to him, following his desires,
and being nourished by his words and by his body.

Jesus is in us and we are in Jesus.
As we talk, meet and share with others,
as we accomplish work and try to live out projects,
as we live with others in family,
in community or as friends and companions,
as we do little gestures of love, kindness, affection and forgiveness,
especially to those who are weak or in need,
we are with Jesus and reveal Jesus to others.
In the words of Cardinal Newman,

> Shine through me, Jesus,
> and be so in me
> that every soul I come in contact with
> may feel your presence in my soul.
> Let them look up and see no longer me
> but only Jesus!

To grow in friendship with Jesus takes time

This life with and in Jesus takes time to grow.
It is a gift of Jesus that we can ask for,
a gift that comes after many inner struggles and inner conflicts.
Paul talks of our flesh being crucified   *Gal 5:24*
so that we are no longer slaves to our compulsions
for power, love, success:
slaves to self-centredness and egotism.

We become free:

> *"It is so that we be free that Christ has set us free."*   Gal 5:1

Free to live simply this friendship with Jesus in the Spirit.

Jesus has already spoken of his leaving and his returning.
His leaving refers to his death; his return refers to his resurrection.
But at the same time he is referring to his presence
and his absence in our lives.
There are times when his presence is more deeply felt,
when we feel guided and held in his love and friendship,
when peace permeates our hearts.
At other times we feel lost, in anguish, as we struggle with inner pain.
Sometimes feelings of guilt and unworthiness rise up in us.
Faith and trust become difficult.
We struggle with ourselves.
These are all signs of our being pruned, stripped,
purified by the Father.
Our faith and trust are being deepened.
The sails of our little boats are not filled with the winds of the Spirit.
We have to row hard,
sometimes against heavy winds of discouragement.
Jesus appears to be sleeping in the boat.
We must learn to wait for Jesus to wake up
and to reveal once again his friendship and his presence to us.

21

Birthed in pain and in God

John 15:18–16:33

To become
a friend of Jesus
is to become like him,
to live as he lived.

This can mean being rejected
and hated
as he was hated.

We will then be "birthed" in God
in a new way
and live
the fulfillment of joy.

Blessed are the persecuted

The words of Jesus are consoling
for all those who struggle for truth and justice today,
who struggle against the powers of evil and oppression
in our world, and are persecuted, pushed aside,
sometimes crushed and killed.

Jesus calls his disciples "out of the world."
They are not "of the world,"
but they will be sent "into the world"
to be a presence of God and of love
where there is an absence of God.

The "world" in the gospel of John has two meanings:
it is the cosmos, the universe,
our "inhabited" earth, loved by God.
It also means the place of the absence of God,
where love is not present and is even feared.
This void of absence becomes indifference to others,
fear of them,
a refusal to share with others.
It can become blatant selfishness, hate, greed and lies,
people locked up in their ideologies and illusions.
This absence is in a part of each culture
and in a part of each one of our hearts.
This absence can be manipulated and filled with evil forces
or filled by God.

Jesus came to witness to the truth
in this world where God is absent and love feared –
the truth of the love of God
and of the value of each and every person.
Some people were attracted to his message of love
and believed that he was a messenger of God;
others violently rejected him and wanted to get rid of him.
He was a threat to them.

They feared him.
Fear is always behind the need to persecute.
As Jesus confronted the powers of evil and hate
hidden in the culture and in the hearts of people,
these powers seemed to get the better of him.
He was condemned to death, eliminated.
But the powers of evil, however, did not win.
Jesus and the powers of love triumphed.

These powers of evil and hatred will also seek to eliminate
the disciples of Jesus:

> *"If the world hates you,*
> *know that it hated me before it hated you....*
> *Remember the words that I said to you:*
> *'a servant is not greater than the master'....*
> *If they persecuted me, they will persecute you;*
> *if they kept my word, they will keep yours also."*   *vv. 18-20*

> *"I have said these things to you*
> *so that [when you are persecuted]*
> *you will not be scandalized....*
> *The hour is coming when whoever kills you*
> *will think that they are offering a service to God...."*   *Jn 16:1-2*

By telling his disciples that they, too, will be persecuted,
Jesus is revealing how they are called to become like him.
They too will accomplish the works of God.
Not just through powerful words and wisdom
but through their weakness, failure and even death.
They will give life as Jesus gave life.
They will conquer the world not in a visible way,
but through their littleness and poverty.
The "hour" of Jesus for which he came
was when he gave his life totally
and when he gave us life through his death.

So, too, all those who are called to give their lives for Jesus,
for truth and for justice, become like him.
They, too, live that hour of Jesus.
Their shed blood becomes one with the blood of the crucified Jesus.
In and through the death of Jesus they, too, give life to the world.
Their blood waters the arid land of our hearts
to bring forth new life.

Most of the members of that first group of disciples chosen by Jesus
were martyred.
Peter and Paul were martyred in Rome.
Paul was beheaded,
and tradition has it that Peter was crucified head down.
So many of the early Christians were martyred by the Romans,
who saw this little "sect" as dangerous,
undermining the authority and power of the Empire,
refusing to worship the emperor and the Roman gods.

The early Christians lived together in community,
sharing their goods with one another,
sharing their lives with those who were rejected by Roman society,
revealing that each person, no matter how poor or weak,
is precious to God.

The message of Jesus grew throughout the world,
because many men and women refused to cower
before insolent, dictatorial might.
They refused to adapt to the pervasive values
and the dominant culture of the times.
Although they experienced fear, they did not succumb to it.
They gave their lives in the name of Jesus.
They accepted being seen as different and strange
as they continued to give witness to the message of truth and justice
of the gospel.
The message of Jesus has been passed on, generation to generation,
thanks to people who gave their lives for the truth.

Dietrich Bonhoeffer,
speaking out against the power of the Nazi regime,
refused the culture of death, the extermination camps,
and the "final solution" of the Jewish people.
Oscar Romero said "no" to a military dictatorship
aligned with the wealthy that was crushing the poor and the landless.
Sr. Luzia Kautidia was assassinated in Mongwa
while helping to transport someone to the hospital.
Pierre Claverie in Algeria continued to proclaim a vision of peace
and dialogue between Christians and Muslims.
There have been many others like them throughout history.

In his book *Il secolo del martirio: I cristiani nel novecento* [They Died for
Their Faith],
Andrea Riccardi tells of hundreds of thousands of men and women
all over the world who have been martyred
in the past hundred years.
His book recounts the horrors of hatred and sadistic torture.
Yet it is also filled with great hope as so many people
have said "no" to lies, injustice and oppression
and "yes" to freedom, truth and Jesus.

Different forms of persecution

Not all followers of Jesus are physically persecuted or killed.
There are many other forms of more subtle, hidden persecution.
There is the persecution of those who strive actively for the rights
of every person, of every culture,
for the rights of minority ethnic groups,
of men and women on death row,
of unborn children,
of people with disabilities who are kept out of sight.
There are those who struggle against organized crime
and all forms of oppression.
Those who side with the poor and the oppressed
can quickly be pushed aside in public life
and be seen as a disturbance.

Even within community life, family life, and at work,
there are forms of persecution,
where some people are rejected, looked down on, put aside.
They live the martyrdom of daily pinpricks.

Nobody likes to be rejected, looked down upon,
made fun of, seen as useless or stupid,
or seen as a danger, a disturbance to the dominant religious or
political order.

There are two dangers in this domain for the friends of Jesus.
The first is the temptation to *make compromises*
with a culture that marginalizes and crushes some people
in order to avoid conflict and rejection.
We are fearful of speaking out about Jesus or about justice and truth.
We are afraid to rock the boat.
We are frightened of what people might think or do to us
if we disturb them or the cultural order.
So we water down faith and the gospel message.

The second danger is the temptation to *like to disturb* this status quo.
When we are rebels at heart and like to shock people,
we can create a fight in order to be in the limelight.
We can do some of these things unconsciously, experience rejection
and then think that we are being persecuted like Jesus was.

The Paraclete will be with those who are martyred

Jesus reassures us:

> "When the Paraclete comes,
> which I will send to you from the Father,
> the Spirit of truth who proceeds from the Father,
> he will testify in my behalf, and you also will testify
> because you have been with me
> from the beginning." Jn 15:26-27

> *"I tell you the truth: it is to your advantage that I go away,*
> *for if I do not go away, the Paraclete will not come to you,*
> *but if I go, I will send her to you."*   *Jn 16:7*

Jesus must go away
so that his disciples can grow in a new way in the Spirit.
If Jesus remained present physically,
they would depend on his physical and external presence,
and the security he gave them.
If he leaves, he will send the Paraclete
who will live inside of them
so that they may be guided, sustained,
fortified by her
and so become like Jesus.
What was true for these first disciples is true for us today.
It is to our advantage that Jesus no longer walks this earth with us
in a physical presence.
He sends to each one of us who so wants it
this new force of love,
which permits us to stand up and witness to the truth
in the name of Jesus,
in the face of difficulties and persecution.

A cry of victory: justice will prevail

Jesus will be judged and condemned to death
during a false trial organized by the supreme religious authorities.
Many of his disciples will also be judged and condemned
by false trials organized by political, military or religious authorities.
The false trial of Jesus will be turned around or vindicated
by the Paraclete, the Spirit of truth,
whom Jesus will send.
Behind this trial is sin,
injustice and a false or evil judgment.
There is sin because the people judging him refuse to believe in him,
to listen to reality and accept it.

Justice will be rendered because Jesus will return to the Father in glory
and there will be a true judgment,
because the evil one, the Prince of the world,
who inspired the condemnations
and the killing of Jesus and of his friends,
is and will be judged.
This is the work of the Paraclete, the Spirit of truth:
to reveal the truth
and to bring to light the evil ways and corruption of the world,
the travesty of justice and the false condemnations.
This is a cry of victory.
Justice will prevail.
Evil will not have the last word.

A new birth in God

The final victory, which for Jesus is the resurrection,
is for the friends of Jesus a transformation in God
where they will *know* the Father
as the Son knows the Father,
where they will *be with* the Father
as the Son *is with* the Father,
where they will be able to say,
"I and Jesus are one,"
as Jesus said,
"I and the Father are one."

But the disciples are not yet prepared
to bear this new and total identification with him.
It is the Spirit of truth who will guide them into the final truth
and lead them into a new and total experience of oneness with God.
The Spirit will reveal to them in an existential way
the unity that exists between Jesus and the Father.
The Spirit of truth will reveal to them
what specifically belongs to Jesus:
that is to say, the unique, total love of the Father for him;

for he is the unique beloved Son.
Everything that the Father has and is belongs to the Son.
So, too, all will be given by the Spirit of truth to those friends of Jesus
who have been led to this inner transformation:

> *"I still have many things to say to you*
> *but you cannot bear them now.*
> *When the Spirit of truth comes,*
> *he will guide you into all the truth,*
> *for he will not speak of his own,*
> *but will speak whatever he hears and*
> *he will declare to you the things that are to come.*
> *He will glorify me,*
> *because he will take what is mine and declare it to you.*
> *All that the Father has is mine.*
> *For this reason I said that he will take what is mine*
> *and declare it to you."* vv. 12-15

Yes, all that the Father has belongs to Jesus.
And all that Jesus has belongs to his friends.

That is why John of the Cross was able to say in a prayer
conceived when he was totally one with Jesus:

> The heavens are mine and the earth is mine;
> the nations are mine; the just are mine;
> sinners are mine; the angels are mine;
> the Mother of God and all creatures are mine;
> God is mine and for me because Christ is mine
> and totally for me.

This total unity with God comes
after a greater experience of anguish, of loneliness, of pain,
of weeping and of mourning.
Here again Jesus is referring to his coming departure, to his death
and to his return in and through his resurrection.

He is also referring to a new and more radical aloneness
in the spiritual and mystical life,
a new and deeper purification of faith
that will prepare the way to a new transformation in God.
In order to reveal this new pain and total joy,
Jesus compares it to childbirth:

> *"Truly, truly, I tell you, you will weep and mourn*
> *but the world will rejoice;*
> *you will have pain, but your pain will turn into joy.*
> *When a woman is in labour,*
> *she has pain because her hour has come.*
> *But when her child is born,*
> *she no longer remembers the anguish*
> *because of the joy of having brought a human being*
> *into the world."* *vv. 20-21*

The Word became flesh in order to lead us into
the heart and "womb" of the Father.
There will be many stages on the road to oneness with God.
We begin as little children born of the Spirit,
born from "on high"
through water and the Spirit,
yet we remain very human,
with our prejudices and compulsions
for spiritual power and recognition,
and educated, formed and rooted in our various cultures.
Our journey in faith will be a growth in trust in Jesus
as he gradually leads us to live in the Father.
Just as we are called to grow in human maturity,
goodness and wisdom,
we are called to grow in union with God,
dying more and more to our self-centred needs.
Then we will live the *final birthing* that Jesus refers to here,
a birthing in the heart of the Trinity.
This will be at the time of our death
when all of us are set in God.

Jesus is referring also to a *final birthing*
that some of his friends will live
as they enter a final transformation in Jesus *in this life*,
even before their death.
Their utter loneliness will be transformed
into a total presence of God.

> "So you have pain now,
> but I will see you again and your hearts will rejoice
> and no one will take your joy from you.
> On that day, you will ask nothing of me."   vv. 22-23

They are set in God.
They will see then that the Father loves them:

> "The Father himself loves you because you have loved me,
> and have believed that I came from God."   v. 27

In *The Dark Night of the Soul*, John of the Cross
speaks about the different stages or steps of love.
The "last step" of what he calls the "secret ladder" of love

> assimilates the soul to God completely,
> because of the clear vision that a person possesses at once
> on reaching it.
> This vision is the cause of the soul's complete likeness to God.
> John the Evangelist says that we know that we shall be like him
> (1 Jn 3:2) not because the soul will have as much capacity as God
> – this is impossible –
> but because all it is will become like God.
> Thus it will be called, and shall be, God
> through participation.
>
> On this last step of clear vision at the top of the mystical ladder,
> where God rests, nothing is any longer hid from the soul,
> and this because of its total assimilation.
> Accordingly our Saviour exclaimed:
> "On that day you will not ask me anything." (Jn 16:23)

Jesus warns the disciples of his imminent, final loneliness,
a loneliness that the disciples and each one of us will live
before our own final union with the Father:

> *"The hour is coming, indeed it has come,*
> *when you will be scattered*
> *each one to his own things*
> *and you will leave me alone.*
> *Yet I am not alone because the Father is with me."*   *v. 32*

Loneliness is the total emptiness of a human heart,
the final and absolute purification
in order to become the place where God resides.
But even in this loneliness, God is present
because Jesus is with us in agony and anguish,
just as the Father is always with him.

> *"I have said this to you so that*
> *in me you may have peace.*
> *In the world you will have distress,*
> *but trust, for I have conquered the world."*   *v. 33*

This is the final message of Jesus for each one of us,
in all our loneliness,
when we feel rejected and abandoned:

> *"Trust, for I have conquered the world."*

Yes, trust, for Jesus is leading each one of us to greater truth
through the Paraclete.
He is leading the whole Church
through time
to a deeper understanding of his message.
He is leading each one of us into the new
through much pain and many deaths.

22

To become one

John 17

*The Word became one of us
to reveal
the face and heart of God
and to lead us all
into a loving communion
with the Father.*

*His yearning,
his prayer is that
we all become one in him:
each one different
each one unique
but together in unity
to the glory of God.*

God's beautiful plan

Having knelt down humbly in front of each disciple
to wash their feet,
having revealed their journey
and the journey of the Church,
through pain and joy
into the heart and ecstasy of God,
Jesus stops.
All has been said.
There is no more place for explanation or discussion.
It is now a moment of contemplation.
Jesus raises his eyes to heaven.
He no longer looks at the earth and at his disciples,
but towards the Father.
He is *with* the Father and *in* the Father,
contemplating the divine plan for creation and for humanity,
a plan that appears to be fulfilled
and becomes a song of thanksgiving.
And yet the plan is not fulfilled.
Jesus prays for its fulfillment:
that people may be healed of their aggressiveness,
hatred and fear
and become one,
one in God.

In the Prologue, John reveals the descending Word
who became flesh
and came into our world of conflict
between light and darkness
to lead all people to the light,
to communion with God.

Some people did not want to walk the road that leads to the light.
Jesus met fear and opposition.
Many wanted to get rid of him.
They clung to their security and power

and refused change and openness.
But even through this opposition, the plan of God is being fulfilled:
Through his death, Jesus reveals his love to the very end.

Now, in this moment of contemplation,
Jesus reveals that the cycle is complete.
It is no longer God descending into flesh
but the flesh of humanity ascending into God.
It is no longer the Word who becomes a human being,
but human beings transformed into God.

All is complete.
The Word of God came from God
and now returns to God,
with all his friends, brothers and sisters in humanity united together.

Jesus glorifies the Father

Jesus says,

> *"Father, the hour has come; glorify your Son*
> *so that the Son may glorify you.*
> *Since you have given him authority over all people*
> *to give eternal life to all you have given to him.*
> *And this is eternal life: that they may know you,*
> *[have an experience of love with you,*
> *be in communion with you],*
> *the only true God and the one you sent,*
> *Jesus, the Messiah."*   *vv. 1-3*

This gospel is the gospel of the glory of God.
Here Jesus contemplates this glory and prays that we all may live it.

But what is this glory?
Glory is the manifestation of the majesty, power,
wisdom and infinity of God.
Creation sings and reveals the glory of God.

Stars and planets millions of light years away.
Galaxies behind galaxies.
Life, the greatness and the littleness of life,
the multitude of different kinds of birds,
fish, fruits, insects and hidden plants,
all intertwined in one glorious whole.
As Gerard Manley Hopkins writes,

> **The world is charged with the grandeur of God.**
> **It will flame out, like shining from shook foil.**

Men, women and children in the beauty of their being
all reveal the power and greatness of the Word,
for all things were created by him
and without him no thing is.   *cf. John 1:3*

God reveals his glory through magnificent,
awe-filled events in history.
When God led the Hebrews through the Red Sea,
as the waters separated
Moses and the Israelites sang:

> *"I will sing to the Lord*
> *for he has triumphed in his glory."*   *Ex 15:1*

Jesus revealed his glory, who he was,
when he changed water into wine at Cana,
when he raised Lazarus from the dead.

> *"If you believe, you will see the glory of God,"*

Jesus said to Martha.

As Jesus kneels down at the feet of his disciples,
as he gives his body to eat and his blood to drink,
he reveals a God who becomes little
in order to dwell in us,
flow and act through us,

give life through us
and transform us into himself.
His humble love is the glory of God.

Jesus reveals that the Father is the Source of all things, all life.
Jesus is the One sent to reveal the Father.
Everything he does and says comes from the Father.
He accomplishes the work of the Father in unity with the Father.

> *"Father, I glorified you on earth*
> *by accomplishing the work you gave me to do.*
> *So now, Father, glorify me in your presence*
> *with the glory that I had in your presence*
> *before the world existed."*   *vv. 4-5*

What is this work that Jesus has accomplished?

> *"I have made your name known*
> *to those you gave me from the world.*
>
> *"They were yours and you gave them to me.*
> *And they have kept your word.*
>
> *"Now they know that everything you gave me is from you.*
> *I have given to them the words you gave me*
> *and they have received them,*
> *and they know in truth that I came from you,*
> *and they have believed that you sent me."*   *vv. 6-8*

Jesus is leading his friends into the glory of the life of God.
We, too, give glory to God
when we recognize that all that is beautiful in us
comes from God.
We, too, become the glory of God
as we bear much fruit,   *cf. Jn 15:8*
as we make known the humble and compassionate God
through our words, our gestures, our lives together.

Irenaeus, the first Bishop of Lyon in France, wrote at the end
of the second century:
"The glory of God is the human person fully alive."
"Alive" with the love of God!

Jesus prays for his friends

Having affirmed and confirmed his friends,
whom he has chosen to found his church,
Jesus prays for them:

> *"It is for them that I pray.*
> *I do not pray for the world*
> *but for those that you have given me*
> *because they belong to you."*   *v. 9*

> *"Holy Father, keep them in your name."*   *v. 11*

> *"I am not asking you to take them out of the world*
> *but to protect them from the evil one."*   *v. 15*

> *"Make them holy in the truth.*
> *Your word is truth.*
> *As you have sent me into the world*
> *so I have sent them into the world,*
> *and for their sake I sanctify myself*
> *so that they also may be made holy in truth."*   *vv. 17-19*

Jesus prays for those who will continue his mission
to reveal the Father and the gift of the Holy Spirit,
that they may be holy
as he is holy.
This holiness does not come as we stretch out towards God,
but as we welcome the Holy One
who comes to dwell in us.

To become holy

We human beings are a mixture
of the presence of God and the absence of God,
of light and darkness,
truth and chaos,
goodness and evil,
openness and closedness.
No human being in himself or herself is holy or pure.
We become holy only through the holiness of God.

By ourselves we cannot bridge the gap that separates
the finite from the Infinite.
God reaches out to us and we become holy
as we welcome God who comes to us.

This implies that we gradually become emptied
of the darkness and selfishness in us,
and liberated from the walls around our hearts
that separate us from God, from others and from our deepest self.

This holiness is not something we can achieve; it is *given*.
It is not reserved for a few strong-willed people,
for austere seekers of God,
for those who have an official role in the Church,
or for those who preach and do advanced theological studies.
It is not reserved for those who are well-known mystics
or for those who do wonderful things for the poor.
Holiness is for all those who are poor enough to welcome Jesus.
It is for people living ordinary lives and who feel lonely.
It is for all those who are old, sick, hospitalized or out of work,
who open their hearts in trust to Jesus
and cry out for his healing love.
"Come, Lord Jesus, come!"

Welcoming God in order to welcome others

As we welcome the loving God in us,
we gradually become liberated from the walls that separate us from
others,
walls that protect us and prevent life from flowing forth in us.
We begin to know and to love others as God knows and loves
them,
to welcome them as God welcomes them.
We become creative with the divine creativity of God.
We become "branches" who dwell in Jesus, the "Vine,"
and who bear much fruit.
Jesus prays for this final accomplishment of humanity,
where the walls of hate and conflict have fallen,
where there are no more divisions or separations,
and we will be *one* in God and with and in each other.

> *"I pray not only on behalf of these,*
> *but also on behalf of those who will believe in me,*
> *through their word,*
> *that they may all be one.*
> *As you, Father, are in me and I am in you,*
> *may they also be in us,*
> *so that the world may believe that you have sent me.*
>
> *"The glory that you have given me, I have given them*
> *[and that glory is the holiness of God]*
> *so that they may be one as we are one,*
> *I in them and you in me,*
> *that they may become completely one*
> *so that the world may know that you have sent them*
> *and have loved them even as you have loved me."*   *vv. 20-23*

In this prayer, Jesus calls his disciples to the summit of love.
From the washing of their feet up until this moment,
we see a deepening in the call to love one another.
After the washing of the feet, he gave his new commandment:
to love one another *as he* loved them.

In that context he called them to abandon any rivalry or competition
and to serve each other, to wash each other's feet,
to help each other to rise up in truth and in the Spirit of God.
A little later we see that to love each other is not just to serve,
it is also to give our lives:

> *"There is no greater love
> than to give one's life for one's friends."*   Jn 15:13

In this prayer, the friends of Jesus are called to an even greater love,
to become one with each other
as the Father and the Son are one in the Spirit.
It is something totally new,
a unity that can in no way be achieved by human means.
It is an openness and tenderness to each one,
that flows from the deepening transformation in God.
Friends of Jesus are no longer just walking towards God,
serving one another,
they are *together, one in God*,
because *God is in them*.

We can understand service, washing each other's feet,
for that is a very human reality.
We can understand giving one's life for one's friends
as a supreme act of love.
But what is this mutual indwelling in God?
To love one another as the Father and Son love each other,
are in each other and dwell in each other?

What analogy can we find that might help us
understand this wondrous unity, this perfect oneness?
First, this oneness is not the fusion
of two people totally dependent on each other,
not knowing the frontiers of their being,
one wrapped up in the other and closed up in each other,
fearful of losing the other,
neither one nor the other knowing who they are.

No, it is the friendship of lovers, their wedding feast of love
when the bride and beloved become one in the sharing of their lives,
giving themselves to one another
and together giving themselves to God and to others.

In love each one is unique and precious;
each one has his or her place;
each one receives and each one gives;
each one has a grateful heart.
There are no more barriers;
each delights in the other,
each is a delight for the other
because in each one is seen the face of God.

> *Arise my love, my fair one*
> *And come away;*
> *For now the winter is past*
> *the rain is over and gone.*
> *The flowers appear on the earth;*
> *the time of singing has come....*

> *My beloved is mine and I am his.*   *Song 2:10-12, 16*

Each one is different
and each one is needed
for the completion of humanity in God.
We are bonded together:
vulnerable, one to another,
open, one to another.
Together we reflect the infinite beauty of God,
the unity in God.
Together we cry out our thanks to God and to others.

We cry out together our desire for God to be glorified
as the source and the end of all beings.

This unity, which comes from the inner life of each person,
is only possible when, stone by stone,
the walls around our vulnerable hearts come down.

Then we no longer judge ourselves as unworthy
and we no longer judge others as unworthy.
We see in them and in ourselves the light and love of God.
There is no longer a void or anguish or terrible loneliness,
but a new life, the very life of God, surging up from within us.
It is an experience of freedom and oneness with others,
an experience of a fullness of life
where one's very identity has mysteriously given way
to a new identity that flows directly from God.

This wondrous unity is a promise of what will be given to us
as we become transformed in God.
On earth we may live glimpses of it,
but most of the time we struggle against the chaos within.
We struggle to keep welcoming people,
to love those whom we do not like or who do not like us.
We struggle to love those who are different or who appear to be rivals.
We struggle to love our enemies, those who hurt us.
We struggle not to judge and condemn people.

Peace comes as we enter this struggle,
as we work for unity
in our family and community,
in our church and between all followers of Jesus,
and between all our brothers and sisters in humanity.

Peace comes as we no longer seek to prove that we are right,
as we live the truth of forgiveness and reconciliation
and accept the light and presence of God
within us and within others.

The Spirit of Jesus gives us the strength to continue on the road
and to love each person as God loves him or her,
so that each one, liberated from sin and fear,
discovers their real person,
precious and important to God, hidden behind their ego,
and the real person of others,
precious and important to God, hidden behind their ego.

Some blocks remain

There is still work to be done by me and by Jesus
in order that I may be free
or, as the writer of this prayer describes it, "disarmed."
These words by Patriarch Athenagoras of Constantinople
are words that I would like to make my own:

> I have waged this war against myself for many years.
> It was terrible.
> But now I am disarmed.
> I am no longer frightened of anything
> because love banishes fear.
> I am disarmed of the need to be right
> and to justify myself by disqualifying others.
> I am no longer on the defensive,
> holding onto my riches.
> I just want to welcome and to share.
> I don't hold on to my ideas and projects.
> If someone shows me something better —
> no, I shouldn't say better but good —
> I accept them without any regrets.
> I no longer seek to compare.
> What is good, true and real is always for me the best.
> That is why I have no fear.
> When we are disarmed and dispossessed of self,
> if we open our hearts to the God-Man
> who makes all things new,
> then He takes away past hurts
> and reveals a new world
> where everything is possible.

Unity among Christians

Today, followers of Jesus from different faith traditions are divided.
Divided in ecclesial structures, in theology,
in models of authority and of the priesthood,
and in forms of worship.
These divisions, many of which originated so long ago,
continue to be horribly painful today.
Christians were torn apart, wars of religion broke out,
people were massacred, burned at the stake.
Jesus, the One who prayed for unity, must have wept.

Today, people of different faith traditions
are working to bring people and churches closer together.

Disciples of Jesus are walking towards greater unity and mutual love.
Jesus reveals that full unity, however,
can only come as God lives more fully in each one of us,
as we become holy through having welcomed the Holy One
within us, and as each of us together
begins to reflect the presence of Jesus in our lives.
We all have work to do to welcome the Holy One within us
and to love as he loves.
Unity does not come from the acceptance of exterior structures
or laws, dogmas or ways of worship.
It surges up from a life that flows within us
and through us all together.
It is hearts and minds bonded together because they are bonded
in communion with Jesus.
It is a song, a celebration of thanksgiving.
It is a sign of the glory of God.
Ecumenism, then, is not to entice people to belong
to one particular church,
but to encourage all, beginning with ourselves,
to love Jesus more dearly
and to follow more fully the charter of life
given to us by Jesus in what is called the "beatitudes."   *cf. Mt 5:1-12*

This unity is not only for those who explicitly follow Jesus,
but for all men and women who are seeking to respect and love
all those who are different
and who seek to live according to the truth
they have perceived in their conscience.
This unity is for all those who are drawn to be close to the weak,
the needy and the oppressed
and to live the path of love and of non-violence.

This unity is a communion
that binds hearts together –
hearts formed in different religious traditions.
In these hearts beats the same yearning for peace, for truth,
the same desire to be held in God.
We are different and at the same time one in our hearts' desires.

Having prayed for all those who believe in him,
from generation to generation, for all times,
Jesus reveals his desire to be with us all, in love:

> *"Father, I desire that those also whom you have given me*
> *may be with me where I am,*
> *to see my glory which you have given me in your love for me*
> *before the foundation of the world."*   *v. 24*

This is our final destiny, which opens the Gospel of John,
when Jesus brought the disciples to the wedding feast in Cana,
and which John the evangelist saw in Patmos:

> *Let us rejoice and exult and give the Lord our God the glory,*
> *for the marriage of the Lamb has come*
> *and his bride has made herself ready....*
> *Blessed are those who are invited*
> *to the wedding feast of the Lamb.*   *Rev 19:7, 9*

Yes, Jesus yearns that we all experience the immense love of God.

> *"Righteous Father, the world does not know you,*
> *but I know you*
> *and these know that you have sent me.*
> *I have made your name known to them*
> *and I will make it known*
> *so that the love with which you have loved me*
> *may be in them and I in them."*   *vv. 25-26*

It will be with this love that flows from the Father
that we go forth to bring life and unity to the world.

23

The King of Love in chains

John 18:1–19:16

*Having prayed for unity,
Jesus enters into the world of conflict.*

*Alone and vulnerable
in the face of worldly
and religious power, Jesus,
the one who came into the world
to proclaim the truth,
the God of love,
is arrested
and condemned to death.*

The Innocent One

Filled with love and kindness for each person,
Jesus is arrested and condemned to death.
His whole being seems to threaten those in power.
The misuse of power continues today.
So many innocent lives, weak and without protection:
children, the elderly, refugees, minority groups, women,
people with disabilities
are pushed aside, treated badly,
sometimes physically or sexually misused and abused.
They cry out for respect, understanding;
their cry for their rights is often ignored by the powerful.
But power will not have the last word.
History tells us those who live by the sword
eventually perish by the sword.
Those who live for truth and justice rise up in truth and justice.

Jesus, the Lamb, crushed by insolent power,
lays down his life in order to give life
and to witness to the truth.
The resurrection of Jesus will announce a new era
where his disciples will be given a new power,
to continue his mission of love
and to transform hearts
through the gift of the Spirit.

The seeds of Judas,
who sought power and hated love.
The seeds of Peter,
who could not accept the Messiah's weakness.
The seeds of some of the religious authorities,
who could not accept the presence of God hidden in the new.
The seeds of Pilate,
afraid of conflict and of being denounced to the Roman authorities.
These seeds are in us all.
Each one of us is capable of hurting weak and innocent people
who threaten and disturb us.

But the seeds of the beloved disciple are also in each of us,
calling us to trust in the folly of love.

The fundamental questions for each one of us are these:
Do I live for truth and justice,
or do I live for the glory and self-satisfaction of power?
Do I feel I exist because of power
or because I believe in love and compassion?

Jesus is arrested

Jesus and his disciples are in a garden near Jerusalem.
A garden usually evokes a beautiful, quiet place of rest.

In this garden, near Jerusalem, there is a confrontation
between Jesus,

>   *"I AM,"*

and Satan, the Evil One,
whom we know had entered the heart of Judas.
Judas leads a whole company of Roman troops and temple police
who come with torches, lanterns and weapons to arrest Jesus.
Judas leads them there because he knew
that Jesus went regularly to this little garden.
As the soldiers approach,
Jesus goes out of the garden, alone,
in order to protect his disciples
and confront the powerful armed men.

>   *"Who are you looking for?"*

he asks them.

>   *"Jesus of Nazareth,"*

they reply. He says to them,

>   *"I AM" [ego eimé].*   vv. 4-5

using the holy name of God announced to Moses.   cf Ex 3

Jesus is "the one who is."
Existence is of his very being.
We human beings do not exist by our own being,
we receive our existence, we receive life.
Jesus is life.
Here "I AM" appears as a weak one.
Truth is so often clothed in vulnerability, not in power.

At this affirmation the men draw back and fall to the ground.
In some way they are stunned by Jesus standing firmly before them,
saying the holy name of God.
They fall to the ground.
Maybe it was a symbolic fall, a shock
that stopped them in their tracks or in holy awe.

Peter, as generous and as immature as ever,
and unable to understand Jesus' message of love and non-violence,
pulls out a sword and cuts off the ear of the high priest's slave!

> *"Put your sword back into its sheath," says Jesus.*
> *"Am I not to drink the cup that the Father has given me?"*   *v.11*

In Holy Scripture, "to drink the cup" means "to suffer."
It is a cup of pain.
It can also be a cup of joy, the cup of communion,
as people drink together from the same cup.
Here it is both a cup of agony and pain
and a cup of communion with his Father.
Jesus said that when his disciples will have left him,
he will not be alone

> *"because the Father is with me."*   *16:32*

Jesus does not want to defend himself using the ways of the world.
Truth shines in all its hidden beauty and vulnerability.
It is the Father who defends him.
Jesus is totally surrendered and abandoned to the Father.

So the soldiers and the Temple police arrest Jesus,
binding him with a rope.
They take him to be tried to Annas, the father-in-law of Caiaphas,
the high priest who, just a few days earlier,
in a prophetic moment,
had proclaimed that Jesus should die for the people.

John speaks of this trial only in a passing way.
It is as if he considers it a non-trial, a false trial.
Hadn't the Sanhedrin already decided to get rid of him?
At different moments in this gospel, however,
Jesus answers accusations that are being made against him.
Maybe the whole gospel represents the trial.
Here, Jesus replies that during his life he had spoken openly
to the whole world in the synagogues and in the Temple,
where all the Jews came together.
He had said nothing in secret.
John wants to affirm the mission of Jesus,
which is to proclaim the truth openly
to the whole world, whatever the cost.

Peter's denial

During the trial, Peter, the one Jesus had named *Céphas* – the Rock,
is asked if he is one of the disciples of Jesus.
Three times he responds to a servant: "*ouk eimé,*"
which can mean "I am not one of his disciples"
but can also mean simply "I am not" or "I have no existence."
Jesus himself had said twice before he was arrested,

> *"I AM" [ego eimé].*   v. 5

He *is* existence.
Here Peter says:

> *"I am not."*   v. 17

He is in a void,
he has no identity,

or rather has only a negative one.
As a disciple, Peter was filled with Jesus.
Now he is empty and lost.
In some ways it is as if he does not exist.

What has happened to Peter?
He has followed Jesus for nearly three years,
seen the miracles, witnessed his healing love.
Peter, who was in awe in front of the transformed Jesus
on Mount Tabor,
now says that he is not a disciple of Jesus,
does not even know Jesus!
Is he afraid of being arrested by the troops?

Or is it something deeper than fear?
Maybe he is going through a kind of breakdown.
He had left everything to follow Jesus
and given his whole life to be with him.
No doubt people in his village had warned him:
"Don't follow that man.
You will see, it will all end badly as it has in so many other cases."
And now, look at Jesus, weak and silent.
He cannot be the Messiah!

Peter believed that the Messiah he had been following
was a man of power who would liberate Israel,
force the Romans to withdraw
and renew the dignity of his people.
Hadn't Jesus raised Lazarus from death?
Wasn't he the victorious King, the great One,
the "One who was to come"?
That was Peter's idea of the Messiah, his ideology.
That is what he wanted and expected for himself,
since Jesus had chosen him to be with him
and share in this same wondrous power.

Now Jesus has lost all power.
He is bound in ropes, dragged away, to be tried like a criminal.
He accepts to be powerless.
Silent, he refuses to speak or to defend himself!
Why doesn't he defend himself?
Peter cannot stand it.
How can the Messiah be weak?
Peter feels cheated, angry and upset.
He is plunged into a terrible disappointment and feelings of despair.
He could not accept Jesus, powerless, washing his feet.
He does not want to be a disciple of this weak Jesus, a weak Messiah!
He is not just denying Jesus
but denying also all that he had seen, heard and lived
during those years with him.
He is denying his own self and his own experience!
That is why he has lost his identity.

From the ideal to reality

Each of us risks not wanting the real, living Jesus,
Son of God and Son of Man,
wanting only the Jesus of our own imagination
and particular ideology
who gives spiritual power and makes us feel important.
A Jesus who does not disturb us or call us to accept our brokenness.
A Jesus who does not invite us to change
and go further on the road of belief, love and gift of self.
Each of us risks being cut off from reality,
imprisoned in our own certitudes,
an ideal that we invent for ourselves and that we cling to for security,
anything that will assure us of our worthiness
and prevent us from recognizing our brokenness and hypocrisy.
Some, imprisoned in a poor self-image,
measure themselves by impossible standards.
Many people enter marriage with enthusiasm
and five or ten years later leave it,
disappointed, feeling cheated,

no longer knowing their partner or themselves.
We can have an ideal image of a person or marriage,
or a community or church,
and then discover the reality.
We run away and blame the other – or others.
The danger is that we choose to see people as we *want to* see them,
not as they really are.

Can we dare to discover God hidden in our world
in all its brokenness and poverty?
Can we dare to accept that we are bonded to people *as they are,*
with all their imperfections,
and that God is hidden in them,
just as he was hidden in the broken Jesus?
Can we dare to discover God
hidden in our own brokenness and poverty?
This is what Jesus is inviting us to accept.
It is the truth that makes us free.

Jesus before Pilate

Jesus is brought to Pilate's palace in Jerusalem.
There, the high priest insists that Jesus be crucified.
Let us now look at each of these principals:
Pilate, the high priests and Jesus.
Pilate, the Roman governor, is the representative of the emperor,
totally in command in those occupied territories.
He is a man of power who despises these conquered people
with their strange religion, rituals and laws.
He loves to make fun of the Jews.
After all, the Roman Empire possesses the world's science,
knowledge, technology and power.

Like all Romans at that time, Pilate has a deep sense of the law.
He wants to impose order according to Roman law,
in the name of the emperor.

He is a rigid, powerful man
but weak inside, like many people who hide behind power.

The high priests,
those representing the Jewish religious authorities,
are filled with confusion, fear and anger.
They want only one thing: for Jesus to be crucified by the Romans.
His presence is too threatening.
They are blinded by the fear
that Jesus might trigger a revolt against the Romans,
who will then retaliate by destroying their nation and the Temple.
Their very identity as a religion, their belief in one God, is at stake.
It is difficult, if not impossible,
for them to believe the miracles they have seen or
to accept that Jesus is the Son of God.
For them this is blasphemy.
They must protect the oneness of God.
Jesus disturbs their spiritual power;
they are losing control of the situation as people flock to him.
Jesus disturbs the social and religious order
by the way he lifts up the poor, the broken, the sinners.
Jesus has to die before it is too late!
So, "they" – an anonymous "they" –
bring Jesus to Pilate but do not enter the palace.
This is to avoid ritual defilement so they can eat the Passover meal.
Pilate is obliged to come and go
between the anonymous "they" outside
and the accused, Jesus, standing alone inside the palace.

Jesus:
chained, silent, serene,
like a lamb led to the slaughter.

Pilate confronts Jesus.
He knows that just a few days before,
the people had hailed Jesus as king,

waving palm branches as he entered Jerusalem sitting on a donkey, and they had cried out:

> *"Hosanna!*
> *Blessed is he who comes in the name of the Lord –*
> *the King of Israel!"*

So Pilate asks:

> *"Are you the king of the Jews?"*   *v. 33*

Jesus replies:

> *"My kingdom is not of this world.*
> *If my kingdom were of this world,*
> *my followers would be fighting*
> *to keep it from being handed over to 'the Jews.'"*   *v. 36*

Then Pilate asks:

> *"So, you are king?"*

And Jesus replies:

> *"You say it. I am king.*
> *For this I was born,*
> *and for this I came into the world*
> *to testify to the truth."*   *v. 37*

When Jesus performed the miracle
of the multiplication of bread and fish,
the crowd wanted to make him king,
but he fled from them.
Jesus did not come to exercise a temporal and social power.
He came to reveal the truth of the God of love
and the Love of God.
It is only now, when he is bound in ropes,
that he accepts the title of king.
He is an imprisoned king, a vulnerable king,
a king with no earthly power.
He is the king of love

who wants to communicate his love
in and through his weakness and vulnerability.
He is a king yearning for the communion of hearts.
This is the truth he has come to proclaim.
Not power for the sake of power, but to build a world of love
at the service of the communion of hearts,
the power of love and compassion that heals, liberates and gives life,
that calls people to live in love with him.

We are all called to live a deep friendship with this vulnerable king.
That is why Jesus came to be with us.
Yet so often we want to be on the winning side
and would like to have a triumphant king,
a triumphant Christianity,
a triumphant church that imposes laws and has global influence.
Like Peter we can be ashamed of our humiliated king.
And like him we can learn from our humiliation.
Perhaps it is only those who are humiliated and excluded
who see in the humiliated king their friend and saviour.

Pilate seems to know that Jesus is not a threat to him
or to the emperor.
Wanting to release Jesus, he says to the anonymous group:

> *"I find no case against him."*   *v. 38*

Pilate seems to think that Jesus is just someone who is a bit off his head,
a dreamy mystic with the illusion of being a king.
He hands Jesus over to be flogged by the soldiers,
maybe hoping in this way to placate the anonymous "they."

The soldiers weave a crown of pointed, piercing thorns
and push it into his head;
Jesus is blinded by the blood that flows into his eyes.
They put a purple gown, a royal colour, around him,
and making fun of him, say:

> *"Hail, king of the Jews!"*   *19:3*

They hit him in the face.
Again Jesus is silent, like a lamb led to the slaughter.
He is a silent, loving king.

Pilate goes out again to the anonymous "they."
He tells them again that he has no case against Jesus.
Then he calls forth Jesus, who is crowned with thorns,
wearing the purple, kingly robe, and says:

> *"Here is the man!"*

They scream:

> *"Crucify him! Crucify him!"*

Playing with the crowd, Pilate wields his power in a mocking way:

> *"Take him yourself and crucify him!"*

He knows that according to Roman law,
the Jews cannot crucify a man.
The anonymous group cries out:

> *"We have a law*
> *and according to that law he ought to die*
> *because he claims he is the Son of God!"*   *vv. 5-7*

Pilate is frightened.
Maybe Jesus has some divine or mystical power
that could cause him some personal harm.
He returns inside and asks Jesus:

> *"Where are you from?"*

Jesus comes from God and is going to God
but Pilate is unable to understand.
Jesus remains silent.

> *"Do you refuse to speak?*
> *Do you not know that I have power over you,*
> *power of life or death?"*

"You would have no power over me
unless it had been given to you from above,"
Jesus replies.   *vv. 9-11*

Pilate is afraid and again wants to release Jesus.
The anonymous group shouts out:

"If you release this man
you are no friend of the emperor.
Anyone who claims to be king
sets himself against the emperor!"   *v. 12*

Why is Pilate so afraid?
He might lose his prestigious posting
if he were denounced to the emperor by the Jewish authorities.
He wants at all costs to avoid trouble and an open conflict.
He acts against all justice and against his own conscience.
He loses his own identity.
He, too, becomes a nobody.
He condemns Jesus.

Before proclaiming the sentence, however,
Pilate says mockingly to the people:

"Here is your king!"

as if this "crazy religious man" is the only one worthy
of being king of such a people.

"Away with him! Away with him!
Crucify him! Crucify him!"
"Shall I crucify your king?" says Pilate again mockingly.

The chief priests shout out,

"We have no king except the emperor!"   *vv. 14-15*

They commit the ultimate blasphemy
because according to their Scriptures, only God is King.

Pilate then hands Jesus over to be crucified.
Jesus remains silent,
no longer free to move.
But Jesus is in fact the only one who is free, totally free,
totally himself, "I AM" –
united to the Father,
speaking and revealing the truth.
He is the King of Love, hidden and silent.

How often in our world today truth is chained,
silenced, hidden, pushed away.
And how often those who speak the truth to abusive power
are silenced.
How often we ourselves have refused to follow our conscience
and the call of truth and justice
because we were afraid of losing our job,
our friends or power of some sort.
Such fear darkens our world
and makes us lose the truth of who we are.

Truth is like a tiny light,
the light of our conscience,
which in a mysterious way is the ruler or the "king"
that governs our being.
It is like the eyes of a child,
the song of a bird,
a gentle flower.
But we are often too busy to notice,
too frightened to listen and to see.
We can even crush this inner conscience,
the ruler or "king" of our being.
We become slaves to our fears and prejudices,
slaves to what others want us to be.
We can keep this king of love and of truth enchained.

24

Jesus: Victim and Saviour

John 19:16-37

Jesus did not run away from pain, he accepted it
and went to the very end
of his mission:to proclaim the truth
of the God of love.

Many rejected him
and his message of love,
not wanting to change
or be changed. Wanting to hold
onto their meagre power
and privileges,
they got rid of him.

But through his wounds and pain
Jesus brings life and hope to all people.
He opens the gates of love
to our broken hearts and world.

A history of oppression

The death of Jesus is one of the most dramatic events
in the history of humanity.
The innocent one,
the one who came to announce universal love and peace,
the one who came to give us life, the fullness of life,
is pushed down into a pit of hatred and rejection,
is condemned to death on a cross.
The one admired for his miracles
becomes an object of ridicule.
His life appears to be a horrible failure.
Hate seems to have conquered love.
But we will see that
the conquered one, the one who apparently failed,
opens up a source of new life,
a new vision for humanity,
a new road to peace and unity.

The history of humanity is one of oppression of the weak.
Continually crushed by the strong, the victims so often are
children abused and neglected,
women abused and raped,
minorities crushed, controlled, cynically ignored,
their cultures left broken,
while many are forced into one form of slavery or another.
The Nazi regime sought to exterminate the Jews.
In Rwanda, in the Balkans, there were different forms of genocide.
The Palestinian people were forced out of their land.
We have in recent years witnessed the introduction
of a new and horrific phrase:
"ethnic cleansing."
And elsewhere, many people with disabilities, seen as useless,
are still being kept closed up in institutions.

On one side, the cruel misuse of power;
on the other, a broken humanity, its dignity lost:
oppressor and victim.

Jesus fulfills his mission

After being unjustly condemned to death
by a frightened and perverse Pilate,
condemned also by the frightened religious authorities of the time,
Jesus walks alone, carrying on his shoulders the huge log of the cross.
He walks to his death serenely, with dignity and in freedom.

He is fulfilling the mission given to him by the Father:
to take away the sin of the world,
to break down the barriers that separate people
from each other,
from God,
from what is deepest within each one.
He is witnessing to the truth:
the truth of love,
the truth of the Love of God and the God of love,
the truth of the importance of each person.

Evil screams and roars.
Truth is a light that shines in the darkness.
Silent,
it draws forth what is deepest within us.

In his final hour
Jesus lays down his life for those he loves,
and for the unity of humanity.
He goes freely to his death,
free to give his life,
free to give us life.

And there in Golgotha, the "Place of the Skull,"

> *"they" [the anonymous "they"] crucified him,
> with two other men, he in the middle.*   v. 18

Jesus is at the heart of history,
the centre of humankind drawing all people to the God of love.

The universal kingship of Jesus

Pilate has an inscription written
and placed above the head of Jesus crowned with thorns:

> *"Jesus of Nazareth, King of the Jews."*

In Hebrew, Latin and Greek,
it proclaims to the whole world that Jesus is king,
the King who will reveal the road to love and to universal peace.

The chief priests do not like that inscription and want Pilate to
change it to say

> *"This man said, 'I am the King of the Jews.'"*

But Pilate refuses, saying:

> *"What I have written I have written."* vv. 19-22

Pilate's words are prophetic,
just as the words of Caiaphas,
when he said that Jesus should be killed
in order to save the whole nation, are prophetic. Jn 11:50
What was written became Scripture.
The kingship of crucified love is proclaimed to the whole world.

The Gospel of John requires me to ask myself:
How prepared am I to bow down before this humble king
and welcome the Source of love and truth
that flows from him?

The naked king

The four soldiers who crucify Jesus
strip him of his clothes.
He becomes the naked King,
stripped of power, mobility and dignity,
to reveal the truth of love in an offering of self.
Truth can be so stark that we turn our eyes away from it.

They decide to cut his outer garment into four pieces,
one for each of them,
but the tunic is seamless, woven in one piece,
probably by the mother of Jesus.
The soldiers do not tear it but cast lots to see who would get it.
The gospel notes with a certain solemnity that they did this
in order to fulfill Scripture:

> *They divided my garments among them*
> *and cast lots for my clothing.*   *Ps 22:18*

The prophet Isaiah said centuries earlier:

> *Like a sapling he grew up before him,*
> *like a root in arid ground.*
> *He had no form or charm to attract us,*
> *no beauty to win our hearts.*
> *He was despised, the lowest of men,*
> *a man of sorrows, familiar with suffering;*
> *one from whom, as it were, we averted our gaze,*
> *he was despised, for whom we had no regard.*
> *Yet ours were the sufferings he was bearing,*
> *ours the sorrows he was carrying,*
> *while we thought of him as someone being punished*
> *and struck with affliction by God,*
> *whereas he was being wounded for our rebellions,*
> *crushed because of our guilt;*
> *the punishment reconciling us fell on him*
> *and we have been healed by his wounds.*
> *Ill-treated and afflicted,*
> *he never opened his mouth,*
> *like a lamb led to the slaughter-house,*
> *like a sheep dumb before its shearers*
> *he never opened his mouth.*   *Is 53:2-5, 7*

Who can believe that this naked man, condemned to death,
is the Word of God made flesh
who liberates us from all the chaos inside us and around us?

Jesus gives his mother to the beloved disciple

After Jesus is stripped of his clothes
and left hanging naked on the cross,
there is a moment filled with gentleness and kindness.

> *Jesus, seeing his mother [standing near the cross]*
> *and the disciple whom he loved,*
> *says to her: "Woman, behold your son."*
> *Then he says to the disciple:*
> *"Behold your mother."* vv. 26-27

The writer adds that from that hour on, the hour of the death of Jesus,
the beloved disciple takes the mother of Jesus
as the Greek says,
"into what belonged to him":
"what was truly his own, the treasure of his heart."

This could appear to be an act of kindness of Jesus.
As a good son, he is thinking of his mother's future.
But other implications of this last gesture of Jesus
are revealed in the full context of the Gospel of John.
Immediately after entrusting his mother to the beloved disciple,
the evangelist tells us:

> *Jesus knew that all was now accomplished.*

What is this mission that Jesus has accomplished
and about which he said to the Father:

> *"I glorified you on earth*
> *by accomplishing the work that you gave me to do."* Jn 17:4

What is this work?
Is it not to bring people, made holy
by the presence of the Holy Spirit, into unity
so that they may be one
as Jesus and the Father are one? Jn 17:21

The final gesture of Jesus is to bring Mary and John into oneness
as he and the Father are one,
to create a covenant of love between them.

Jesus does not say to the beloved disciple,
"Behold my mother."
He says:

> *"Behold your mother."*

By giving his mother as the mother of the beloved disciple
Jesus is calling her to give life to the beloved disciple,
to bring Jesus to birth, as it were, within him,
so that the disciple may dwell in Jesus and Jesus in him.
And in the same gesture,
the beloved disciple is being called to become Jesus for his mother,
for she has only one son: Jesus.
Here is the supreme unity of love and communion.

Origen, a prominent theologian,
was born about 80 years after the death of John the Evangelist.
For him, this moment is essential
to a full understanding of the Gospel of John.
In the introduction to his commentary, he writes:

> Nobody can really understand this gospel
> unless they too have reclined on the heart of Jesus
> and received Mary as mother as the beloved disciple did.

Those "fathers of the church" who followed Origen
loved to make a comparison between
Mary giving birth to Jesus through the power of the Holy Spirit,
and Mary giving birth through the power of the Holy Spirit
to the beloved disciple,
to all the beloved disciples,
and to the Church, which is the Body of Christ.

The final cry of thirst and the death of Jesus

After entrusting Mary to the beloved disciple,
the Gospel of John says:

> *knowing that all was accomplished,*
> *Jesus said in order to fulfill Scripture:*
> *"I thirst."*   *v. 28*

In biblical language, "thirst" implies anguish and loneliness.
Jesus, scorned, stripped and mocked.
Jesus, who has lost all dignity,
nailed to the wood of the cross.
Jesus, wracked by pain, his strength and power
ebb away with each moment.
Jesus, abandoned by disciples and friends,
remains in communion with his mother.
In some mysterious way,
in his birth and in his death,
he needs her presence, her love.
Her trust and love are his strength,
joy and consolation.
A woman of compassion, she remains standing at the cross
when others had fled in fear and doubt.
With and in Jesus she offers all to God.

Now, with Jesus giving his mother to the beloved disciple,
it is as if he is saying to her:
"Do not look at me, look at my beloved disciple.
He will render me present to you."

Jesus is now totally alone.
He cries out

> *"I thirst!"*
> *I am in anguish!*

And in this anguish, Jesus is giving his life:

> *"That all may be one, as the Father and I are one,"*

creating unity becomes his final gesture.
Responding to his cry of thirst,
"they," again the anonymous "they,"
who in this gospel have no real identity,
give him some vinegar on a sponge.
Jesus says:

> *"It is accomplished!"*

All is finished.
His mission has been fulfilled.

> *Then, inclining his head, he delivers up the Spirit.*   *vv. 28-30*

These mysterious words can be taken in different ways.
The Greek does not just say that he inclined his head
and gave up his last breath.
It suggests that he inclined his head
and *gave [parédokem] the Spirit.*
His last act, then, is to give the gift of the Spirit.
He *breathes out* the Spirit,
as later he will breathe on the disciples and also give them his Spirit.

Blood and water flow from his side

The Feast of the Passover is to begin soon.
The Jewish authorities want the bodies of the crucified
to be taken down and buried.
So, they

> *ask Pilate to have the legs of the crucified men broken*
> *and their bodies removed.*   *v. 31*

One might ask, what the link is between breaking legs and death?

When you are hanging by your arms on a cross,
you can only breathe as you push up with your legs.
If you cannot push yourself up because your legs are broken,
you will be asphyxiated and die in a horrible anguish.
During the hours on the cross,

Jesus had to keep pushing up with his legs
and his nail-pierced feet in order to breathe.
He was in excruciating pain, his voice hardly audible.
In order to hear him, his mother
and the beloved disciple had to stay close.

The soldiers break the legs of the two men on either side of him,
but when they come to Jesus they

> *saw that he was already dead*
> *and did not break his legs.*
> *Instead one of the soldiers pierced his side with a spear*
> *and at once blood and water came out.*　　　　*vv. 33-34*

With great solemnity the beloved disciple affirms and testifies
to what he has seen.

> *He who saw this has testified*
> *so that you also may believe.*
> *His testimony is true*
> *and he knows that he tells the truth.*　　　　*v. 35*

In the blood and the water flowing from the side of Jesus,
the evangelist sees a symbol of hope.
Water symbolizes the Spirit.
With Nicodemus we are called to be "born again," from "on high,"
through water and the Spirit.

Jesus promised the Samaritan woman
that living waters would flow from her heart
if she drank of the waters he gives.

There was the great cry of Jesus in the Temple
during the Feast of Tents:

> *"You who are thirsty, come to me and drink."*　　　　*Jn 7:37*

The water flowing from the heart of Jesus is the sign of his love
and of the gift of the Spirit

that is to be given to all who are willing to receive it.
This water heals, cleanses and gives life.
This water transforms "closedness," negativity, hate and violence
into openness, gentleness, love
and forgiveness.

The water flowing from the pierced heart of Jesus
reveals in a symbolic way
the transmission of life, the life of God,
which is one of the fundamental themes
of the Gospel of John.
It reveals God's desire to break down the walls
that separate us from God,
imprison us in ourselves and prevent us from being fully alive.
God yearns to liberate us,
to live in us and for us to live in God
in an eternal embrace of ecstasy.
It is this unconditional love of Jesus,
giving himself to us totally in all his vulnerable being,
which opens us up to receive his life, the life of God,
and be reborn.

A ray of hope

This horrifying story of violence, hatred and cruelty ends
with an immense ray of hope:
death does not have the last word!
Violence and hate have been transformed
into tenderness and forgiveness
through the power of God, the Word of God made flesh.
Waters of life begin to flow.
People will now be able to receive these waters
of love and communion
and find inner liberation.
As disciples they will become a source of peace for our divided,
broken world.

But this gift of the Spirit is not given without pain.
The pain and death of Jesus, freely accepted,
are followed by the pain and death that his disciples willingly accept.
Just as life flowed from the pierced heart of Jesus,
life will flow from the pierced hearts
of those who will suffer in the name of Jesus.
Disciples of Jesus throughout the ages
suffer rejection, are mocked, laughed at, pushed aside,
sometimes tortured and killed for their faith, for truth and justice.
They become like Jesus.
Paul tells his disciples:

> *I rejoice in my sufferings for your sake*
> *and in my flesh I complete what is lacking in Christ's affliction,*
> *for the sake of his body, the Church.*   *Col 1:24*

Disciples who suffer in the name of Jesus become a source of life
for the church and for the world.
In 1982, Oscar Romero was assassinated by the military in El Salvador
because he sided with the poor,
with those who had no land.
He denounced the oppression of those in power.
Shortly before he was killed, Romero said:
"Even if my blood is poured out,
it will give life to others in El Salvador."
He is one of countless many who have given their lives
proclaiming the message of love of Jesus.

Living failure

Hearts are wounded,
psyches and bodies broken.
Many people today are living with a sense of failure
and can find no meaning to their lives.
The mystery of Jesus is that he descended into failure and pain
and let himself be trampled upon.
Through this failure and pain he brought life to us.

A grain of wheat has to die in order to bear fruit.
Grapes have to decompose in order to ferment and produce wine.
My hope is that those who live with a sense of failure,
who do not have the faith of the martyrs and witnesses
who preceded us,
may discover the gentle presence of God within their hearts and lives.
My prayer is that this presence will reveal to them
that God loves them today,
and that knowing this, they can give life and hope to others.

I have the privilege of knowing some people who suffer a lot of pain.
Although there are moments when this pain is alleviated
it is never fully cured.
I think of a young woman in Paris
who goes in and out of a psychiatric hospital
in a terrible state of confusion.

She, like others who suffer in so many different ways,
finds meaning in her pain through her faith and her love for Jesus.
In her anguish and confusion she can live brief moments of peace,
in the knowledge that these moments of peace
are given by and offered to God.

Those who suffer will, I hope, find the help they need
to alleviate their pain and anguish
rather than become closed up in themselves,
trapped by an overwhelming sense of worthlessness and depression.
We all have to struggle not to give in to this pain
or to be engulfed by it.
When everything has been done to ease this pain,
we can learn to be with Jesus
and try to turn our pain into prayer and offering.

Yet many men and women continue to be crucified today,
living in what seems to them senseless pain,
a pain that takes many guises.

Many are victims of injustice,
in refugee camps,
prisons, hospitals, institutions, slum areas, living on city streets.
Many are rejected, thrown out of society;
they cry out for someone who might alleviate their pain.
They struggle to find dignity and freedom.
Many lose faith.
They call out to men and women of compassion
to stand beside them,
like Mary, at the foot of the cross.
They need to experience this presence of love.
My hope is that their pain,
held in the pain and blood of Jesus
and transformed by the compassion of Mary,
will become a source of life for them and for others.

They lay the dead body of Jesus in the tomb

Joseph of Arimathea and Nicodemus

> *took the body of Jesus*
> *and bound it in linen cloths with the spices*
> *as is the burial custom of the Jews.*
> *Now in the place where he was crucified*
> *there was a garden,*
> *and in the garden a new tomb*
> *where no one had ever been laid.*   *vv. 40-41*

All is finished.
Jesus is dead.
Hope has yet to be born.
The disciples' hearts are deadened by pain.
The heart of Mary of Magdala, who was also with Jesus at the cross,
is wounded by another, inner death,
a death of sadness.
Her beloved has gone.

25

Called to forgive

John 20

The one who was rejected,
who was put to death,
has risen up in love.

And the disciples rise up
from despair to hope.

Not to reveal power
but to reveal
the compassionate
and liberating
love of God.

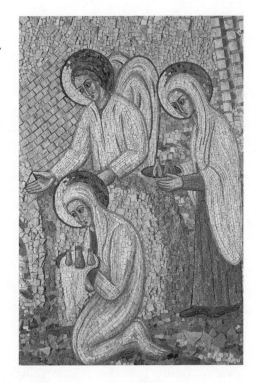

The meeting with Mary of Magdala

Early in the morning on the first day of the week,
Mary of Magdala goes to the tomb
where they have laid the body of her beloved Jesus.
Her heart is broken.

> *"I sought him whom my soul loves.*
> *I sought him but found him not.*
> *I called him but he gave no answer,"*   Song 3:1

cries the bride in the Song of Songs who prefigures Mary.
She wants to be the first to come and anoint the body.
But who will take the stone away?
And when she arrives at the tomb, what does she find?

The stone has been taken away!
The body of Jesus has disappeared.
Someone has stolen the body of her beloved!
The tomb is empty,
as empty as her heart.
She runs to Simon Peter and to the other disciple,
the "one whom Jesus loved," crying,

> *"They have taken the Lord out of the tomb*
> *and we do not know where they have laid him!"*   Jn 20:2

At Mary's cry of alarm, Peter and the other disciple go running to
the tomb.

Everybody seems to be running in this early-morning light.
Running out of fear?
Running because they are confused?
Running because Jesus has disappeared?
But where is the body of Jesus?
The evangelist reveals in a delicate way
the relationship between the two disciples:

The two were running together,
but the other disciple outran Peter
and reached the tomb first.
He bent down to look in and saw the linen wrapping lying there,
but he did not go in.
Then Simon Peter came, following him and went into the tomb.
He saw the linen wrappings lying there
and the cloth that had been on Jesus' head,
not lying with the linen wrappings
but rolled up in a place by itself.
Then the other disciple, who had reached the tomb first,
also went in and he saw and he believed,
for as yet they had not understood scripture
that he must rise from the dead.   *vv. 4-9*

Peter, heavy with sadness and guilt,
is confused and runs slowly.
The other disciple, the "beloved," seems less troubled.
He had followed Jesus to the cross
and so is more sprightly.
But he is respectful and lets Peter go into the tomb first.
Peter – "Céphas," the Rock – is still the leader,
even though he has denied Jesus.
Peter sees the cloth that had been over the head of Jesus
folded up in a corner.
No thief would have stopped to fold this cloth!
The other disciple, in a flash of insight, understands:
Jesus is surely risen.
Peter remains confused and blocked.
He does not yet believe.

> *And Mary stood weeping outside the tomb.*

The disciples leave Mary alone with her grief.
They do not understand her pain.
They seem confused before a woman's tears.
Unable to respond to her, they run home.

Mary, weeping, bends over to look into the empty tomb.
She sees two angels in white sitting where the body of Jesus
had been lying.
They say to her:

>*"Woman, why are you weeping?"*

She replies:

>*"They have taken away my Lord
>and I do not know where they have laid him."*   *vv. 11-13*

She is so sure that Jesus is dead, really dead.
Blinded by her tears and depression,
she is unable to question the meaning of these two angels.
When she had said this, she turned around
and saw Jesus standing there,
but she did not know that it was Jesus.

>*Jesus said to her, "Woman, why are you weeping?*
>*Whom are you looking for?"*
>*Supposing him to be the gardener, she said to him:*
>*"Sir, if you have carried him away,*
>*tell me where you have laid him*
>*and I will take him away."*   *vv. 14-15*

Jesus says quietly:

>*"Mary."*

He calls her by her name,
she who was wildly searching for his dead body.
Yet it is Jesus who finds her.

There is such tenderness in his voice, such love.
"It is Jesus!
He is alive!
It is truly the Beloved!"
She cries out:

>*"Rabboni!"*

Her tears of grief disappear under the passionate force of her love.
She throws herself at his feet and clings to him.

Jesus says to her:

> *"Do not cling to me*
> *because I have not yet ascended to the Father....*
> *But go to my brothers and say to them:*
> *'I am ascending to my Father and your Father,*
> *to my God and your God.'"*   *v. 17*

There is something so humble in the story of the resurrection.
The risen Jesus does not appear triumphant over the Temple
to signify to everyone his victory
and to humiliate those who humiliated him.
He appears to Mary of Magdala, the loved one, the forgiven one,
alone in a garden.
Jesus shares a simple, heart-to-heart relationship with her,
a gentle moment of eternity.
He does not appear with power but with a gentle love.

Calling Mary by her name, he echoes the words of the prophet Isaiah:

> *"Do not fear for I have redeemed [liberated] you.*
> *I have called you by name and you are mine....*
> *You are precious to my eyes and honoured*
> *and I love you."*   *Is 43:1, 4*

Mary discovers a new relationship with Jesus.
She must not try to possess him and cling to him,
or seek to be the only one loved by him.
She must not hold on to the past but live in the present moment
in a new, more interior relationship with the risen Jesus.
This relationship is a mutual indwelling, he in her, and she in him,
and it will be given fully at Pentecost with a new gift of the Spirit.

Jesus does not want her to cling to him.
He sends her forth to the community,
to those men with whom she must surely be angry,
who lacked compassion for her when she was upset.
Hadn't they abandoned Jesus at the cross?
Yet Jesus often sends us where we do not want to go!
How difficult it must be to go from an intimate encounter with Jesus
to the larger community with all its needs and expectations!
Mary runs and announces to these men that she has seen the Lord
and that he has called them his "brothers."
But they do not believe her.
In Mark's gospel we hear that Jesus

> upbraided them for their lack of faith and stubbornness,
> because they had not believed those who saw him
> after he had risen.   Mk 16:14

Jesus defends Mary in front of these men who do not understand.

Or maybe they do not want to understand!
Their minds are swirling with all kinds of anxiety.
Aren't they the chosen ones?
Aren't they the ones who will be in the government
and rule over the church?
How could Jesus appear to this woman before appearing to them?
This cannot be possible!
In recounting this exchange between Jesus and Mary of Magdala,
John is telling us something important
about the role of women in the Church.

What else does John tell us about Mary?

Who is this woman who was all alone,
in the dark of the early hours of the day,
weeping and wailing, frantically seeking the dead body of Jesus?
And why does the evangelist devote so much time to her?

The answer takes us to the heart of the message of Jesus.
The Gospel of John shows how this woman is an important sign
for all of us.

Mary does indeed represent each one of us.
Like her, we run here and there frantically,
each one of us alone, feeling empty,
wailing and weeping for a key to peace,
seeking a dead body,
a Jesus who lived some two thousand years ago.
Then Jesus, whom she seeks,
finds her and calls her by name.
So, too, each of us is waiting to be found and called by our name.

Although Mary of Magdala appears infrequently in the gospel,
she has great importance in this scene of the risen Jesus.
Luke speaks of her as being with the twelve chosen ones
who accompanied Jesus.   *Lk 8:2*
He says that seven demons had gone out of her.
Magdala, on the Lake of Galilee,
was the place where the Roman soldiers camped.
Mary of Magdala is Mary of the Roman camp.

In the Hebrew Scriptures,
to turn away from God and from God's covenant of love
was compared to adultery or prostitution.
The prophet Hosea welcomed his wife back again
after she had left him to enter into a life of prostitution.
This was a prophetic sign of a compassionate and forgiving God
who welcomes back those loved ones who have strayed.

Now John tells us that at the foot of the cross
and in the early morning light of the resurrection,
we find this woman,
Mary of the Roman camp.
She is forgiven and loved.

She symbolizes each one of us
who has strayed from God's love
and yet is forgiven.
She has become the "beloved" of God,
and is the first to meet the risen Jesus.
The loving words of God given to Hosea's forgiven wife
are now for her:

> *Therefore I will allure her*
> *and bring her into the wilderness*
> *and speak tenderly to her....*
> *I will take you for my bride forever.*
> *I will take you for my bride in righteousness and in justice,*
> *in steadfast love and mercy.*
> *I will take you for my bride in faithfulness*
> *and you shall know the Lord.*   *Hos 2:14, 19-20*

The meeting with the disciples

That same evening, Jesus appears to the disciples,
who are hiding behind locked doors,
frightened of the religious authorities.
Clearly, they have paid no attention to the wildly excited Mary,
who told them she has seen Jesus.
Jesus appears to them, saying:

> *"Peace to you!"*   *v. 19*

Then, to prove that it is truly him, not a ghost,
he shows them his hands and his feet
and the gaping wound in his side.

How is it that Mary of Magdala earlier and the disciples now
do not recognize Jesus right away?
Mary recognizes him only when Jesus calls her by name.
The disciples recognize him only when he shows them his wounds.
I think they are blinded by their unfulfilled expectations
and their feelings of loss and despair.
In much the same way, we can also be blinded by our fears and tears.

Jesus simply says to them:

> *"Peace to you!"*

The peace Jesus gives is not the peace the world gives.
It is an inner peace that flows from his presence.
Jesus comes to his disciples and gives himself to them,
revealing his forgiving love for each one.
He does not criticize or judge them for their fears
and their moments of infidelity.
He does not make any critical remark to Peter, who denied him.
He does not make anyone feel guilty.
Jesus confirms his choice of them:
they are his beloved ones
and he is there for each of them.

When we are frightened, don't we, too, hide
behind the locked doors of our hearts,
unable to reach out towards others?
Yet, Jesus comes to each of us through these locked doors and says:

> *"Peace to you!"*

At a level that is deeper than all that is wounded and fearful in us,
Jesus reveals that he loves us and forgives us for all our inconstancies.
We are unique and precious to him.
We are the beloved children of God.
Jesus will always be with us
in all the pain and joy we will live in the journey of life.

Jesus sends them forth to transmit the forgiveness of God

In a short, concise passage, the author of this gospel reveals to us
the mission statement of the risen Jesus to his disciples:

> *"Peace to you.*
> *As the Father sent me,*
> *I send you."*
> *He then breathed upon them.*
> *"Receive the Holy Spirit.*

Those whose sins you forgive, are forgiven;
Those whose sins you retain, are retained."   *vv. 21-23*

In this short encounter, Jesus transforms the group
of frightened and confused individuals
into a community of love
where the disciples become covenanted together.
They are called to become like Jesus
and to continue together the mission given him by the Father:
to reveal the merciful face of God,
the compassionate and forgiving God,
and to give life, eternal life, to all who accept him.
God took the initiative to liberate us
when we were trapped behind the barriers of fear and sin.

The disciples will continue to give this life
to those who are hindered by these barriers.

"Truly, truly," said Jesus,
"whoever receives one whom I send, receives me,
and whoever receives me,
receives the one who sent me."   *Jn 13:20*

Jesus is showing his disciples their responsibility,
something that is both terrible and beautiful.
They are to be transformed by the Holy Spirit
and sent out into the world
to love people as Jesus loves them
and to give their lives for them
because each person in the world is precious and beautiful to God,
even if that beauty is hidden behind layers of fear, chaos and sin.

If disciples become like Jesus and dwell in him,
they will liberate people from violence and hatred
and the barriers of sin.
Some people, however, will refuse to receive the disciples of Jesus,
just as some people refused Jesus himself.

Their barriers remain.
Those who welcome Jesus in the disciples
will enter the community of love of Jesus.
Their barriers of fear will disappear as they meet Jesus.

But we must be careful.
Some people refuse to welcome disciples of Jesus
because of the example we set.
We are not sufficiently transformed by the Holy Spirit.
Neither do we live and witness the life of Jesus.
We *talk* Jesus
but do not *live* Jesus.
We talk about love
but do not live love.
People will know we are disciples of Jesus
by the way we love one another
in community, in church.

This mission to forgive and to liberate people
by the gift of the Holy Spirit
concerns not only ordained ministers,
who have a special role to welcome people
into the community of believers
and in some cases offer the sacrament of reconciliation.
It also concerns *all* the disciples of Jesus.
As followers of Jesus, we are *all called* to be a presence of Jesus,
to free people from barriers of fear and sin,
by the power of the Holy Spirit living in us and loving through us.
We are all called to become a fountain of grace
as was the Samaritan woman.
We are all called to be men and women of forgiveness.
We must remember the words of the prayer Jesus gave us:

> *"Forgive us our trespasses*
> *as we forgive those who trespass against us."*   Mt 6:12

Thomas caught in doubt

One of the disciples, Thomas, nicknamed "the Twin," was absent
when Jesus appeared to the other ten.

> *So the disciples told him, "We have seen the Lord."*
> *But he said, "Unless I see the marks of the nails in his hands*
> *and put my fingers in the marks of the nails*
> *and my hand in his side, I will not believe."*　　　　　*v. 25*

Thomas refuses to believe what all the others announce
unanimously: "We have seen the Lord!"
He seems cut off from them, angry with them.
Maybe he is jealous or hurt
because they lived something special when he was absent.
He tells them that he will only believe
if he can put a finger in the wounds of Jesus.

One week later, when Thomas is with the other disciples,
Jesus reappears and says:

> *"Peace to you."*

Turning to Thomas he says:

> *"Put your fingers here and see my hands.*
> *Reach out your hand and put it in my side.*
> *Be not doubting but believe."*　　　　　*v. 27*

It is moving to see how Jesus meets and accepts Thomas just as he is.
Jesus accepts the challenge without complaint or criticism.
He responds to Thomas' need and cry
even if this need comes from a lack of trust.
Moved to tears,
Thomas places his hand into the side of Jesus with love and respect
and cries out:

"My Lord and my God!"
"Have you believed because you have seen me?" said Jesus.
"Blessed are those who have not seen and yet believe." vv. 28-29

This scene ends on the note of belief and trust,
as John writes to all his readers who have not seen the risen Jesus:

> *These things are written so that you may come to believe*
> *that Jesus is the Messiah, the Son of God,*
> *and that through believing*
> *you may have life in his name.*   *v. 31*

The gospel is written so that we may believe and have life, a new life,
the very life of God that flows from God.
O happy fault of Thomas who did not believe,
so that our belief may be founded upon his doubts,
which called forth this new apparition of Jesus!

The wounds of Jesus

In these two apparitions,
we can contemplate the risen body of Jesus,
a body that reveals the wounds inflicted upon him.
A gaping hole remains in his side, big enough to fit a hand;
a hole remains in his hands and feet big enough to fit a finger.
These wounds are there for all ages and all time,
to reveal the humble and forgiving love of Jesus
who accepted to go to the utter end of love.
The risen Jesus does not appear as the powerful one,
but as the wounded and forgiving one.

These wounds become his glory.
From the wound in his side flowed the waters that vivify
and heal us.
Through his wounds we are healed.   *Is 53:5*

Jesus invites each one of us, through Thomas,
to touch not only his wounds,
but those wounds in others and in ourselves,
wounds that can make us hate others and ourselves
and can be a sign of separation and division.
These wounds will be transformed into a sign of forgiveness
through the love of Jesus
and will bring people together in love.
These wounds reveal that we need each other.
These wounds become the place of mutual compassion,
of indwelling
and of thanksgiving.

We, too, will show our wounds
when we are with him in the kingdom,
revealing our brokenness
and the healing power of Jesus.

26

Meeting Jesus every day

John 21

In our daily lives
of work
friendship
prayer
and for some
– at times – loneliness,
Jesus is present,
calling us to grow
in faith and in love.

He asks each one of us:
"Do you love me?"
He asks us to follow him.

Everything seems so ordinary

The conclusion of the Gospel of John is very gentle.
We are back in Galilee,
the home of Jesus and his disciples.
All the surprising, exciting, wonderful, stimulating and tragic events
are over.
We are in the ordinariness of simple daily life.
Peter tells the others that he is going fishing.
Maybe he and the others are a bit bored and
somewhat uncertain about what is going to happen.

What better than to go fishing?
Six other disciples join him.
They work all night but catch nothing. Not one fish!

As dawn breaks, they are not far from the shore.
A stranger calls out to them:

> *"Children, do you have a bit of fish?"*
> *"No!"* they cry out.
> *"Throw out the net on the right side of the boat*
> *and you will find some,"* says the stranger.   vv. 5-6

They do so and their net is instantly filled with a heavy load of fish,
so heavy that they cannot drag the net into the boat.
The "beloved disciple" recognizes the stranger as Jesus
and says to Peter:
"It is the Lord!"
Peter puts on his clothes because he is naked,
plunges into the lake
and rushes towards Jesus.
The other disciples bring the boat to shore,
dragging the net filled with fish.

When they reach the shore and disembark,
they see a little charcoal fire with fish and bread on it.
Jesus says to them:

> *"Bring in some of the fish you have caught."* v. 10

Simon Peter goes over, drags the net filled to bursting with fish,
but even with such a haul the net holds and does not tear.
Jesus says:

> *"Come and have breakfast."*
> *And he took the bread and gave it to them,*
> *so too with the fish.* vv. 12-13

Everything seems so ordinary, even this miracle.
They just put the net on the other side of the boat
and were lucky!
This is not the same as the extraordinary event at Cana
or the multiplication of bread and fish.
Those events were seen by everybody.
Here, Jesus is on the shore, and has prepared breakfast
for these hungry, tired men.
All is so simple, so loving.
Jesus cares so much for them.

Do we believe that Jesus cares for us?
Before Cana and the meeting with John the Baptizer,
Jesus had lived a seemingly inconspicuous life in Galilee
with Mary and Joseph and their neighbours.
He had done nothing out of the ordinary.
He had lived a simple life of family, of community,
of prayer, of work,
sharing with neighbours, being close to the weak and the poor,
going to the synagogue and on pilgrimage
with others from the village.
The Word became flesh in order to reveal a very human life
rooted in the earth, in culture, in faith and in loving relationships.
Now, after the resurrection, we are back in Galilee
in this simple life of togetherness and work.

Why does the evangelist choose to tell this simple, touching story?
As I read the Gospel of John again and again,
I believe that he is telling us about the presence of the risen Jesus
in *our* ordinary lives.

The evangelist wants us to remember that
Jesus meets us wherever we are.
We do not have to do extraordinary things,
but to love and serve others in the name of the risen Jesus.
It all sounds simple, though in reality it is not.
In our everyday lives, conflicts arise so easily.
Relationships can be difficult.
How do I work with others?
How do I nourish friendships?
How do I accept the unexpected and the accidents of life?

And in this closing section of the Gospel of John
we are also being shown the future of the Church.
Up until now the gospel has talked about Jesus:
his life, death and resurrection.
Here the disciples are together in unity.
The Church is community.
The disciples are in the boat, which is a symbol of the Church, *together*.
Often the waters are stormy, sometimes they are dangerous,
but Jesus is always present.

Peter is clearly the leader,
but he does not recognize Jesus at first.
He needs the beloved disciple in order to recognize Jesus.
Leaders can be so taken up with responsibilities and leadership
that they need someone at hand who has a clear vision of things.
When Peter is helped to see that it is Jesus, he plunges towards him,
he takes risks, jumping into the lake.
He keeps his eyes riveted on Jesus.
All he wants to do is to be with Jesus, for without Jesus he is insecure.

Peter immediately obeys Jesus when he tells him to haul in the net.
He doesn't tell others to do it, but does it himself.
He becomes the servant-leader.

Peter is confirmed as the servant-leader

At the outset of this gospel, Jesus chooses Simon Peter
as "Céphas," the "Rock" upon which the future community
would be built.
Peter has the temperament and characteristics of a leader.
He intervenes in the name of the group of the twelve
to announce his belief in Jesus.
He also tells Jesus now and again what he should or should not do
and he tries to save him from being arrested.
Finally, when Jesus becomes vulnerable,
this strong but weak man collapses
and affirms that he is not a disciple of Jesus.
He denies Jesus three times.
The "Rock" clearly is no longer a rock!
Does that mean that Peter has lost his role as the "rock"?

On that Easter morning when Mary of Magdala
rushes to the disciples,
she clearly seeks Peter as the leader of the group
even if he has denied Jesus.

What does Jesus think of this?
Is he going to defer leadership to the beloved disciple
who remained faithful to the end and was at the cross?

After breakfast, Jesus takes Peter aside and asks him:

> *"Do you love me more than these others?"*

Peter has learned his lesson.
He does not reply as he had before:
"Of course, and I will give my life for you."
He has been humbled by his experience;

he knows his weakness and his compulsions.
All he can say, perhaps with a faltering voice, is

> *"You know that I love you."*

Jesus tells him:

> *"Feed my lambs."*

Again Jesus asks him:

> *"Do you love me?"*

Peter responds in the same way.
Jesus tells him:

> *"Tend my sheep."*

For a third time, Jesus asks if Peter loves him.
Peter is upset with the three questions and says:

> *"Lord, you know everything.*
> *You know that I love you."*

Jesus replies:

> *"Feed my sheep."*   *vv. 15-17*

Peter is grieved that Jesus repeats the same question three times.
Jesus is reminding him of the three times Peter had said:

> *"I am not his disciple."*

Jesus is confirming Peter as the leader.
Peter is forgiven.
Jesus wants this man, who is now more humble,
to be the shepherd of the flock.
The lambs and the sheep do not belong to him,
they belong to Jesus.
It is not for him to control them
but to help them to be in communion with Jesus,
to listen to Jesus.

The flock is not an industry or a commercial enterprise
of which he is the manager
and which must be efficient and produce results!
The flock is made up of people called by Jesus to grow in love.

But Peter can only guide, nourish and be responsible for people
in the name of Jesus *if he loves Jesus,*
and I dare say *if he loves Jesus passionately*
and is prepared to give his life for Jesus.
We can only assume a responsibility in the name of Jesus
if we love Jesus and become his friend.
This is not something devotional or sentimental.
It is a commitment to help people
to whom we are not especially attracted
to grow in their love of Jesus
and to work with them.
Not seeking to control them but to liberate them.

Peter is called first of all to feed the little ones, the lambs –
to care for them, be with them:
those who cannot fend for themselves,
who are lost and lonely,
who are weak, sick and hungry,
who are excluded from society.
That is the heart of his demanding mission.
The poor are at the heart of the Church.
But their cry can disturb us.
It is not always easy to be with them.

Peter must feed them with what?
With Jesus,
because in his being and in his words,
Jesus is food for each one of us disciples.
It is the food of his body given in the Eucharist,
the food of the word of God,
the food of his love revealed in the humble love of the shepherds,

those servant-leaders who lead those
who are lonely and broken to Jesus.

Peter is also called to lead those who are growing in faith
in the right direction towards a greater trust in Jesus,
and to become like Jesus.

Then Jesus tells Peter:

> *"Truly, truly, I tell you,*
> *when you were young, you used to fasten your own belt.*
> *When you grow old, you will stretch out your hands*
> *and someone else will fasten a belt around you*
> *and take you where you do not wish to go."*
> *He said this to indicate the kind of death*
> *by which he would glorify God.*
> *After that he said: "Follow me."*   *vv. 18-19*

Peter is called to follow and imitate the Good Shepherd,
to guide the flock,
to wash others' feet,
to nourish them
and to give his life for those who have been entrusted to him.
He is not there for his own privileges and glory,
he is there for Jesus, only for Jesus.

We, too, are called to be humble shepherds

Jesus will help us also to become truly caring persons
and to look after those who have been confided to us.
We must remember, however,
that although they are entrusted to us,
they belong first and foremost to Jesus.
Our role is to guide them to Jesus, guide them to truth and love.
We are called to be humble servant-leaders.

This conclusion about shepherding
and the presence of Jesus in our daily lives

is important because it also touches on the future of the Church
and the world.
Like Jesus, the first believers were persecuted and killed.
To be a follower of Jesus is a dangerous undertaking.

This passage reminds us to be humble shepherds,
not seeking power, wealth or our own glory
but to be servant-leaders,
ready to give our lives and to share our lives with the poor,
to live simply with the poor,
to serve Jesus,
who remains present in the daily ordinariness of our lives
and who calls us to become "beloved."

Peter and the beloved disciple

There is a fascinating incident
between Peter and the beloved disciple,
who in a way represents all of us who are called to dwell in Jesus.
This incident can help us to see the role and limits of a shepherd.
If we are called to follow a shepherd,
we are called first and foremost to follow Jesus.
Peter knew that Jesus loved this disciple in a special way,
and at the cross had entrusted Mary to him as his mother.
Peter has been confirmed as the rock, the leader and the shepherd,
but what about the beloved disciple? What is going to happen to him?

> *Peter turns and sees the disciple*
> *whom Jesus loved following them,*
> *so he asks, "Lord, what about him?"*

Jesus answers in an ambiguous and mysterious way:

> *"If it is my will that he remain until I come,*
> *what is that to you?"*
> *Then he adds, "Follow me."*   *vv. 21-22*

What is the relationship between Peter and the beloved disciple?
What does it symbolize?

Jesus seems to be saying at first:
"He is none of your business. You, follow me."
But perhaps the meaning is deeper than that.
Let us remember how deeply united the two disciples are.
They are frequently together, united in the love of Jesus.
They are different and at times can appear as rivals,
one running faster than the other!
Peter has been confirmed as the shepherd
who will feed and tend the flock of Jesus,
who is the Good and Wonderful and Perfect Shepherd.
His role is to lead people to Jesus
so that they may dwell in Jesus, and Jesus in them,
and so that they may become beloved disciples
inspired and guided directly by Jesus and by the Holy Spirit.
Peter's role is humble but necessary.
He is called to be a sign and a source of unity for the flock.
The Church on earth needs a shepherd and shepherds,
to help each one be faithful to their call.

Peter has his role, just as the beloved disciple also has his role.
Both have been called by Jesus.
When all is complete, Jesus will be the only Shepherd
and all will be beloved in him
in the glory of the Father.

What does Jesus mean when he talks about the beloved
"remaining" or *"dwelling"*?
The evangelist writes:

> *The rumour spread among the brothers and sisters*
> *that this disciple would not die.*
> *Yet Jesus did not say to him that he would not die*
> *but "if it is my will that he remain until I come,*
> *what is that to you?"*   *v. 23*

How will John "remain" until the final coming of Jesus?
Could it be that as the Church grows throughout the world
and over time, it will need to grow in depth

and discover more clearly the message
contained in the Gospel of John?
Could it be that this mystical life revealed by John
will be a source of unity for all Christians?
Could it be that, up until Jesus comes,
there will always remain disciples who, like John,
will take the Mother of Jesus as their own?
The Gospel of John concludes with a message about communion
and unity that reveals the deepest desire in the heart of Jesus.

The possibility of peace and truth

John finishes his gospel by signing his "name":

> *This is the disciple who is testifying to these things*
> *and has written them and we know that his testimony is true.*
> *But there are also many other things that Jesus did;*
> *if every one of them were written down I suppose*
> *that the world itself could not contain the books*
> *that would be written.*   *vv. 24-25*

We may have difficulties believing
in the signs or miracles of Jesus that John talks about in this gospel.
One miracle, however, we cannot deny:
that a man who was condemned to death by the Romans,
and a few uneducated people who left the shore of a lake
to follow him and were scattered after his death,
would finally humble not only the Roman emperor
but all the empires of the earth.
It is this miracle that invites us to believe that
peace and truth are possible.
Even if the influence of Christian churches today has diminished,
the message of universal love given to us by Jesus
is the deepest truth and the strongest force
that can bring peace to our world.

There are different levels of truth in the Gospel of John.
There is the actual account of what happened,

such as the marriage feast in Cana,
and then there is the symbolism of the marriage and
what Jesus reveals through this story as a kind of parable
to help us believe and live the new life he came to bring us.
If the Holy Spirit is the principal author of this book
who inspired the beloved disciple to become the author of it,
then the Holy Spirit is also in each one of us
as we read it, understand it,
deepen our appreciation of it
and try to live the message it contains.

★★★

The interpretation I have given of this Gospel of John speaks of
what is in my own heart,
with my particular experience of faith, life and prayer
rooted as well in what many wise and holy people
of the past and present
have taught me by their words, their lives or their writings.

In the Gospel of John,
I have come to see that to pray is above all to dwell in Jesus
and to let Jesus dwell in me.
It is not first and foremost to *say prayers,*
but to live in the *now* of the present moment,
in communion with Jesus.
Prayer is a place of rest and quiet.
When we love someone, don't we delight in being with each other,
being present to one another?
Now and again we may say a word of affection,
we will be attentive to each other and listen to each other,
but it is essentially a place of silence.
The great Spanish mystic John of the Cross once said,
"Silence is the way God speaks to us."

I learned the silence of prayer and the prayer of silence
with my spiritual father, Père Thomas Philippe.
He helped me to find silence in myself.
It is true that this silence is the fruit of the presence of God; it is peace.

This is what Jesus is telling us with his words:

> *"I leave you my peace,*
> *I give you my peace."*

These insights that I share in this book
come from the life of Jesus in me,
what Jesus teaches me in prayer, in study.
They also flow from my life with people who are weak
and who have taught me to welcome Jesus
from the place of poverty in me.
This interpretation of the Gospel of John cannot be separated
from who I am, with all that is broken in me
and from the ways Jesus has guided my life.

To read this Gospel is to share the good news for the poor.
To experience poverty and the cry of the poor
is to be led into a deeper understanding
of the gospel of Jesus.

What is important, however, is that we read the gospel
not as an academic exercise, but as if it were a letter from a friend
telling us of the love and life of Jesus
and calling each one of us to abide in him.

My hope and prayer is that we,
as faltering followers and friends of Jesus,
will continue seeking to dwell in him
– just as he seeks to dwell in us.
This seeking will challenge each of us to open ourselves
to the pain of humanity
and to become friends with those who are weak, broken, rejected
and in need.
Together, I pray, we may rise up
in the new life promised to us all
where we will know God.

Sources

Quotation from André Chouraqui is taken from the Introduction to *L'Univers de la Bible,* Éditions Brépols-Lidis, 1982–1989.

Quotation from Luc de Villers is taken from *Revue Thomiste,* April 1982.

Quotations from Etty Hillesum are taken from *Etty: The Letters and Diaries of Etty Hillesum 1941–1943.* Ottawa/Grand Rapids, MI: Novalis/Eerdmans, 2003.

Quotation from Victor Hugo is taken from Jean Mambrino, *L'Hesperie, pays du soir,* Éditions Cahier Arfuyen, 68370 Orbey, France.

Pope John Paul II's comments in Assisi, 2003, are taken from Letter of John Paul II to All Heads of State and Government of the World and Decalogue of Assisi for Peace, from the Vatican, 24 February, 2003.

Cardinal Walter Kasper's comments are taken from *The Tablet,* May 17, 2003.

Quotation from Martin Luther King is taken from *Strength to Love,* Philadelphia: Fortress Press, p. 22.

Quotation from St. Francis is taken from Admonitions in *Francis and Clare: The Complete Works,* Regis Armstrong, ed., in the *Classics of Western Spirituality* Series. Paulist, 1982.

Quotation from Andrea Riccardi is taken from *Il secolo del martirio – I cristiani nel nocento* (Mondadori) Milan, 2000.

Quotations from St. John of the Cross are copyrighted by the Institute of Carmelite Studies, Washington, DC.

Quotation from Patriarch Athenagoras (ecumenical patriarch of Constantinople from 1948–1972) is taken from Jean Vanier's translation from the French of Athenagoras' poem "I am disarmed," which appeared in *Revue Tychique,* no. 136, November 1998.